CORK'S
ST PATRICK'S
STREET
A HISTORY

12107. - PATRICK STREET, CORK.

CORK'S ST PATRICK'S STREET

A HISTORY

Antóin O'Callaghan

The Collins Press

First published in 2010 by
The Collins Press
West Link Park
Doughcloyne
Wilton
Cork

Photographs on pp 11, 39, 42, 47, 50, 74, 105
114 (both) and 192 courtesy of the author.

Antóin O'Callaghan has asserted his moral right to be identified as the author of this work.

British Library Cataloguing in Publication Data

O'Callaghan, Antoin.
Cork's St Patrick's Street : a history.
1. St. Patrick Street (Cork, Ireland)--History. 2. Cork
(Ireland)--History.
I. Title
941.9'56-dc22

ISBN-13: 9781848890572

Design and typesetting by Stuart Coughlan / edit+

Typeset in Adobe Garamond Pro
Printed in Italy by Printer Trento

Contents

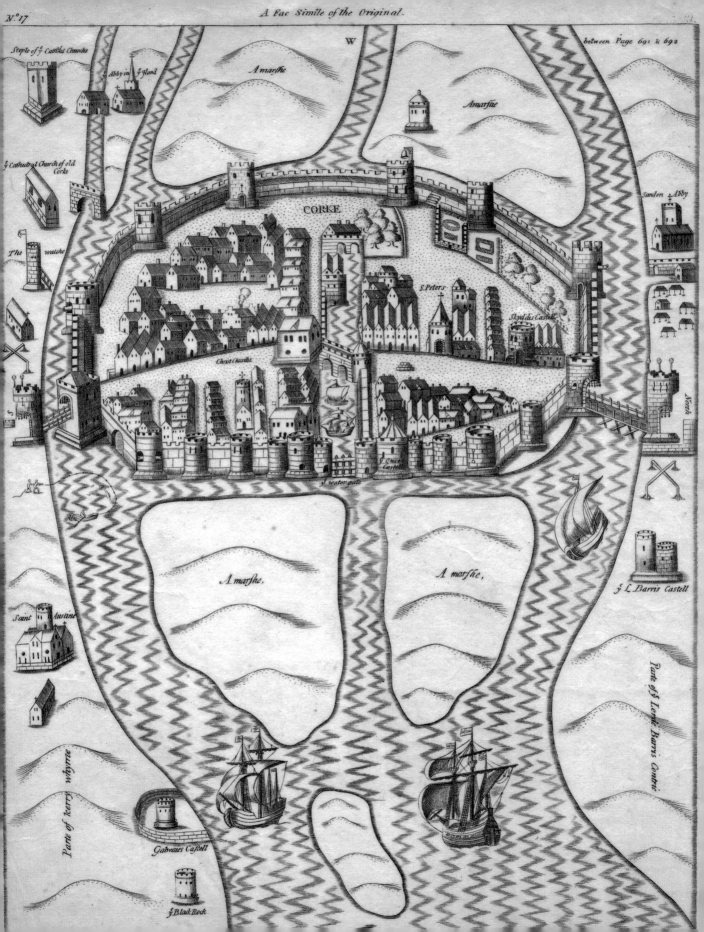

Steple of y̆ Cattlick Churche

Abby in y̆ Iland

W

A marshe

A marshe

y̆ Cathedral Church of old Corke

CORKE

Sanden Abby

The watche

S. Peters

Skyddis Castell

Christ Churche

S

North

y̆ Quene Castell

y̆ water-gate

A marshe.

A marshe,

y̆ L Barris Castell

Saint Austane

Parte of y̆ Lorde Barris Cuntrie

Parte of y̆ kerry whyrre

Galwaies Castell

y̆ Black Rock.

Introduction

On 22 September 2004, Catalan architect Beth Gali was present for the official opening of the newly refurbished St Patrick's Street in Cork city, which she had designed. The ceremony was the culmination of years of planning and work that had gone into the creation of an open and spacious city centre of which the citizens could be proud. Beth Gali's design sought to achieve a pedestrian-friendly space for the future whilst also incorporating an acknowledgement of Cork's past.[1] The natural curve of the one-time river channel was retained and the iconic figure of Fr Mathew kept his prime position on the street. Many names of those trading on the street have also been there for generations and so the ordinary Cork people who come into the theatre that is St Patrick's Street every day are following in the footsteps of their forebears. To them all, one thing remains unchanged. It is their St Patrick's Street, known affectionately to all as 'Pana'.

St Patrick's Street developed in the 1780s when the city was expanding beyond the old medieval walled core into the outlying marshlands. The river channel that ran where the street is today was arched over and what had been 'the Long Quay' became St Patrick's Street. But why was it so named? Seeking an answer to that question was one reason why I began to study the history of the street that took over as the city's main street from the aptly named North and South Main Streets. The results of my endeavours prompted more questions than they answered. Who were the people that created and named the street? Had their motivation in choosing to name it after St Patrick any particular local or national historical context? How

Facing page: early seventeenth-century map of Cork showing shipping on the river channels between the islands.
(Courtesy Cork City Library)

has the street changed over the course of more than 200 years? Has the street an identity and what is the place of St Patrick's Street in the history of Cork?

St Patrick's Street in Cork will be considered from a number of historical perspectives. Chapter 1 will give a brief outline of the city's development through the ages, from its origins as an early monastic settlement into a medieval walled town and then a commercially successful Atlantic seaport in the seventeenth and eighteenth centuries. Some of the dynamics most relevant to this process, including trade and the reclamation of the marshlands, will be highlighted, as will be the prehistory of the area today known as St Patrick's Street.

In Chapter 2 the 'Place and Identity' of the street will be examined, including how it came to be named after the national saint and became a legacy that was passed on to future generations. Research has led to an acceptance of 1783 as the starting date of the street and this is confirmed by an examination of contemporary newspapers in that year and those before it. This book, however, will further reveal the precise week in which an announcement regarding the development of the street was made and then followed almost immediately by the first public usage of the name 'St Patrick's Street'. A physical portrait of the street will also be undertaken to reveal something of its enduring culture through time; the degree of affluence on the street and its place as the centre of transport in the city. It is a natural instinct to want a sense of what the street looked like early in the course of its history, but since photography did not begin until the latter half of the nineteenth century other methods will be pursued to achieve this goal, including consideration of evidence from earlier times that remains on the street to this day as well as contemporary written accounts.

The street was completed with the opening of the first St Patrick's Bridge in 1789. Chapter 3 tells the story of the bridge from its construction in that year to its destruction by a flood in 1853. A temporary wooden bridge was then located at the site until a permanent replacement was built in the 1860s.

Chapter 4 looks at the 'People of St Patrick's Street': those who formed and shaped the street and gave it an identity; those who inherited that legacy and reshaped it to suit their own needs and times; and the men and women for whom St Patrick's Street was a central part of their lives. No profile of the people of St Patrick's Street would be complete without reference to

a number of key individuals, from the largely unheralded social activist William Thompson, who grew up on the street, to a variety of successful business people. This chapter will also ask how St Patrick's Street became so central to people's lives when it is nowhere near the centre of political power at City Hall, has no church or cathedral, and is some distance from the various sports grounds. The answer lies in the mass gatherings of the people. When they wanted to celebrate or protest, to pray or to praise, they came together on the main street of the city to make their statement. One such gathering was in October 1864, when 100,000 people attended the unveiling of a monument to one of the greatest Corkmen, Fr Theobald Mathew. Today it is known simply as 'the Statue'.

Crowds gathered on a ruined St Patrick's Street following the burning on the night of 11 December 1920.
(Courtesy Michael Lenihan)

A commercial portrait of the street will also be undertaken in Chapter 5, using primarily the trade directories. This analysis will trace its progression from an area where a number of business strands were located to one that is almost completely devoted to retail. It will graphically illustrate that progression from 1787, when 10 per cent of the listed businesses were retail outlets, to 1997, when the figure was 80 per cent. Furthermore, examination of the valuations of the properties, using those of the Pipe Water Company of 1809 and *Griffith's Valuations* of the 1850s will show that the street was from the outset a place of high status and value.

In Chapter 6, one of the most famous and violent weeks on St Patrick's Street is examined: June 1870, when a tailors' strike erupted into street-battles with police and considerable damage was done to the premises on the street. Despite this turmoil, many changes and developments occurred in the latter half of the nineteenth century and these are dealt with in Chapter 7. Between 1891 and 1920, too, a number of significant events occurred in Cork's history that form the basis of Chapter 8: St Patrick's Day parades were reinstated with official political involvement; many of the businesses on the street attended the international exhibition of 1902; King Edward VII processed through St Patrick's Street; and the city was spared the destruction that was wrought on Dublin in 1916. That good fortune, however, would change four years later.

The so-called 'Burning of Cork' on the night of 11 December 1920 was a major event in the history of St Patrick's Street. The scale of destruction caused by the British Auxiliaries through arson and violence was immense and entire sections of the street's south side were completely destroyed. For the people of Cork gathered on the street the next morning, what lay before them in a rubble heap was not just brick and stone but all that the centre of the city meant to them. Within seven years, however, the street was resurrected from the ashes. Chapter 9 tells the story of the street's destruction and reconstruction. From the outset a determination to restore Cork city commercially was as important as the desire to have an aesthetically pleasing streetscape. This story of the restoration of St Patrick's Street gives an insight into Cork society at the time and is arguably more important than that of the burning.

Chapter 10 looks at the street as experienced by the people of Cork through the remainder of the twentieth century; the changes in the shops and various premises on the street; the arrival of new forms of transport and entertainment; and how St Patrick's Street became central in the lives of all Cork people. Finally, Chapter 11 looks at the changes that have occurred on the street in the first decade of the twenty-first century.

In the course of this book a number of key words are proposed as crucial to the attempt to locate St Patrick's Street in the history of Cork. The street, created partially through *investment*, has an *identity* that is clearly associated with its *name* in the minds of Cork people. It is a *legacy* not just in stone and brick but also in tradition and custom and is *central* to the lives of Cork people.

A series of pictures is also presented throughout the book to contribute a visual element to the narrative, substantiate the findings, recollect the past and thereby perpetuate memories. Image and imagination are thus united in the interpretation of the photographs that tell of St Patrick's Street's past. The pictures have two other dimensions. As an archive they both store and disseminate information. As evidence they arguably prove a lived experience.[2] Four factors determined the picture-selection process. Firstly, the pictures represent different eras in the history of the street; secondly, they represent an event or events in the linear narrative of the street's history: thirdly, the pictures are chosen to best support the arguments outlined in this book: lastly, material chosen is generally available in the public domain. Some of the pictures are taken from archive film footage of Cork, footage of the 'Burning of Cork', a tourist film made in the 1930s, and more modern film including work on the recent redevelopment of the street and the opening which Beth Gali attended.

Catalan architect Beth Gali, who was responsible for the early twenty-first century redesign of St Patrick's Street.

1 Early History

Celtic Beginnings

The origin of Cork city lies in the era of monasticism that prevailed in Ireland following the mission of St Patrick. The year 606 has been suggested as a likely date for the foundation of its first monastery, after a holy man called Finbarr came to a place known as Corcach Mór Mumhan, the great marsh of Munster, and settled on the slopes overlooking a series of marshy islands in the valley below.[1] This date, however, is highly speculative.[2] What is certain is that by the end of the seventh century a monastic settlement did exist in Cork, the *Annals of the Four Masters* recording the death of 'Suibhne, son of Maelumha, successor of Bairre of Corcach' in the year 680.[3] Donnchadh Ó Corráin has written of how Cork, along with Kildare, Clonmacnoise, Clonard and others, was one of the great monasteries of the period.[4] Thus it must be seen as part of an island-wide development of settlements that were monastic in nature.

Celtic society at this time was 'tribal and rural in nature' with many local kingdoms (*túatha*) scattered throughout the land, not answerable to any central authority.[5] This has been suggested as one of the reasons for the development of a monastic rather than a diocesan form of religious structure.[6] Some monasteries were founded on land donated by local kings. The abbotship was often hereditary and relations with the royal dynasties very close – often familial. The abbot was responsible for both the monastery itself and the lay society associated with it: the pilgrims, penitents and 'monastic tenants' who lived on and cared for the monastic

Facing page: eighteenth-century map of Cork showing shipping on the main river channel. (Courtesy Cork City Library)

13

lands.[7] To these people the monks provided spiritual and educational services and in return payment was made with produce and labour.[8] The monasteries, therefore, 'ruled by aristocrats … and important centres of economic activity', were central to the surrounding lay society.[9] Ó Corráin suggests 'it is fair to assume that they [the abbots] controlled economic resources in accord with their dignity'.[10]

Into this brief profile of Celtic monastic character, Cork sits comfortably. Jefferies describes how it was 'controlled by Abbots of the royal dynasty [of Munster]'. He goes on to say how they 'governed the rich lands of the Uí Meic Iair … located between Cork and Ovens'.[11] Thus the settlement at Cork was closely associated with the hinterland and benefited from the resources available. With regard to study and learning in Cork, Ó Corráin has written that it can be traced 'with certainty to the beginning of the eighth-century' while for Bolster 'Cork was to Munster – a guiding light, an oasis in the desert, to which flocked the sons of neighbouring chiefs and many others'.[12]

From this period in Cork's history, the legacy to future generations included a 'centre role' in a region of rich agricultural land capable of yielding a harvest of wealth. It also included the tenets of Celtic Christianity, from St Patrick through St Finbarr to future generations; a faith continuum to which both sides of the Catholic/Protestant divide would still claim attachment a millennium after Cork's foundation.

Viking Times

The Viking period for Cork resulted in further development of the settlement's 'centre' role in the region and also a shift from being a monastic settlement to an urban one: a town. Much of this change was achieved through a process that many centuries later would again prove crucial to the development of the modern city – reclamation of the marshlands.

From the Scandinavian lands to the northeast, following their plunder of Scotland and England, the Vikings attacked the monasteries in Ireland. The first penetrations came from the Norwegians at the turn of the ninth century. Historians are agreed that Cork was plundered a number of times following the first Viking experience *c.* 820 but there is disagreement as to the situation thereafter.[13] From about 850, however, across the country 'the great raids of the ninth century were over'.[14] The second phase of penetration came primarily from the Danes early in the tenth century and this time many who came stayed on. Their assimilation into Irish society over the ensuing century can be sketched in broad strokes. Across the country groups formed alliances with local kings and were 'drawn more and more into Irish affairs, playing their own parts in the complex and shifting alliances of the little kingdoms'.[15] Others formed bases in harbours around the coastline and developed centres of trade, including Waterford, Wexford, Cork, Limerick and Dublin. With time 'the population of the Norse towns turned Christian and finally in speech and habit almost Irish'.[16]

It is not surprising that the Vikings formed a town at Cork given the excellence of the harbour, its inland location to which larger vessels could navigate and the suitability of the surrounding hinterland. According to O'Sullivan, 'the absence of a substantial town somewhere on the Lee, convenient to the harbour, would be contrary to the ordinary development of all the civilised communities of Europe'.[17] As elsewhere 'the Vikings who settled at Cork arrived at some kind of understanding with the leading men of the neighbouring ecclesiastical community'.[18] The urban development established by the Vikings was located on the southern of the two islands that eventually formed the medieval town. Excavations have uncovered a 'wooden walkway extending from the south bank of the river and conceivably across it to the south island, very close to the South Gate Bridge'. Just downstream was 'the little wooden harbour … where small ships and boats put in'. This was used by 'Cork's Hiberno-Viking merchants' engaged in trade and was 'in close proximity to major routes extending north and south of the [River] Lee'.[19] Connecting these two areas was the spinal main street that today we know as the North Main Street and South Main Street.

The settlement at Cork was no longer just an ecclesiastical centre but a trading town which was central to the whole south Munster region. Major route ways connected the surrounding hinterland to the town which now had a distinctive urban shape centred upon a main spine. It can be concluded that the creation of an infrastructure for the boats that moored at the small harbour, and for the town itself, required some reclamation of the marshlands. This was not a process that only the Norse in Cork engaged in. In Dublin, 'within a century, the Vikings had started to reclaim land from the [River] Liffey to make a stable waterfront'.[20]

From the Viking period 'the gift of the Norsemen to Ireland was her own coastline, her sea-port towns, the beginning of her civic communication and her trade'.[21] In Cork, one crucial legacy was the earliest reclamation of the marshlands in pursuit of urban development, a legacy that would be embraced and advanced in the modern city.

The Normans

The arrival of the Normans in the 1170s brought to Cork the third element in what Bradley and Halpin have called the 'fusion of many diverse cultural traditions' that contributed to the emerging culture of the main town in south Munster.[22] Over the previous century Cork had developed under Norse influence into a seaport from which cloth, corn, honey, wine, furs, hides and fish as well as slaves were traded.[23] Such was the importance of Cork that Diarmaid McCarthy, King of Desmond, chose it as his capital in the twelfth century. When he finally surrendered the city to the Normans in 1177 its importance was consolidated by King Henry II's granting of a charter to the city and of the surrounding lands to his knights Robert FitzStephen and Milo de Cogan.[24] Thus did Henry II lay the foundation for what he hoped would be considerable future benefits accruing to the Crown. The royal charter would 'promote the fortunes' of Cork to this end.[25]

Similar processes were occurring across Europe where a 'massive migratory movement' was 'at the root of urban growth'. From the tenth to the thirteenth centuries economic trends were improving with merchants investing capital in pursuit of commercial profits.[26] 'The chartered borough was one of the standard methods of economic development employed throughout medieval Europe.'[27] Two migratory movements, those of the Vikings and the Normans, had brought Cork to this point in its history. Cork's charters were a royal declaration of administrative governance as well as a means of facilitating investment and economic development and marked 'the participation of Cork' in this European movement.[28] The city's second charter, granted in 1242, encouraged merchants to acquire holdings in the city by granting them freedom from tolls and customs and a monopoly of trade within their own jurisdiction.[29] Thus, merchants ensured the continued development and prosperity of Cork through imports – including wine from France – and exports, both of which strengthened during the thirteenth century. For the export of certain commodities (wool, woolfells and hides), O'Sullivan ranked Cork second of the four main city ports: Dublin, Cork, Waterford and Limerick.[30] Other exports included wheat, beef, pork, fish and malt.[31] The aggregate effect of this trade was to create a prosperous place with 'on-going improvements being made in the fabric of the city'.[32] It can be concluded that with economic expansion and a degree of fiscal and administrative organisation stemming from the early charters, Cork's merchant class grew wealthier through trade which was largely based in agricultural production.

1250–1599

In the following centuries the fortunes of Cork were directly associated with that of the surrounding hinterland. When, as happened in the fourteenth century, famine, disease, climate change and war impacted on the region and agricultural productivity fell dramatically, the effect upon the city was calamitous. Not alone was its prosperity effected, with customs returns dropping from £400 to £118 between 1276 and 1332, but the area could 'no longer provide sufficient food to feed the people of the city'.[33] The merchants, however, are recognised as having contributed greatly to Cork's survival. According to Jefferies: 'its merchants continued to provide an indispensable service' and 'to engage in significant levels of trading'. [34]

Physically, Cork's most dominant feature was its walls, built towards the end of the twelfth century and a constant drain on the city's resources.[35] Within the city, although rich and poor lived side by side, the better houses were those of the merchants and from the fourteenth century on these were being built of stone 'with slate or stone tiled roofs'.[36] The spinal main street stretched from the north to the south bridges, and from this ran the multitude of laneways, lined either side by houses, where the majority of the residents lived.[37] A river channel ran through the centre of the town, beneath the Middle Bridge and along where Castle Street is located today. In medieval times this was the quayside that served the port of Cork and it is shown on a number of the earliest maps of the city.[38] From these maps it can be seen that one possible access channel to the port was that which flowed where St Patrick's Street is today, between two marshy islands to the east of the walled town.

Reclamation and Expansion: 1600–1780

The seventeenth and eighteenth centuries were periods of dramatic change across all aspects of Cork life. The population increased dramatically; civic

> aforesaid Mayor and Sheriffs and Com...ality of the aforesaid city and their successors that ... City ...ork and all and singular the houses, ...ds, water and watercourses, soil and foundation... standing, lying, being and extending from the outside part of the wall of the said City of Cork on all sides whatsoever for the space and circuit of three miles according to the form of the statute passed in our Kingdom of England, to be measured within the space of one year after the date of these presents . . . from the said extern part of the Wall of the City of Cork to be measured to a great stone or other plain and remarkable sign to remain for ever . . . . the same may and shall be one County of itself, distinct and separate from our County of Cork, and from every other county whatsoever in our said Kingdom of Ireland . . . and that it shall for ever hereafter be named and called by the name of the "County of the City of Cork" (excepting

Text taken from the charter of 1608 granted by King James 1.

administration and political representation became exclusively Protestant domains; and there was a huge increase in the volume of trade as well as a change in its nature and content. All of these factors were directly associated with investment and land reclamation beyond the city walls.

Against a backdrop of the Catholic Counter-Reformation, the Battle of Kinsale in 1601 and the Elizabethan plantations, religious tensions became an increasingly significant part of Cork life. Mark McCarthy has argued that Cork's Catholic families 'certainly maintained a form of resistance' to the attempted imposition of the Protestant religion on them by the Crown and that 'hostility to the English state in the city of Cork at the beginning of the seventeenth century clearly went under the banner of Counter-Reformation.'[39]

A rebellion in support of King Charles I against his adversaries in Parliament began in Ulster in October 1641, spread southwards to Munster and resulted in the expulsion of the majority of the Catholic population from Cork city on 26 July 1644, on which day also 'the civil authority ceased in Cork'.[40] Although some wealthier Catholics were allowed to stay in the city at first, further orders of expulsion were issued the following month. In time many Catholics returned to the city, only to be re-expelled under the Cromwellian regime of the late 1640s.[41] By the end of the 1650s, 'the real estate and resources of Cork city and county had been transferred into the possession of the Protestant English community'.[42] Civic administration was completely in Protestant hands and a census of

Ireland in 1659 showed that almost two-thirds of the Cork city population were categorised as English.[43]

Parish	English	Irish
Christ Church	415	287
St Peter's	265	122
Total	680	409

The supremacy of the English Protestant population within Cork city was challenged in 1686 when the Catholic King James II ordered that his co-religionists have their status restored. When the Protestants in the city failed to comply he reconstituted the Corporation and gave the Catholics a two-thirds majority. It was a short-lived victory. Cork was besieged during the war between James and William of Orange in 1689–90, the walls severely damaged by cannon mounted in the suburbs and the city taken after less than a week's resistance.[44] Protestants regained control of all aspects of city life and 'rigorously excluded' the Catholic population.[45] Catholics would remain excluded from official civic authority for a century and a half.

The tumultuous events of the early 1600s, the 1640s and the war of 1689–90 interrupted but by no means halted the advancing prosperity of Cork during the seventeenth and eighteenth centuries. The periods of peace allowed people in the hinterland to restore their scattered flocks; there was also a marked improvement in inland transport facilitating the movement of produce to the city and Cork grew to the status of an Atlantic European port.[46] Key events that contributed to Cork's development during this period included the granting in 1608 of another charter to the city, privilege number four of which stated: 'our aforesaid City of Cork and all … standing, lying, being and extending from the outside part of the wall of the said City of Cork on all sides whatsoever for the space and circuit of three miles … shall be one county of itself'.[47] This was a significant milestone on Cork's journey to becoming a modern city. Other factors included the transferring of slaughterhouses to outside the walls in the early 1600s, a sign of increased trade in meat as well as early moves beyond the old medieval core.[48] The Cattle Acts of the 1660s, meanwhile, preventing the import of Irish cattle to Britain, forced producers to seek new markets, which they did successfully through increased trade with the expanding transatlantic British empire and the Caribbean.[49] The trade in victuals and animal by-products grew sharply and the quality and relative cheapness of the Cork product drew large fleets of shipping to the port resulting in more employment for large numbers of people who now migrated to the city, thereby changing the nature of trade and increasing the population.[50]

The growths in population and trade that took place in Cork during the seventeenth century were major factors behind the most significant development of the period: the reclamation of the marshlands beyond the old medieval walls. An early seventeenth-century map of the city gives an indication of movement into the marshlands (Figure 1). Item thirteen on the map's legend locates an entrance fort on the North-Eastern Marsh while item fourteen is listed as a walkabout. In a map of the city dated 1690 (Figure 2), that same marsh is shown built upon and at the eastern end an area is marked 'custom house'.[51] This is significant, showing that the decisions taken by the elite controlling group reflected what they perceived to be the requirements of the city, i.e. their own personal priorities of facilities for trade including a new Custom House and the development of warehouses and quayside space to accommodate increasing volumes of shipping which as early as the 1680s had grown to a figure of fifty ships owned by Cork merchants alone.[52]

In promoting such developments the Corporation leased the marshlands to willing developers.[53] Thus, men such as Aldermen Timothy Tuckey and Noblett Dunscombe obtained possession of entire islands

Figure 1 *(Left)* Early map of Cork, 1610, showing 'Entrance Fort' and 'Walk-About'. (Courtesy Cork City Library)

Figure 2 *(Right)* Map of Cork, *c*. 1690, showing built-up marshland beyond the walled town including the 'Custom House' location. (Courtesy Cork City Library)

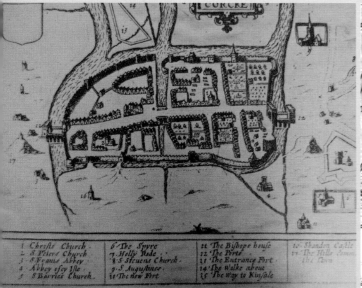

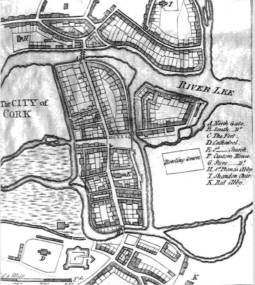

on which they developed streets, quaysides and warehouses.[54] Other investments occurred too. The Hoare brothers, who were involved in politics and trading, became the first bankers operating in the city.[55] With the lapsing of the Navigation Acts a number of Cork merchants set up a sugar refinery.[56] Some of the infrastructure developments are seen on Carty's map of 1726: on the North-Eastern Marsh, ships at the quaysides; six streets leading to a quay on the channel that ran where St Patrick's Street is today; five running to the main north channel (Figure 3); on Dunscombe's Marsh, five blocks for development with streets leading to another quay on the south side of today's St Patrick's Street (Figure 4). All of these developments symbolise not just the physical element of a changing city but also the willingness on the part of entrepreneurial merchant traders to invest in such changes. Another symbolic event was the closure of the old Watergate in 1714.[57] This was followed by the infilling of Daunt's Square thereby connecting the quays and the water channel of today's St Patrick's Street to the old city.[58]

Thus investment and development were clearly taking place in the marshlands and these were of sufficient value to merit inclusion in wills as early as 1709. On 30 May that year Jonathan Perrie willed 'his dwelling house on North East Marsh in parish Christ church'; in 1728 Henry Lumley willed 'his estate on the Marsh of Cork'; in 1737 Jane Craggs willed her 'dwelling house, garden, etc. situate without the Watergate of City of Cork'.[59]

Figure 3 (Left) Section of Carty's map, 1726, showing shipping and street development to the north of the St Patrick's Street channel.
(Courtesy Cork City Library)

Figure 4 (Right) A different section of Carty's map, 1726, showing street development on Dunscombe's Marsh, to the south of the St Patrick's Street channel.
(Courtesy Cork City Library)

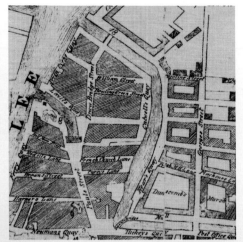

Figure 5 A section of Smith's map of Cork, 1750, showing streets to the north and south of the St Patrick's Street channel and Hoare's and Calwell's Quays. (Cork City Library)

Figure 6 Part of Rocque's Map, 1759, showing streets north and south of the St Patrick's Street channel. (Cork City Library)

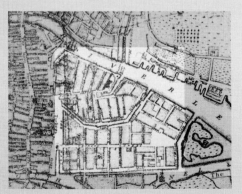

Figure 7 Connor's 1774 map of Cork showing location of newly developed centre to the east of old walled city. The highlighted area shows the fully built-up North-Eastern and Dunscombe's Marshes. (Cork City Library)

The eighteenth century saw a continuation of this development of the new city as what Mark McCarthy called 'speculative merchant capital' continued to be invested.[60] Trade continued to be the mainstay of Cork's wealth and success.[61] In a ledger from the Hoare Bank, accounts for trade journeys to places such as Lisbon and Jamaica are recorded, listing as cargo some of the main items exported from the city at the time such as beef and butter.[62] In a map of Cork dated 1750, both sides of the channel where St Patrick's Street is today were operating as quaysides and were named on the map as Hoare's Quay and Calwell's Quay (Figure 5).[63] In Rocque's map of 1759 seven streets are shown leading to Calwell's Quay (Figure 6), while in the later Connor's map, both islands either side of the St Patrick's Street channel are shown fully blocked (Figure 7). The infilling of city streets beyond Daunt's Square had begun and the Grand Parade channel is shown as a wide and spacious street.

Conclusion

Just as in Celtic, Viking and Norman times, Cork, at the end of the late medieval period, reflected dynamics and changes occurring elsewhere. As Dublin expanded eastwards, so also did Cork.[64] As the population grew nationally so too did Cork's. In economic terms the southern capital developed more rapidly than many other places. Thus, from a position whereby Cork during the sixteenth century 'was inferior to the other three Irish towns [Dublin, Limerick and Galway] in cross-channel shipping', it was by the end of the seventeenth century 'the second city in trade and magnitude'.[65] While Cork's merchant fleet 'was growing rapidly', 'the number of ships owned by Galway merchants had fallen'.[66]

In religious terms also, Cork was an example of the broader national situation with Catholics excluded from virtually all positions of power and control. However, 'Catholic tradesmen and merchants in the towns fared better under the penal laws than did their co-religionists in rural areas'.[67] A 'spirit of tolerance grew' and 'based upon economical motives', Catholics having garnered wealth, particularly from the provisions trade through connections to the rural hinterland, 'it was necessary for the members of both religions to find some way of living together'.[68] In Cork the formation of a Committee of Merchants in 1769 for the furtherance of trade, consisting of both Catholic and Protestant members, symbolised that in an environment where the severity of the penal restrictions on Catholics was waning, expediency won over other considerations. The development of the Masonic Lodges with membership determined by social status rather than religion 'for those Protestant and Catholic gentlemen who for whatever reason were uncomfortable with the dominant political values' was another such symbol.[69] Finally, a declaration of loyalty to the crown in 1776 (the year of the American Revolution) signed by 160 Cork people, largely merchants and approximately a quarter of whom were Catholic, is a further example of the inclusion of Catholics in matters of shared interest.[70]

In just over a thousand years, Cork developed from one of a number of early monastic settlements to the second city in the land; a wealthy trading port on the Western European/North American highway, benefiting from the produce of a rich hinterland. The forces that shaped the city were many; among the strongest were economy and trade. Early Viking reclamations helped form a trading town; after dark periods in the fourteenth and fifteenth centuries, the merchant community was highlighted as greatly assisting a degree of recovery. In the post-Kinsale period 'the 1610s, 1620s and 1630s proved to be a time of lasting military stability … accompanied by morphological, demographic and economic expansion'.[71] The latter half of the seventeenth century saw an extended and highly profitable provisions industry develop, while following the siege of the city in 1690 and the Jacobite War, 'the pace of physical recovery was vigorous'.[72] The wealth generated by the Cork trading operations continued to grow as the eighteenth century progressed and this both facilitated and demanded investment by a politically dominant merchant class to the east of the old walled town. A modern phase of marshland reclamation and dockland development ensued. Increasing volumes of shipping moored at newly developed quaysides on the reclaimed marshlands. Crucially for modern Cork, the river channel that ran where St Patrick's Street is today was flanked either side by newly developing areas of the expanding city. The infilling of this channel would join together the two former marshy islands and at once create a new centre for Cork and a new main street.

2 Place and Identity

The addition of the Cross of St Patrick to those of St Andrew of Scotland and St George of England in 1801, thereby creating the 'Union Jack' flag of the Kingdom of Great Britain and Ireland, can be interpreted in a number of ways.[1] For Ascendancy Protestants, it symbolised their union with Britain.[2] That the Cross of St Patrick was added indicated that he was identified with and symbolised their particular brand of Irishness.[3] For those who rejected the Act of Union of 1801, both Catholic and Protestant, the addition of the cross seemed a betrayal.[4] No longer did they have an Irish identity of their own; rather it was now embedded in a greater United Kingdom.[5] St Patrick, it is clear, was accorded different status by the different sectors in society; a political figure, brother-knight to St George and St Andrew to the Protestant Ascendancy, but also patron of a Catholic majority seeking equality and emancipation and a hero of the lower orders who celebrated with gusto his feast day on 17 March each year.[6] Thus, both before and after the Act of Union, an important feature for each group in Irish society was their own narrative of identity; who they were and what their place was in a changing world.

Narratives of Identity

Edward Relph has written that in the relationship between community and place 'each reinforces the identity of the other' and that 'people are their place and a place is its people'.[7] Despite being written almost 200 years after the Act of Union, Relph's analysis of place and identity is still valid for discussion of that period in Ireland. The majority of the population, both

Facing page: **St Patrick's Street in the 1870s.**
(Courtesy Amy and Chris Ramsden, The Day Collection)

Catholic and Protestant, saw themselves as Irish and set about creating appropriate narratives of identity. The creation of that identity was a crucial element in the second half of the eighteenth century.

For Relph, the three elements of the identity of a place were its physical characteristics; the activities, or what occurred in the place; and the meanings, which are the perspectives with which people or groups see a place. Since people shape a place, are the actors who perform upon the stage that is a place, and hold the viewpoints and understandings that constitute the meanings of a place, it can be said that people and place are absolutely interconnected. It follows that for a given set of people, 'a place' becomes 'this' or 'our place' whether in the macro (a continent or a country) or the micro (a town or a street). People identify with their place and it becomes part of their identity. Statements of that identity are expressed through the use of symbols, for example, flags and iconography. One of the most significant elements of identifying a place is the name it is given: giving it a name 'turns a space into a place'.[8] Through her extensive work on the iconography of the Dublin streetscape, Yvonne Whelan adds to the conceptual framework within which people, place and identity can be examined. She argues that physical form has a powerful role in the construction of identity. It is the product of agents active in social, political and institutional processes and symbolically reproduces the cultural norms and values of dominant groups in society. Signs and symbols 'play a crucial role' and among these are public statuary, architecture and, crucially, street names.[9]

O'Connell Street in Dublin is more than just the main street of the capital; it is the main street of the nation.[10] First laid out as Drogheda Street by Henry Moore, Earl of Drogheda, during the expansion of the city eastwards from the old medieval core in the eighteenth century, an important landowner, Luke Gardiner, developed a tree-lined walkway on Drogheda Street which was then renamed Sackville Street after Lionel Cranfield Sackville, Duke of Dorset and Lord Lieutenant of Ireland from 1731–7 and again from 1751–5.[11] The context of the street naming convention employed in this Dublin example illustrates that it was 'major power brokers' after whom the developments were named, thereby perpetuating 'in the streetscape and in the minds of the inhabitants the memory of historical figures or events deemed worthy of remembering by those in charge'.[12] As elements of the cultural landscape, street names, statues and monuments all play a powerful role in forging narratives of identity. In the lead-up to Independence, a crucial strategy on the part of nationalists was the renaming of streets in an attempt to expunge the British identity and create a new narrative identifying with a glorious nationalist past. In this manner Dublin's Sackville Street became O'Connell Street.[13]

Similarities abound between Dublin and the situation in Cork. In both places expansion eastwards during the eighteenth century led to the creation of a new city centre and a new main street. The Wide Street Commissioners were appointed to oversee these developments in both cities; in Dublin in 1757 and Cork in 1765.[14] Street names have also been altered in both cities in pursuit of a new nationalist narrative of identity: Sackville Street to O'Connell Street in Dublin and George's Street to Oliver Plunkett Street and King Street to MacCurtain Street in Cork. There is, however, a strain in the comparison because Cork's main street was and still is St Patrick's Street – named after the national saint as opposed to a 'major power broker' and unchanged through its history. This chapter looks at the context in which Cork's main street came to be called St Patrick's Street.

St Patrick's Street, Cork

The infilling of the river channel that ran between the North-Eastern and Dunscombe Marshes, flanked by Hoare's, Calwell's and the Long Quays, led to the formation of St Patrick's Street, a process that took a number of years to bring to completion. Research has led to an acceptance of 1783 as the correct date for the beginning of this work. Examination of the *Hibernian Chronicle* for that year and those before it reveals that the first public usage of the name St Patrick's Street occurred in 1783. Now, from another contemporary newspaper published in Cork – the *Volunteer Journal or Independent Gazetteer* – this book shows that the first usage of the name in the public forum occurred on Thursday 22 May 1783, immediately following an announcement regarding the formation of the street as well as calls for the naming of the new developments.

The *Volunteer Journal or Independent Gazetteer* (the *Journal*) was printed and published by John and Robert Baldwin of Marlborough Street. On Monday 31 March 1783, a notice appeared in the *Journal* saying that the Baldwins 'respectfully acquaint their friends and the public that their printing office is removed to the new house, number 9, next door to Mr Seymour's on the Long Quay'.[15] Over the following weeks a series of notices appeared offering a variety of items for sale at this premises. On Thursday 3 April the *Journal* had details of 'an elixir' that could be obtained. That advertisement was repeated on 7 and 10 April. On Thursday 24 April a reward was offered by Robert Baldwin at No. 9 Long Quay for information regarding a stolen or strayed small red-and-white spaniel. On Monday 28 April *Walkers and Exhams Magazine* for March was offered, and this was repeated on Thursday 1 May. Other businesses also advertised as operating on the Long Quay. On Monday 31 March Hardy & McGrath's auction room on the Long Quay advertised a grand china auction. On Thursday 3 April (and repeated on 7, 10, 14 and 17 April) George Seymour advertised his wares for sale at No. 8 Long Quay.[16]

Then, on Thursday 1 May 1783, the following item appeared under the Cork notices.

> We are happy to inform our readers that there is a probability of having the Long Quay dock arched over, the ensuing summer, nearly as far as the Crooked Billet Quay. The work is now going on with vigour, a presentment of 600L [pounds] having been obtained last assizes for this very useful purpose.[17]

Thus was it announced that the infilling of the river channel that would in time become St Patrick's Street was under way. In the *Journal* of 5 May, a letter signed by 'A Citizen' called for the naming of the new street developments, of which the following is an extract:

> Gentlemen …
>
> The present laudable spirit of improvement, I observe, has induced the Society of Arts and Sciences, lately established here, to encourage a general survey of the city in order to lay down an accurate map of its streets, lanes, alleys and quays etc. which will doubtless be of general utility: but when we consider that nearly one half of the streets, lanes, quays etc. are now destitute of names to distinguish them by, it were much to be wished that before the completion of the undertaking, proper names were fixed for them, and such exhibited in large letters on a board at the corner of every street (as in London and Dublin), which might be done at a small expense, but without it, no map that can be published of the city of Cork will be intelligible.
>
> A Citizen.[18]

On both Thursday 15 May and Monday 19 May, 'the printers hereof, No. 9 Long Quay' advertised *Walkers and Exhams Magazine* for sale. Then, on Thursday 22 May – the next edition of the *Journal* – the following notice appeared.

> Just arrived and to be had at the printers hereof, No. 9 St Patrick's Street (formerly Long Quay), Walkers Hibernian Magazine or Compendium of Entertaining Knowledge for April 1783.[19]

St Patrick's Street had arrived.

In the editions of 26 and 29 May and 2 June, the same notice appeared. By 23 June and in the following editions, John and Robert Baldwin advertised as being located at No. 9 St Patrick's Street with no further reference to the Long Quay.[20] In another contemporary newspaper, the *Hibernian Chronicle*, notices still appeared for businesses on the Long Quay. Deane & Co. advertised rock salt from their Lime and Salt Works on Maylor Street, the Long Quay.[21] Newfoundland Train Oil was offered for sale 'at the cellar under the auction room on the Long Quay'.[22] On Monday 14 July the death of a Mrs Freeman was recorded at her house on the Long Quay. Although these latter notices are dated after the aforementioned date of 22 May in the *Journal*, the name of St Patrick's Street was nonetheless becoming the norm.[23] In a notice regarding a collection to be taken in the city for the relief of the poor, Dr Townsend and Messrs Seymour, Coppinger and Gregg were appointed to collect on St Patrick's Street.[24] On 23 October Robert Travers was offering to lend £400 from his St Patrick's Street offices. On 10 November the death of James Cunningham, a wine and spirit merchant, was recorded at St Patrick's Street, while on 22 December Thomas Sheehan, a nursery and seeds man, announced he was moving his business from the Exchange to the Grand Parade corner of St Patrick's Street.[25]

Context

1 January 1780 was the day appointed for celebrating both the British victory at the Battle of Savannah during the American War of Independence and also the Act of Parliament that granted free trade to Ireland. Throughout the country there were great festivities and in Cork, following parades and the firing of salutes, 'the military, naval and several

other gentlemen had an elegant entertainment provided for them at the King's Arms Tavern'.

> That night there was the most general illumination known for many years. One house represented Hibernia in a dejected manner, but supported by St Patrick who was looking up to a cherubim coming from England with FREE TRADE and pointing to a distant view of commerce to Africa, Europe and America, which pleases the patron of our isle so much that he salutes the angel with a kaad meel a faltera [*sic*].[26]

The scene described is full of symbolism. Firstly, 'Hibernia in a dejected manner' showed that Ireland was an unhappy country because she did not hold her rightful place in the world as symbolised by 'commerce with Africa, Europe and America'. The coming of 'FREE TRADE' would bring her to that rightful place. St Patrick supporting Hibernia illustrated that the patron saint had a crucial role as champion, protector and icon of Ireland. Of great significance was that this scene took place in Cork city. Thus Cork was a participant in the national event and, most importantly, those Cork people responsible for the illuminations recognised the role of St Patrick in society at that time.

From the mid-eighteenth century, three factors in particular had contributed to changing undercurrents in Irish society. Firstly, a perception of increased security under the Hanoverian regime on the part of the Protestant ruling elite; secondly, a Protestant middle class disillusioned by the corruption, decision-making and policies of the ruling elite; and thirdly, a rising Catholic middle class growing wealthy through trade and commerce. These three factors were closely interrelated. The middle-class Protestants felt increasingly removed from their Ascendancy co-religionists and disillusioned with the regulation and order imposed from above.[27] The introduction of trade restrictions against Ireland, for example, was seen as a statement by England that Ireland was a single all-inclusive entity, at least in trade. Protestant and Catholic alike were all 'Irish'.[28] In an era that saw a new commercial spirit developing, this resulted in the Protestant Irish becoming alienated from Britain over the economic constraints imposed upon them.[29] So also with the growing numbers of Catholic merchants whose wealth was increasing at this time. 'From the early 1760's Dublin Catholic merchants were playing a part in the commercial affairs of the country through participation in the Committee of Merchants.'[30] They were increasingly accepted into mainstream society as the ruling elite became more secure and oversaw a relaxation in the administration of the Penal Laws. Nevertheless, excluded from the civic and administrative decision-making process, they also resented externally imposed controls. The political elite at the top of Irish society preserved their existence through acceptance and compliance with the external controls in return for peerages and pensions.[31] In the rest of society, along with commercial discontent, there was also political discontent.

This rising spirit of disaffection contributed to the rise of the mainly middle-class Patriot movement of the 1760s.[32] The goal of this group was an accepted independent Irish identity within the British family. S. J. Connolly says that among the Protestant Irish, political autonomy was sought.[33] For Lecky, the position of Catholics was improving and a spirit of nationality had arisen.[34] Seeking to assert their identity, these sections of society embraced their Gaelic heritage. 'Buy Irish' campaigns were organised and there was an expectation that the upper echelons of society would, for the sake of local manufacturers, dress themselves in clothes made in Ireland.[35] There was also a marked increase in the celebration of St Patrick's Day, which in 1760 became a banker's holiday.[36] For many it was a 'popular holiday, an occasion for sports, recreation and drinking'.[37] A number of new societies such as the Ancient and Most Benevolent Order of the Friendly Brothers of St Patrick also developed.[38]

The use of the name St Patrick in this way illustrates that at this period in Irish history, the appropriation of the name and entity of the patron saint was employed by the different elements in society, citing him as their champion and protector, and representative of their unique and true Irish heritage and thus their identity. The Protestant Church in Ireland claimed to be the Church of St Patrick.[39] 'The Church of Ireland as a bulwark of the establishment, never failed to emphasise that its doctrines were conducive to order and stability in the eighteenth century and Patrick was invoked to legitimise this.'[40] Preaching in St Patrick's Cathedral, Dublin on 17 March 1756, Rev. William Henry said that St Patrick's banishment of the snakes was the banishment of wrath and strife and that the Church of Ireland alone could maintain order in the country.[41] Writing on the history of the Church of Ireland a hundred years later, the Rev. Arthur Edwards stated that 'every Irish bishop and clergyman … can clearly trace his spiritual authority and ecclesiastical descent from its ancient church of St Patrick'.[42]

St Patrick as represented in a nineteenth-century stained-glass window in St Vincent's Church, Sunday's Well.

(Courtesy sandraocallaghan.com)

The Catholic Church, too, claimed to be descended from St Patrick. William Gahan, an Augustinian preacher, said 'the holy Catholic religion, which was planted by St Patrick above thirteen hundred years ago … has been carefully transmitted to us, whole and entire, unchanged and uncorrupted'.[43] The new Catholic church built in Waterford in 1764 was named after St Patrick.[44] In 1795, the establishment of a seminary for the education of Catholic priests under the patronage of St Patrick illustrated both that his status in Ireland was accepted by the authorities and that he was the model for the Catholic priest that would emerge therefrom.[45] St Patrick was to the fore in all aspects of Irish life: patron of many societies; protector of social order; founding father to both sides of the sectarian divide. St Patrick became the icon for Ireland and Irishness.[46]

As support for the Patriot movement grew, they realised that some form of mass movement was needed to add weight to their claims. Furthermore, with a volatile international situation and the threat of invasion from France, it was both a statement of loyalty to the Crown and an assertion of Irish independence when a Volunteer movement was set up, beginning in Ulster in 1778 and spreading throughout the country. While the Volunteer movement was a Protestant one, Catholic leaders, keen to be involved in all aspects of public life, were quick to support the endeavour. In a number of areas Protestants welcomed Catholics into the movement.[47] The Volunteer mass gatherings and military displays were 'a great psychological affirmation of citizenship, of patriotism, of exclusive identity'.[48] These statements were clearly read by the government in London and along with other factors, such as a deteriorating economic situation, led to the granting of free trade to Ireland in 1779. There was joy and celebration throughout Ireland at this achievement. In Cork, the illumination showing St Patrick supporting Hibernia and welcoming free trade made a statement about Cork's position in the matter.

Henry Grattan said in the Irish House of Commons that 'while the Crown of Ireland was inseparably united to that of England, Ireland was by right a distinct kingdom'.[49] In 1782, with the amending of Poyning's Law and the repeal of the Declaratory Act, Ireland effectively achieved legislative independence. Two consequences of this were that 'in the exhilaration surrounding the events of 1778–82, enthusiasm for all things Gaelic reached new heights' and recognising the dynamics then occurring in Ireland, the London government sought to embrace events and control them.[50] To achieve this, an Order of Knights was instituted equivalent to those of the Garter and Bath in England and the Thistle in Scotland. The cream of the elite would receive this honour and thus remain in the King's gratitude. The patron chosen, thereby giving him the highest profile as protector of the Protestant political order, was St Patrick. The Order would be known as the Most Illustrious Order of the Knights of St Patrick.

The idea for this Order is attributed to George Nugent Temple Grenville, third Earl Temple, Lord Lieutenant of Ireland since September 1782 and brother to the Chief Secretary in London, William Grenville.[51] In a letter dated 2 January 1783, Earl Temple wrote to his brother with a list of suggested names – all of whom were Earls – who would receive the Order.[52] On 5 February, Earl Temple again wrote to his brother in London, this time informing him that 'half Dublin is mad about the Order' and expressed his hope that the installation would take place on 17 March, St Patrick's Day.[53] On 9 February he wrote that 'Clements the jeweller undertakes to have the collars and badges done in time for the 17th'. Concerned that the right impression would be given he wrote on 16 February that 'the *Gazette* writer, in announcing the Illustrious Order of St Patrick has left out the Most which shocks our Irish'. He urged that this be rectified. Finally on 7 March he wrote that 'all our preparations are ready'.[54]

On 17 March 1783, the installation of the Most Illustrious Order of the Knights of St Patrick took place in the Great Ballroom of Dublin Castle which at His Majesty's pleasure 'should be styled the Hall of St Patrick, which was done by proclamation'.[55] It was reported that 'all ranks of people in the streets to see the Knights etc pass and repass [*sic*] in their carriages to and from the Castle … formed a scene that is indescribable and which will long be remembered with pride and satisfaction by thousands of the sons and daughters of Hibernia'.[56]

Across society, St Patrick was identified as the iconic representative of Ireland and of Irishness. But this was not incompatible with allegiance to the Crown. It was no different in Cork. As early as 1758, one society with St Patrick as patron – the Most Ancient and Benevolent Order of the Friendly Brothers of Saint Patrick – had a branch operating in County Cork. Its secretary, John F. Harris, called for a meeting at the house of the widow Roycroft in Bandon on St Patrick's Day of that year.[57] Throughout Ireland Catholics sought to reassure the ruling order of their loyalty and in 1759 the Earl of Shannon conveyed a declaration of loyalty to the Lord Lieutenant, to which 124 leading Cork Catholics had penned their names.[58] The royal family was first prayed for in Roman Catholic chapels on 8 February 1768.[59] In September 1778 'the Bishop of Cork accompanied a great number of clergy and above 700 respectable Roman Catholics to take the oath of allegiance'.[60]

Cork at this time was a rapidly developing urban centre facilitating the growth of a large middle class. 'Legal and professional services for those who could afford to patronise the professions had been heavily concentrated in the city in the eighteenth century.'[61] The nature of the commodities available in the city suggested a select clientele.[62] Many of these commodities were imported; the main items of export from Cork – butter and other items of the provisions industry – created great wealth in the city and the formation of a Committee of Merchants in March 1769 was both a statement of the city's increasing commerciality and the desirability of non-denominational trade associations. The Committee of Merchants included both Catholics and Protestants from the outset.[63] Such was the dedication of Cork's commercial sector that the embargoes of the 1770s resulted in no fewer than four petitions being sent by the merchant community seeking free trade for their operations.[64] Here again, Cork was very much in step with the rest of the country.

The Rev. C. B. Gibson listed fifteen cavalry and thirty-six infantry units of the Volunteers operating in County Cork by 1782, and although David Dickson says that only a minority of the ninety-odd corps operating in south Munster welcomed Catholics, a number of these were in Cork city including the City Cavalry Corps and the Cork Boyne Corps.[65] Resolutions appeared in the *Hibernian Chronicle* of 28 March 1772 from the Bandon Corps 'that we look upon religious toleration as highly advantageous to society' and on 3 June from the Cork Boyne Corps 'that respectable men of every denomination be admissible into the Volunteer corps of the province'.[66] Yet again Cork was mirroring the national situation and this was reinforced, particularly in relation to St Patrick, when on 17 March 1783, the very day that the Knights of the Most Illustrious Order of Saint Patrick were being installed in Dublin, a number of Corps attended a ceremony at the Capuchin Friary. 'This day at the Capuchin Friary a sermon was preached by the Catholic priest, Rev. Arthur O'Leary, before a great number of the armed societies of this city. His subject was in part a beautiful and glowing description of the most interesting passages in the life of Saint Patrick.'[67] During the ceremony he referred to 'our honoured Volunteers' as 'the sons of Saint Patrick'.[68] One final connection with St

Patrick and between Cork and the national situation was that the Earl of Shannon, who was officer commanding the True Blue Cavalry and the True Blue Infantry (both of Cork) was on that day honoured as a Knight of the Most Illustrious Order of Saint Patrick at the ceremony in Dublin.[69]

It was at this time and in this context – that of an Irish identity being promulgated across all sectors of society and St Patrick being given a new status as champion, patron, protector and icon – that Cork named its new street, St Patrick's Street.

Decision Makers

According to Angela Fahy, 'Cork was a city dominated socially and economically in the eighteenth century by a merchant community' who were for the most part Protestant and Quaker and 'the Catholic population who made up 80 per cent of those living in the city had little opportunity to participate'.[70] Even among the minority Protestant community, however, power was in the hands of a small group known as the 'Friendly Club'. This exclusive group of Freemen was set up in the 1760s to retain power and control in the changing society of the time and comprised 'an exclusive body of about 350 – all Protestants, mostly Tories'.[71] This body controlled almost all matters in the city and it would have been from amongst these people that any decisions regarding the development of St Patrick's Street emanated.[72] 'The senior sheriff for the year was the club's president and one of his functions was to select the city's grand jury', those who adjudicated at the assizes.[73] As seen earlier it was money from the assizes that was granted for the infilling of the river channel to create St Patrick's Street.

Three bodies were closely associated with the creation and naming of St Patrick's Street. Firstly, the Corporation, consisting of the Mayor, the Sheriffs, Recorder, Common Speaker, Aldermen and as many Burgesses as required to make up a total of twenty-four. Those serving were selected from among the Freemen to which access was controlled by the Friendly Club. A number of decisions taken at Corporation meetings illustrate its involvement in the St Patrick's Street project. On 13 November 1781 they sought from Parliament an order 'enabling the Grand Jury at Assizes to be held for said City, to present money for arching over … for widening streets and public passages'; on 29 July 1785 £50 was made available to the Mayor 'towards purchasing the buildings which obstruct the passage of St Patrick's Street.[74] Secondly, a body whose very name would suggest that it was involved in the development of St Patrick's Street: the Commissioners for Making Wide and Convenient Streets, or more commonly the Wide Street Commissioners, established in Cork by Act of Parliament in 1765.[75]

There are no early records of Wide Street Commissioners proceedings, however, and apart from O'Sullivan's account, where he records that the Mayor, Recorder, Burgesses, etc. as well as John Hely Hutchinson and Henry Sheares were numbered among the Commissioners, no other work names those who were actually appointed. O'Sullivan goes on to say that because there was no provision in the Act of Parliament for funding, 'the work accomplished by them during the remainder of this century must have been practically nothing'.[76] A different interpretation to O'Sullivan's is possible. Modern historians credit the Wide Street Commissioners with the laying out of South Terrace, Dunbar Street and the widening of Castle, Tuckey and Shandon Streets prior to receiving funding in 1817.[77] The Wide Street Commissioners for Cork were established by the Act, 5 Geo. III, Ch.24, Sect.XII:

> And whereas many of the streets lanes and passages of the said city of Cork and the suburbs thereof are too narrow, by means whereof the trade of the said city is generally obstructed, be it enacted by the authority aforesaid that the Mayor and Recorder of the said city of Cork for the time being, the Right Honourable John Hely Hutchinson Esq. William Ponsonby Esq. Henry Sheares Esq. the several Aldermen of the said city for the time being, Hugh Lawton Esq. Francis Carelton Esq. Stephen Denroch Esq. Riggs Falkiner Esq. Bayle Rogers Esq. Walter Travers Esq. William Verling Esq. Simon Dring Esq. Luke Grant Esq. Kevan Izod merchant, Godfrey Baker merchant, Henry Wrixon Esq. and William Butler Esq. shall be and are hereby appointed commissioners for making wide and convenient streets, ways and passages in the said city of Cork and the suburbs thereof.[78]

On 20 March 1783 a notice appeared in the *Hibernian Chronicle*.

> The Commissioners for Widening the streets of the City of Cork, give notice to the several owners and persons in the grounds and houses formerly known by the name of the Cork Arms and extending from

thence to Paul's church and yard, that they intend to meet at the Council Chamber of the City of Cork, on Tuesday the twenty-fifth day of March, instant, at eleven o'clock in the forenoon, to treat with them for the purchase of their respective interests in the aforesaid grounds and houses; where the Commissioners request such owners or persons interested, will attend, otherwise the Commissioners must proceed to value the same, pursuant to the powers vested in them by law.
March 17, 1783.[79]

Some weeks later, an editorial appeared in the *Volunteer Journal* regarding a suggestion to the Committee for Making Wide and Convenient Streets and Avenues from several inhabitants of North Main Street.[80] Thus, in 1783, precisely at the time when the creation of St Patrick's Street began and was first named, the Wide Street Commissioners were certainly active. The significance of the identity of the Commissioners now becomes relevant.

Between 1765 and 1783 fewer than fifty people were named in Caulfield's *Council Book of the Corporation of Cork* as having served as Aldermen on the Corporation.[81] Under the legislation, these served as Wide Street Commissioners. Thus the Mayor, Recorder and Aldermen for 1783, along with those others named in the 1765 legislation or their successors, were the Wide Street Commissioners for 1783 and so both the Corporation and the Commissioners were largely the same people. Comparing them with the nearest directory available, that of Richard Lucas in 1787, at least three – John Thompson, Kevan Izod and John Webb – were listed as resident on St Patrick's Street; Richard Kellett was based on Drawbridge Street, adjacent to St Patrick's Street; and Vesian Pick, who served on the Corporation from 1778 (although he was not an Alderman until after 1796), was also listed as St Patrick's Street. Thus among the Wide Street Commissioners and the Corporation, there was the same minority who were either at the time or within four years living on St Patrick's Street and in whose interests it was to see it develop.

The development of St Patrick's Street was not a short term project; rather, it took a number of years to bring to completion. On 30 July 1787 Mayor Samuel Rowland gave notice that because of the decayed and ruinous condition of the old drawbridge at Drawbridge Street and 'as it now ceases to be of material utility on account of the arching in Patrick Street, to nearly approaching it' the timbers of the bridge were to be sold at auction.[82] Six months earlier, in January 1787, a committee had been appointed 'to receive proposals for building a bridge over the northern channel of the river'.[83] The development of St Patrick's Street, begun in 1783, can be said to have been brought to its final conclusion on 29 September 1789 with the opening of the new bridge whereby it was possible to enter the new street at one end, traverse its length and exit the other.[84]

The opening of the first St Patrick's Bridge, as reported on 1 October 1789 in the *Hibernian Chronicle*, introduces the Ancient and Honourable Fraternity of Free and Accepted Masons in the Province of Munster. In the latter half of the eighteenth century and early decades of the nineteenth century, a number of Masonic lodges in Cork had names which clearly associated them with the broad context within which, this chapter has argued, was located the development and naming of St Patrick's Street. Hibernian Lodge No. 95, originally constituted at Cashel, County Tipperary, transferred to Cork in 1750 and held its first meeting in the Globe Tavern where it continued to meet until 1776 when it moved to Hanover Street. Shamrock Lodge No. 27 was reconstituted on 20 December 1750 and St Patrick's Lodge, which had existed during the eighteenth century, possibly in Dublin, was revived in Cork in June 1808 under Master John Wrixon.[85]

Some of these were among those lodges that, having left the Corporation Chamber, processed through St Patrick's Street to the bridge and were met by the Wide Street Commissioners and the architect, who put the keystone of the last arch into place, performed the opening ceremony and, most significantly, 'called upon the Commissioners to mention the name intended for the new bridge, which being communicated, the Grand Almoner emptied his chalice of wine upon the keystone and in the name of the Ancient and Honourable Fraternity of the Free and Accepted Masons of the Province of Munster, proclaimed it St Patrick's Bridge'.[86] Thus are connected the three groups who had an involvement with the development of St Patrick's Street from its commencement in 1783 to its completion with the opening ceremony of St Patrick's Bridge in 1789. At the request of the Corporation, money from the assizes, granted by the Grand Jury (itself appointed by the leader of the Friendly Club), paid for the development. The Wide Street Commissioners were active at the time and consisted largely of the same membership as the Corporation, including the Aldermen and the Mayor. Departing from the Corporation

Chambers, the Fraternity of Freemasons, some of whose lodges had names associating them with St Patrick, paraded through St Patrick's Street and at the new bridge called upon the Commissioners to say its name.

This perspective on the earliest development of St Patrick's Street set out to examine when, why and by whom the project was undertaken. What can be concluded is that the project took place in a context whereby the patron St Patrick was an integral part of a developing national identity, acceptable to both the ruling Protestant minority and the Catholic majority whose place in society, although improving, was still largely one of powerlessness. Cork was manifestly associated with this context. The most symbolic statement of that context was the founding of the Order of the Most Illustrious Knights of St Patrick in March 1783. Eight weeks later a major new infrastructural development began in the city and almost immediately was called St Patrick's Street. This, however, did not conform to the naming convention, as in Dublin for example. The elite minority who held the reins of political power in Cork were Protestants, mostly from the merchant community, who for a number of years, while never willing to cede power to Catholics, had tolerated an increasing degree of Catholic involvement because commerce deemed it appropriate. The naming of the new street after St Patrick, which was in keeping with a national context and acceptable to both Catholics and Protestants, was most appropriate.

Flags in the Mason Lodge on Tuckey Street in Cork.

A Physical Portrait

1. On 18 January 1787, the Mayor of Cork, Samuel Rowland Esq., following a very dangerous fire at the premises of the merchant John Shea, expressed his astonishment that 'the fire engines belonging to the several parishes are now kept in such a wretched condition'. He also noted that pumps were 'much wanted in different parts of the city that are now arched over and thro' which the river formerly flowed open and unconfined for their benefit heretofore'.[87]

2. On 17 September 1801, the *Hibernian Chronicle* editorialised that 'nothing requires the interference of the Police so much as the shameful impunity with which car-men are allowed to drive their cars through the streets. Instead of leading their horses, they uniformly sit on their cars, by which disagreeable abuse no less than three children were driven over in Patrick's-Street last week'.[88]

3. Misfortune befell a lamplighter in October 1807 when he 'fell from his ladder on Patrick's-Street by which his back was broke'.[89]

4. On 10 December 1825, a notice appeared in the *Constitution* newspaper offering 'excellent building ground in St Patrick's Street to be let for building on'. The ground was situated between French Church Street and Academy Street, of length 58 feet 6 inches fronting onto St Patrick's Street, commanding three fronts, and ideally suited for speculation in 'an Arcade, Bazaar or extensive building'.[90]

These four reports form an introductory narrative to a physical portrait of the street encompassing the street surface, transport, services, and buildings, each of which has provided a permanent contribution the street's narrative of identity.

Street Surface

The infilling of the river channels between the reclaimed marshy islands marked the final phase in the development of a new city centre for Cork. This process involved the arching over of the channels and then the creation of a surface on top. At no point in the creation of St Patrick's Street was the course of the river channel altered. Thus, today's distinctive curved shape of St Patrick's Street is directly attributable to the course of the river channel that runs beneath.[91] The width of the street is also a function of the river channel, its complete confinement dictating the spatial dimensions of the street.[92] It was through archaeological excavations during the 1990s that a greater appreciation of the composition of the street surface was achieved.

Over time various infrastructural developments required modifications to the street surface such as the laying of tram tracks in the 1870s and the 1890s. Resurfacing work was done in the 1880s and in the 1930s (following the closure of the tram service) the wooden sett blocks forming the road surface were salvaged as fuel when a more modern surface dressing was applied.[93] Subterranean service ducting during the twentieth century, requiring access points, was also a factor in the changing street surface. In the late 1990s, as part of the installation of a new main drainage system in the city, archaeological excavation of St Patrick's Street was done under licence, revealing the constituent elements of the ground beneath the street. Trenches of 1.36m at the western end and 4.35m at the eastern end were dug, each to a maximum width of 2m. 'The only archaeology noted was nineteenth century drainage features' and most of the stratigraphy exposed was identified as backfill from the infill of the river channel. The culverting of the channel itself was constructed of red sandstone.[94] The revealed stratigraphy consisted mainly of four layers: the existing hard surface; a grey gravel foundation; dumped material consisting largely of eighteenth- and nineteenth-century material including pottery, bone, oyster shell and stone; and clay mud which came to 1.3m below the present-day surface. The nineteenth-century services exposed were supported on red brick.[95]

In the recent development of the street, to Beth Gali's design, the accommodation of these services posed difficulties. Among the challenges was 'to re-orient the access chambers … so that the rectangular covers aligned with the pattern of the stone in the finished footpath'.[96] The 2003–4 redevelopment of St Patrick's Street sought to return as much of the

Trams, transport, lamp-standards and buildings, all part of the physical make-up of St Patrick's Street. (Courtesy Michael Lenihan)

street as possible to the pedestrian. It was decided to make the traffic lanes 4m wide with a service lane of 2.4m to accommodate bus stops, taxi ranks and loading areas. Sett stone paving for the surface area was the preferred choice; the principal advantages were their long life and the ease of lifting and replacing for access below the surface. During the research phase, the Dutch town of S'Hertogenbosch, as well as projects in Scotland, Spain, France and Ireland (Dublin and Galway) were examined. Based on the data gathered, as well as the density of pipe service at shallow depths below the paving – a consequence of the river channel further down – it was decided to use a fully reinforced concrete base to the paving. The research also indicated another potential problem – cleaning. Vehicular areas collect a film of rubber and oil requiring frequent costly cleaning; chewing gum in the pedestrian areas poses similar problems. One alternative was the use

Stone surfacing at the base of the Fr Mathew Statue in the Beth Gali redesign of the street.

of bituminous material for the main traffic lanes.[97] The architect declared herself comfortable with the appearance of this, although stone surfacing for certain of the traffic areas – such as the crossing of side streets and around the Fr Mathew Statue – would be employed also. The choice of colours and the use of heavily patterned stone for the pedestrian areas made chewing gum less conspicuous.[98] While serious consideration was given to the use of Irish stone, the quarries were not in a position to provide the quantities at an economic rate and, apart from some Kerry Red Marble, suitable materials were sourced from northern Spain.

Transport

With the opening of St Patrick's Bridge in September 1789, a second crossing on the north channel of the river became operational. However, the bridge was accessible only upon payment of a toll and the list of such tolls gives a snapshot of the nature of transport operating into and out of St Patrick's Street at the time. Eleven categories of tolls were put in place under the legislation 26 Geo. III, C.28, Sect. XXVI and of these, six applied to transport drawn by animals.[99] These were evenly divided into two groups: those having 'vehicles of burthen' and those not so listed. The 'of burthen' category referred to goods transportation, while the others referred to passenger transportation. The individual ratings within each group were based upon the number of animals used. For passenger categories, tolls were placed on 'every coach, chariot, berlin, chaise, chair or calash', while the goods vehicles tolled were 'every wagon, wain, cart or carriage of burthen or other carriage with either four or two wheels'.[100] Thus, a variety of vehicles drawn by one, two, four or up to six horses, for both people and goods, plied their way on St Patrick's Street and were a physical presence on the street from the very start. In 1803, to avoid accidents, people were advised to drive on the left side of the road, as in other cities.[101]

St Patrick's Street was one of the newly created wide and spacious city streets to which a number of middle-class merchants moved and where they now lived in high-status residences.[102] However, one consequence of the opening of St Patrick's Bridge was the development of suburbs to the northeast of the city.[103] For many decades only the wealthiest – those who could afford their own horses and carriages – could possibly live in these areas.[104] With developments in transport such as the rail services

Horse-drawn tram system of the 1870s. Note the absence of electric cables and the shadow of the horse in front of the tram.
(Courtesy Michael Lenihan)

and the improvement of road conditions, however, increased numbers of the middle class moved to the suburbs.[105] As a consequence, increasing levels of transport to and from the city centre became part of the physical fabric of the city. A commercial portrait of St Patrick's Street follows in a later chapter and will show that it was a street of high-value properties and where the more exclusive retail outlets were located. Furthermore, the commodities sold there were of a luxury nature geared to the middle and upper classes. Developing transport systems then, which served the suburbs where these classes resided, naturally connected to St Patrick's Street. None of the public transport systems that developed during the nineteenth and twentieth centuries transited North Main Street or South Main Street and so it was St Patrick's Street that became the centre of Cork's public transport systems.

One such system was the short-lived horse-drawn tram, which was introduced on 12 September 1872.[106] It received little support from the public and disappeared from the streets again in 1875. In 1876, the tracks, only recently laid, were removed and St Patrick's Street returned to its previous appearance. The electric tram system which began in December

1898 lasted until 1931. Not alone were tram tracks and cars again a feature on St Patrick's Street, but the poles carrying the electric cables now ran the length of the street in the centre.[107] 'Tram stops dotted St Patrick's Street.'[108] The owners of the system were the Cork Electric Tramways and Lighting Company Ltd and the fleet consisted of thirty-five cars. These were the first horseless carriages operating on St Patrick's Street and the existence of the system meant that Cork was now on a par with other great cities.[109] 'Cork was the eleventh city in Britain and Ireland to have electric trams. London did not have them until three years later (1901).'[110] As with the horse-drawn trams of a quarter of a century earlier, the Fr Mathew Statue at the north end of St Patrick's Street was the hub of the new service.[111]

By the 1920s, a new form of public transport appeared on St Patrick's Street: the omnibus, introduced when Captain A. P. Morgan from London imported five Daimler double-decker buses. Within a short time six more operators appeared and this led to the battle of the buses, different services racing each other to get to the next stop.[112] This competition led to price cuts which soon put the services in difficulties. By 1931 the Irish Omnibus Company had bought out the other services and, no longer able to compete,

Electric trams on St Patrick's Street. Note the curved nature of the street.
(Courtesy Michael Lenihan)

Tram ticket showing that the word 'Statue' was all that was needed to indicate the city centre. (Courtesy Michael Lenihan)

the electric trams ceased in 1931 with the loss of 230 jobs.[113] For the buses as for the trams, the Fr Mathew Statue on St Patrick's Street was the centre of the system.[114] This was manifest in two ways. Firstly, buses on occasions had in their destination window simply 'Statue'. Whatever about visitors, Cork people instinctively knew which statue and where.[115] Secondly, the fares were denoted with 'Statue' as their start point. For example, 'Statue to Blackrock' was 3½ d while 'Statue to South Gate Bridge' was 1½ d.[116]

Transport forms have been an integral part of the physicality of St Patrick's Street throughout its history, both for the presence of the vehicles themselves and the associated infrastructural works, whether tram tracks, electric poles or bus stops, and this continues to be the case today.

Services

A number of other features on the street merit inclusion in this physical portrait, for example the street lighting, which at the time of the accident that befell the lamp-lighter in 1807, consisted, as throughout the city centre, of oil lamps.[117] From their introduction in the mid-eighteenth century, they were regularly criticised as being unsatisfactory and so in 1822 responsibility for lighting the streets was vested in the Wide Street Commissioners.[118] In 1825 they contracted the London United Company to provide gas lighting throughout the city.[119] This in turn lasted until the 1930s when gas was replaced with electricity for the lighting of the city streets.[120]

Part of the physical make-up of St Patrick's Street, the standards for these street lamps varied in design over time. For many years after the demise of the trams, the street lamps still followed a central line on the street with one lamp extended across each of the traffic lanes going north and south. The Dutch journalist Kees van Hoek, writing in 1945, described how underneath the 'wide street's tall centred lamp-posts, the long rank of taxis shine as if fresh from the showroom'.[121] By the 1970s, the centre line had disappeared and the lamp posts were located along the pavements with two lamps still splayed either side of the centre post. In the recent redevelopment of St Patrick's Street, and based on the principle that 'lighting in public spaces is more than just a functional necessity – it makes a significant impact on the ambience of the space at night-time – as well as an architectural statement', the Flannery lamp, named after local schoolgirl Sarah Flannery, European Young Scientist of the Year in 1998, was specially designed for Beth Gali's plans.[122] It consists of two linked poles standing scissors-like with an assembly of lamps capable of casting light in multiple directions.[123] The lamps were also designed to remind the public of the shipping masts with which the space was graced when it was a waterway, in times past. The lighting, however, did not meet with universal approval, prompting Beth Gali to make a statement in their defence at the official opening in September 2004: 'For the lights I tried to bring the spirit of the harbour into the city. We have to find new monuments for our cities. They can be lights, street-furniture or whatever'.[124] Thus, Beth Gali and the design team sought to use apolitical iconography to reintroduce elements of the street's past identity in the creation of the new streetscape.

Buildings

Significant elements in the physicality of any space are statuary and buildings. Limerick's Treaty Stone and St John's Castle recall great events in that city's past; the Pikeman Statue in Wexford commemorates the 1798 rebellion and the Padraic Ó Conaire statue in Galway and that unveiled to Sean Ó Riada in Cúl Aodha in August 2008 recall icons of the Irish cultural past, both recent and not so recent. While Dublin's O'Connell Street has many monuments, among them those to the great nationalist leaders Daniel O'Connell and Charles Stewart Parnell, as well as the apolitical Millennium Spire, St Patrick's Street in Cork is devoid of similar icons. It has, however, what is known simply as the Statue, a monument to Fr Mathew, the Apostle of Temperance, erected in 1864. While O'Connell Street in Dublin has the iconic General Post Office, synonymous with the 1916 rebellion and the fight for independence, St Patrick's Street has no such nationally recognised buildings. Nevertheless, entire sections of the street were burned in December 1920 in the episode known as the 'Burning of Cork'. Both of these stories will be told in later sections of this book. For this physical portrait, however, some other aspects of the buildings on the street will be briefly examined.

Prior to 1783, the junction of Academy Street and St Patrick's Street was where the Crooked Billet Dock joined Traver's or Caldwell's Quay.[125] At this junction today stands the most prominent feature of early St Patrick's Street, the merchant houses at Nos. 92–93. Built prior to the infilling of the river channel, the main entrance was on the first floor – to which

Steps that once led down to shipping moored alongside the merchant housing, when St Patrick's Street was still a river channel.

Top: Nineteenth-century bow-fronted housing on St Patrick's Street. (Courtesy sandraocallaghan.com)

Centre: Three bow-fronted houses, between two of which was the entrance to the Wesleyan Chapel. (Courtesy sandraocallaghan.com)

Bottom: The merchant houses at nos. 92 and 93, Le Chateau Bar and Barter's Travel Agency of today, in the night lighting of the twenty-first-century street. (Courtesy Peter Carr)

steps led – while the stores were located below at ship level.[126] Today a public house operates in the old stores area of No. 93 and to the rear of No. 92, entered into beneath the old steps. It is owned by the Reidy brothers who continue the traditions operating there since 1793.[127] Further along the street, towards the north channel, are three bow-fronted four-storey commercial buildings dating to the late eighteenth century.[128] Between Nos. 100–101 was the entrance to the Methodist church which began there in 1805.

From the foregoing it can be said that the buildings were four storeys in height and had a dual functionality; from the first storey up they served as residences and working space with warehouse/storage space beneath.[129] With the development of the street towards the end of the eighteenth century a more decorative appearance was brought to bear with the construction of bow-fronted properties.[130] A number of premises began to develop as shops. William Mercer at No. 3 St Patrick's Street advertised material for ladies' petticoats and the new Vandyke stockings in 1795.[131] In the *Cork Mercantile Chronicle* in 1804 Richard Ronayne announced that his warehouse at No. 32 St Patrick Street 'is now very effectively supplied with every article in the wine, spirit and grocery trade'. In the same paper John Odell was advertised as a bookseller and stationer at No. 6.[132] By 1807, of seventy-four listings for St Patrick's Street, twenty-four, or just over 30 per cent, were retail operations.[133] These physical characteristics were commented upon by contemporary visitors to the city. Mirza Abu Taleb Khan, known as the Persian Prince, visited Cork in 1799 and commented on the four-storey regular houses, adding that they had handsome doors and glazed windows. He also detailed the nature of the contents of the 'shops'.[134] An added physical dimension illustrating that Cork

Left: **Three different building types in one block illustrating the irregular building lines of the street.**
(Courtesy sandraocallaghan.com)

Rigth: **The block advertised for development in the *Constitution* in 1825.**
(Courtesy sandraocallaghan.com)

and St Patrick's Street embraced developments elsewhere in Europe was the glazing. Glazing of shopfronts began towards the end of the seventeenth century, was prominent in London and Paris by early to mid-eighteenth century and half a century later the newly emerging St Patrick's Street followed suit.[135] However, Dutch Navy captain Cornelius De Jong, who visited Cork in 1802, noted the recently infilled streets and some houses, 'although new and recently built, in comparison with those in other European cities, they do not deserve to be called beautiful'.[136]

Robert Graham of Redgorton in Scotland, writing in 1835, described St Patrick's Street as 'the handsomest street', having buildings 'totally irregular, of all heights and sizes' but having 'a great deficiency of ornament'. The general line was broken with buildings at times receding and advancing; some are weather-slated and 'the best are built of English brick, when they do not go to the expense of stone'.[137] Today those same physical features can be seen on the street. The block advertised for development in December 1825 is where The Moderne (Nos. 89–90) and Spectra Photo (No. 91) are today and is totally out of line with the block to the west finishing with the Ulster Bank (No. 88). Height discrepancies can also be observed along the length of the street on both sides.

A number of points recorded by Archibald Stark in 1850 serve to illustrate physical developments on St Patrick's Street in the latter half of the nineteenth century. Describing it as similar to Dame Street in Dublin, it was, he said, home to 'some of the principal establishments of the city and the shops are as large, as well appointed and managed as those of Dublin'.[138] He also described how 'you are reminded of the existence of the *Cork Examiner* by the colossal yellow letters that are emblazoned with the civic arms' and that there was 'on either side of the street a succession of

Woodford Bourne & Co. carved in the facade of the building at the Daunt Square end of the street.

commodious premises'.[139] These observations are significant. His noting of 'commodious premises' marks the beginning of a trend whereby businesses increasingly occupied more than single premises on the street. In *Aldwell's Directory 1844–1845*, there is only one such listing (Charles Cahill, Nos. 18–19).[140] *Slater's Directory* of 1856, has two; *Laing's*, from 1863, has six; *Guy's*, of 1875, 1891, 1893 and 1907 have nine, ten, twelve and fourteen respectively.[141] Thus certain businesses on St Patrick's Street were developing through consolidation, absorption and expansion.

The 'colossal yellow lettering' symbolised another physical feature emerging on the streetscape, constituting both an advertisement and a statement of identity. Names displayed on buildings became part of the street's narrative of identity, creating icons of the street and indeed the city – both buildings and institutions. The *Cork Examiner* lettering proclaimed its existence; Woodford Bourne, cast in the facade of Nos. 64–65, marked the western entrance to the street; the London House at Nos.14–15 declared St Patrick's Street to be part of the empire. In 1919 this was replaced with another iconic sign: Roches Stores.[142]

The face of St Patrick's Street changed considerably during the course of the twentieth century, particularly following the destruction of large sections of the street by fire in December 1920. A civic survey undertaken by the Town Planning Association was published in 1926 and established 'an agenda for planning and development that lasted for sixty years'.[143] 'Out of the *Cork Civic Survey of 1926*' came the '*1941 Town Planning Report*' which recommended the creation of a new street from St Patrick's Street to City Hall, one reason for which was the increasing volume of traffic on St Patrick's Street, Grand Parade and South Mall.[144] This never happened, however, as it would have necessitated the demolition of a number of

buildings on St Patrick's Street and changed its physicality dramatically.

Another draft development plan from 1969 was reviewed in 1974. This led, in the late 1970s, to the establishment of the Land Utilisation and Transportation Study (LUTS), one important aspect of which was office and shopping development in the core of the city. A 33 per cent growth in shopping space was envisaged between 1976 and 1991 through redevelopment of the core area – St Patrick's and the surrounding streets. However, 16 per cent of all buildings in this central core were in a poor condition or worse.[145] A number of initiatives were undertaken. The 1990 Derelict Sites Act was employed and led to the clearing of many derelict buildings and the creation of development space. *The Shop Fronts and Advertisements Design Guidelines, 1990*, ensured that 'shop fronts on listed buildings should be consistent with the age and style of the buildings', and this formed the basis of design features for the future in St Patrick's

Entrance to the *Cork Examiner* offices at No. 95 flanked either side by the London and Newcastle Tea Company and O'Flynn's Butchers.
(Courtesy Amy and Chris Ramsden, The Day Collection)

Street and throughout the city-centre core area.[146] Thus were buildings such as Nos. 94–95 St Patrick's Street, with three-storey bay frontages dating from the middle of the nineteenth century (and where the *Cork Examiner* was founded) declared valuable and restrictions placed on any work that could be done to them.[147] As a consequence, some of the various period influences as they affected St Patrick's Street were protected and preserved.[148] This preservation, however, was partially abandoned so that the 2009 developments on the street saw some of these previously 'valuable' structures demolished to facilitate the construction of new retail and office accommodation. The O'Callaghan developments at Academy Street and Opera House Lane, leading to Emmet Place from St Patrick's Street, saw the removal of the building where the *Cork Examiner* had previously resided.

The physical nature of St Patrick's Street is a crucial part of its narrative of identity. This portrait has concentrated on four specific elements of its physicality: its shape and surface, transport, services and buildings. Each has added a permanent dimension to the street's narrative of identity and impacted on the lives of the people, giving them more pedestrian space for comfort, a centre of transport from the suburbs, and spacious comfortable shops. That these developments also occurred coincident with similar ones elsewhere places St Patrick's Street in a broader Irish and European context.

Conclusion

In this chapter on 'Place and Identity', the choice of St Patrick's Street's most basic statement of identity, its name, was firmly placed in a national context whereby, for a broad spectrum of society, association with St Patrick was a fundamental part of their narrative of identity. Cork sat comfortably in this context and many with power and influence were involved in various bodies such as Volunteer Corps and the Freemasons, bodies which themselves had associations with St Patrick. This chapter also dates the naming of the street to within a matter of days and shows that this occurred shortly after the installation of a new Order of Knights for Ireland, named after St Patrick.

Physical aspects of the street are examined and show that part of its unique identity was the retention of the shape of the river channel that ran beneath. This had consequences for later developments on the street, for

Parchment associated with St Patrick's Lodge and having an address on Maylor Street. (Courtesy sandraocallaghan.com)

example the depth to which services could be laid. This physical portrait also shows how the street became the centre of the city, with developing transport systems bypassing the older North Main Street and South Main Street and radiating to the suburbs from a St Patrick's Street centre. From this perspective one can say that St Patrick's Street in Cork has a unique identity which also connects the city with national identity, not just in being named after the patron saint, but in the context and timing of that naming.

3 St Patrick's Bridge

An Expanding City

As we have seen, it was during the latter half of the eighteenth century that many of the streams dividing the islands in the valley where Cork developed were bridged over, with a consequent expansion of the city centre. Along with this, some areas on the hills surrounding the city were also being inhabited, among them Dillon's Cross, Strand Road (now Lower Road) and other parts of the northeastern quarter. The residents of these areas were possibly among the first to seek a downriver crossing from the North Gate Bridge, the sole access road to the northern hills. Whether or not they would have been successful on their own will never be known; they were helped in their demands by the fact that the city's commerce was rapidly developing along with the city itself.[1]

Events many thousands of miles from Cork city were to have a bearing on commercial development at this time. The port was used as a rendezvous for shipping going to and coming from the West Indies and the east coast of America, up to and during the American War of Independence. Wool-combing, cloth-weaving and branches of cotton manufacture, as well as other industries such as paper-making and glass-blowing were all important to the city during the 1760s and 1770s. Later, the provision of meat for the navy, along with tanning, brewing and glue-making, were vital industries. None of these was the most important, however. Since the middle of the seventeenth century, the butter trade was the principal source of wealth for many merchants in Cork and it was exported to every part of the world in firkins, the circular casks used for holding the product.

The fact that many of these industries were based in the north side of the city was one important factor in the St Patrick's Bridge story. Another was that the stream following the course of today's St Patrick's Street was covered in during the 1780s. O'Sullivan's *Economic History of Cork* tells us that the rapidly expanding victualling (provisions) trade was another factor necessitating a new bridge. Thus, the Corporation of the day was called upon to build a bridge across the north channel of the river where the St Patrick's Street stream joined the main channel of the River Lee. This action would bring to completion the project whereby St Patrick's Street itself was built.[2]

Opposition to the Project

The idea for the bridge did not go without opposition. Many businessmen, particularly those in the Mallow Lane (now Shandon Street) and Blarney Lane areas where the provision and slaughtering industries were concentrated saw the project as a threat to their interests. So too did the operators of the many ferries plying the river near the proposed site of the new bridge. They began a campaign to prevent the project from going ahead and opposition mounted to such an extent that a public meeting was organised for 1 May 1785 at twelve o'clock to be held at the Corporation. One of the principal arguments made was the poor logic of placing a bridge downstream from the Custom House. (At that time it was located in today's Municipal Art Building on Emmet Place, which was constructed in 1724.) The organisers of the opposition drew up a petition calling for the defeat of a project which, they claimed, would be the ruin of thousands.

Finance Raised

The petition was sent to Parliament in response to representations from the Corporation in favour of the bridge, which were made during 1784 and 1785. The opposition was in vain, however, and in 1786 legislation was approved for raising the money required for the building of a bridge at a site downstream from the Custom House where the St Patrick's Street stream joined the River Lee. The public were given the opportunity to benefit financially from the construction of the bridge. Money for the project would be raised by the issuing of debentures, or loan-stock, and the rate of interest was set at 8 per cent. The Corporation itself invested £1,000. Tolls were to be placed on the bridge to meet this financial requirement. The tolls were to last for a period of twenty-one years and anything over and above the interest and maintenance costs would be used to pay off the principal owing. There was no shortage of willing investors and the project quickly got under way.

Michael Shanahan was a sculptor and architect working in the city at the time and he was appointed architect and chief contractor to the project.[3] He was a considerable figure in the architectural world; among his clients were the Earl of Bristol and the Bishop of Derry. *Hodder's Directory* of 1805 listed him as working out of White Street.[4] It was during the first half of 1788 that he set about organising the project.

Angry Flood

On 25 July 1788, the foundation stone for the new bridge was laid and over the next six months the bridge began to take shape. The arches reached out from the quay walls and the population marvelled at the feat of engineering. Then, disaster struck. A flood of the like not seen in the city for many years swept through the valley on 17 January 1789, submerging everything in its path in a matter of hours.[5] The entire city from the Mayor's residence (the present-day Mercy Hospital) to the lower reaches of the harbour was completely covered, forming an inland lake. Only the vigilance of the citizens prevented a major catastrophe. The new bridge, however, was in ruins. A boat which had been moored at today's Carroll's Quay (then the Sand Quay), broke its moorings and crashed against the unfinished centre arch of the bridge and destroyed it.[6] Shortly after this, the other arches came down and nothing remained of the work of the previous year. With the sweeping away of the bridge, Michael Shanahan was ruined. He could not continue the project and departed for London. There, he met a man named Hargrave and outlined his sorrowful tale. Hargrave took over the contract and, together with Shanahan, travelled back to Cork to continue the project.[7]

The happy result of this endeavour was the christening of the new bridge on 29 September 1789. The *Hibernian Chronicle* of 1 October gives the following description of the events as they occurred on the day.

> On Tuesday the Key-stone of the last arch of the new bridge was laid by the Ancient and Honourable Society of Free Masons of this city. The morning was ushered in with the ringing of bells; an immense crowd assembled in the principal streets before the hour of eleven. About twelve the procession of the different Lodges, dressed with their jewels and the insignia of the respective orders, preceded by the band of the 51st regiment, began in the following manner:
> Army Lodge,
> Grand Tyler with drawn sword,
> Grand Almoner bearing a chalice of wine.
> Two Grand Deacons, the Bible supported by two other Grand Deacons,
> The Chaplain of the Grand Lodge,
> Lord Donoughmore, Grand Master of All Ireland,
> Joseph Rogers Esq. Provincial Grand Master of Munster attended by two Grand Wardens, secretary etc.
> Tyler of Lodge No.1.
> Two Deacons of do.
> Master, Wardens Secretary etc. of do.
> After whom followed 14 Lodges with their Masters and Wardens in regular order.

The lodges referred to were those of the Society of Freemasons who were prominent in the city. The *Hibernian Chronicle* again takes up the story:

> The procession moved from the Council chamber amid the acclamation of the rejoicing multitude, through Castle Street, down the new street called St Patrick's Street, and advanced to the foot of the new bridge, which was decorated on the occasion with the Irish

standard, the Union flag, and several other ensigns – here they were saluted with nine cannon, the workmen dressed in white aprons lining each side of the bridge; the procession advanced up to the centre of the last arch where they were received by the Commissioners and the Architect. The last key-stone which was previously suspended; and which weighed 47 hundred, was then instantly lowered into its berth – and the Bible laid upon a scarlet velvet cushion adorned with tassels and gold fringe was placed upon it – His Lordship, as Grand Master, thereupon, in due form gave three distinct knocks with a mallet; the Commissioners were then called upon to mention the name intended for the new bridge, which being communicated, the Grand Master emptied his chalice of wine upon the key-stone and the Grand Master, in the name of the Ancient and Honourable Fraternity of the Free and Accepted Masons of the Province of Munster, proclaimed it St Patrick's Bridge. The whole body of Masons, composed of upwards of 400 of the most respectable gentlemen of city and county gave a salute three times three which was returned by nine cheers of the populace and the firing of nine cannon. After this the procession marched over the bridge and its portcullis, surveyed them, and was again saluted with nine cannon. They then returned back in the same order to the Council chamber.[8]

So it was that Cork city received its new bridge with a ceremony that we, over two centuries later, can only regret not seeing. The bridge itself was narrow and humpbacked, had three elliptical arches topped with open balustrades, and was constructed of limestone. A gateway for shipping – the portcullis – was located at the northern end of the bridge. Hargrave and Shanahan were the heroes of the day and the shareholders who had invested in the debentures were well pleased with themselves. Their enterprise soon proved profitable, helped no doubt by the efficient management of the toll collecting which had passed into their hands.

Tolls Trouble

Whatever about the maintenance of the bridge itself, the care of the shipping gateway was vital to the merchants who operated upriver. A large amount of shipping passed through here, docking on the quays between the new bridge and the North Gate Bridge. These merchants, as well as the people who passed over the bridge proper, felt much aggrieved at the expense they had to bear for so long a time. On the other hand, those who had purchased debentures in the project were in favour of the portcullis and the tolls, upon which depended returns on their investments.[9] These diverse perspectives on the tolls issue were illustrated in advertisements in the *Cork Mercantile Chronicle* in August and September 1806. On 13 August, under a heading of New Bridge, one advertisement read:

> Such persons as feel interested in keeping the Portcullis on the New Bridge open are earnestly entreated to meet at the Council Chamber at one o'clock tomorrow to consider the best manner of opposing the application now made to shut up the same.[10]

On 10 September:

> The Holders of Bridge Debentures will be paid one year's annuity to the fifth of July last by Samuel Randall Wily, Batchelor's Quay, Cork.[11]

Meanwhile, the tolls for the ensuing year were advertised on 13, 25 and 29 August.[12] Those opposed to the portcullis and the tolls formed a committee, continued their lobbying and eventually pressurised the shareholders into forgoing any further profits and putting the tolls up for auction, thereby clearing any outstanding principal owing. This would eventually lead to the bridge becoming free to all users in 1812. The portcullis, however, remained in operation.

Though the merchants were successful in achieving their goal regarding the maintenance of the portcullis, the days of shipping passing St Patrick's Bridge to berth upstream were slowly ending. The Custom House, which had operated since 1724, was replaced after 1814 by a new one further downstream.[13] As a result, it was not necessary for shipping to travel as far up the river as previously. Furthermore, there was a general belief in the city that the portcullis section of the bridge was not just a nuisance, but dangerous as well. In March 1812 the Court D'Oyer declared it so and sought for it to be replaced.[14] Thus there was a general call for the closure of the portcullis and the filling in of the stream that ran beneath it. Although this was opposed by the merchants, an Act of Parliament was passed in 1822 allowing the closure. There followed a legal battle and in

1824 the portcullis was removed finally with payment of £1,200 to the affected members of the commercial community.

Proposed By-Law

At a Harbour Board meeting held on 2 May 1849, the issue of who was responsible for the upkeep and maintenance of the bridges in the city was discussed. This occurred following damage being inflicted on St Patrick's Bridge when a vessel under tow crashed into and damaged one of the parapets. At the meeting it was stated that there were three public bodies – the Grand Jury, the Harbour Board and the Wide Street Board – involved but that none of them was responsible for the care of the bridge. A suggestion was made that the repair could be done cheaply with 'a plain rubble wall'. However, the Harbour Master wanted the job done properly and that would cost in the region of £40. Board member Mr Harley warned that public money being used in this way was a bad habit for public bodies to engage in. He had previously contacted the Admiralty regarding other bridge matters and the officials there had suggested the Corporation was responsible for the bridges. Eventually, Councillor Meagher moved that £50 should be provided by the Harbour Board to repair the bridge but that by-laws should be enacted restricting the operation of towing vessels in order to ensure such an incident could not damage the bridge again. The Harbour Master, however, said that if tow boats were to be restricted from bringing shipping upstream, there could be occasions when strong westerly winds would prevent certain vessels from reaching the Custom House. To peals of laughter, Councillor Meagher suggested that the westerly winds be made subject to the proposed by-laws.[15] It is unlikely that anybody remembered that humour four years later, in November 1853.

Another Catastrophic Flood

November 1853 brought disaster again when, following a violent storm, an enormous flood swept through Cork city. By ten o'clock in the morning Great George's Street (now Washington Street) was completely submerged. Many people were trapped in the upper floors of their homes; a blacksmith is said to have floated downstream as far as Anglesea Bridge on the south channel where some sailors threw him a rope and rescued him. Quay walls collapsed with the pressure of the onrushing waters but one structure, the

The destroyed St Patrick's Bridge following the flood of November 1853.
(Courtesy DeBurca Rare Books)

North Gate Bridge, stood firm. Its huge parapets caused the water on the western side to rise six feet higher than the downstream side; when this great volume of water eventually rushed past the bridge, carrying with it significant quantities of debris, including large trees, it wrought the destruction of St Patrick's Bridge, less than a mile away. The bridge was swept away and with it the lives of between fifteen and twenty people. A small group of men and boys were leaning over the bridge, fascinated by the swirling waters beneath; they were never seen again. Of four women journeying to the northside of the city, two were lost.[16]

Cork was devastated. The Mayor, John Francis Maguire, away in Dublin on business, heard of the disaster and rushed back to the city to take charge of the situation. He increased the number of ferries crossing the river and then arranged for a temporary pontoon bridge to accommodate the requirements of the citizens until more permanent plans could be made. John Benson, the city engineer, was then instructed to draw up the plans and by the following day was able to present to the Corporation drawings for a timber bridge, which he recommended should be placed

50 feet away from the existing bridge site to facilitate reconstruction. Estimated construction time for the bridge was a month. At a cost of 'about £2,000' and paid for by the Harbour Board, five weeks after the disastrous flood, on 7 December 1853, Benson's Bridge was officially opened to the public by the Mayor.[17] Before the end of the year, the Corporation took the decision to apply to Parliament for permission to replace St Patrick's Bridge, as well as the North Gate Bridge which had contributed so largely to the destruction of the former. That permission was granted in 1856 when the Cork Bridge and Waterworks Act was drafted into law allowing the Corporation to borrow money for the replacement of the bridges. Before that could happen, however, a number of serious issues arose as to what type the replacement bridge should be, what material it should be constructed from and the means of financing the rebuilding. These issues ran for a number of years, eventually leading to a large public meeting being held in the city in December 1855.

Controversy

As in 1849 it was not long before the issue of who would pay for the repair of the bridge reared its head. At a Harbour Board meeting on Wednesday 11 January 1854, a letter from the Attorney General was read which stated that 'respecting the Wide Street Board and the Grand Jury, the Corporation are the proper party to repair or reconstruct St Patrick's Bridge'. He also advised that 'the Harbour Commissioners not interfere' but that 'if in constructing a new bridge or new arches, a plan could be adopted which would improve the navigation, the Harbour Commissioners may fairly defray any additional expenses that arise therein'.[18]

A week later, the Corporation appointed a committee to prepare legislation for the replacement of the bridge, while a report on the cause of the destruction was presented to the Harbour Board by Henry Hennessy, MRIA, librarian at Queen's College, Cork. Hennessy's report outlined that the quantity of rain registered at the college for a fortnight before the flood was 9.86 inches compared with 3.87 inches for the same period a year previously. This gave rise to over 2 billion extra cubic feet of water in the river. Hennessy concluded that the primary causes of the destruction were excessive and continued rainfall, from which resulted the saturated condition of the basin of the River Lee for some time anterior to the flood and the sudden and extraordinary fall of rain during the night immediately before the flood, whereby an immense volume of water was superimposed on the already saturated catchment area of the river. Significantly, the report also said that swelling produced by bridges and weirs, among which was the North Gate Bridge, was a secondary cause.[19]

An editorial in the *Cork Examiner* of 28 January brought to the attention of the public that, in order to finance the rebuilding of St Patrick's Bridge, the bridge committee proposed 'an application to Government for the continuance of the existing tax on coal entering the port, which tax is not higher than five pence on each ton'. 'By consenting to continue it, they [the members of the government] will themselves be free from applications for grants, and the citizens of Cork will be saved a world of anxiety as to where all the money is to come from.' The editorial also agreed with a call from members of the Harbour Board that serious consideration should be given to making the replacement a swivel bridge.[20] Over the following month the coal tax proposal became complicated. Not all imported coal was landed within the borough of Cork – some was put ashore in Queenstown (Cobh) and near Midleton. The authorities in these locations decided that if Cork was to seek a continuance of the tax for the improvement of the city, they would seek to obtain a percentage, for the benefit of their own localities. At a meeting of the Corporation on 15 March 1854, the High Sheriff said that such was the extent of the claim from a number of places outside of the city, that 'they would put a gloss on the transaction that is not altogether correct'. With these claims lodged in opposition to the city receiving all of the tax, 'it would be idle to go on'. He therefore announced that he would move at the next meeting that no further steps be taken in this matter. Furthermore, he said, 'Benson's Bridge is a very good one and will certainly last twenty-five years'.[21] So ended the coal tax proposal, but the swivel one continued for some time longer.

The Bridge Type Controversy

What type should the new St Patrick's Bridge be? That was the question occupying the minds of the councillors and the citizens. Ideas and suggestions were many and varied, with some people suggesting that since Benson's timber bridge would last for many decades, why not use the money for building completely new bridges and let the next generation worry about replacing St Patrick's Bridge.[22] St Patrick's Bridge, however, was always going to be replaced and the main decisions to be made were whether the bridge should be constructed of timber, iron or stone and whether it should be a swivel bridge or not. Many arguments were made in favour of and against the different types, but in the end a stone bridge was decided upon because there was plenty of limestone available locally and employment would be given to the local stonecutters and stonemasons.[23] (In fact almost 100 of these people would be employed on the project.) Were an iron bridge to be built, it would be more costly and most of the money would leave the area. A fixed rather than a swivel bridge was selected and one of the arguments that John Benson made in favour of this was that, in the event of armed insurrection, the mechanism could be jammed by the rebels, thereby preventing troops from the barracks gaining access to the city via the shortest possible route. Benson, however, had prepared plans for all three types of bridges.[24]

At a Harbour Board meeting on Wednesday 3 May 1854, the chairman, Mr Donegan, pointed out that St Patrick's Bridge was falling 'day after day into dilapidation'.[25] On Wednesday 10 May, an editorial in the *Cork Examiner* said that 'it is high time that the vacillation was at an end and that some plans were determined'.[26] Following this the Corporation asked John Benson and another engineer, Mr J. Long, to do a full report for them. The inspections for this took place on 11 and 12 May, following which John Benson recommended that 'the present wreck should be taken down and that a flat bridge, with a spacious archway should be constructed in its stead'.[27] Long, in his report, largely agreed with Benson. When read to the Corporation, Alderman Lyons said that 'whatever discrepancy there might appear between the reports, there was in reality no difference'. He further pointed out that while specifications and plans would be prepared 'there would no doubt be a war about swivels'.[28] In a supplementary report to the Corporation dated 31 July, Benson further recommended that 'the injured piers be entirely rebuilt on a new foundation several feet below the present deepest bed of the river'.

It took some time for the plans to be drawn up and in April 1855 it was proposed to a joint Harbour Board and Corporation committee that 'it would be advisable to have erected on the site of St Patrick's Bridge a solid bridge as level as possible, width sixty-four feet and a deeper foundation than the former one'.[29] The same notice was read to the Corporation on the following Monday, but the issue became acrimonious. Some members still agitated for a swivel bridge and when pressed, one of them, Mr Fitzgibbon, acknowledged holding property above the bridge. A Mr Lambkin declared himself 'perfectly disgusted with the personal motives which people bring into every public question. It is really monstrous.'[30] The end result was that the issue was postponed until the next meeting. Reporting on the matter, the *Cork Examiner* did not deal with the personalities involved but came down firmly on the side of a swivel bridge. On 4 May it declared that 'the proposal to replace St Patrick's Bridge with a swivel rather than a fixed structure affords perhaps the greatest opportunity which has ever offered for improving the City of Cork'.[31]

The issue remained dominant for the summer months of 1855, until September, when at a Corporation meeting, not only was the swivel bridge again proposed and rejected but there was another proposal to finance the bridge through a coal tax – exclusive of the coals landed in those areas that had previously opposed the plan. This prompted a letter to be published on 1 October saying that the proposal was 'pregnant with mischief' and that in opting for a solid structure the Corporation was 'highly unjust towards the owners of property situated contiguous to the quays above St Patrick's Bridge and the north west portion of the city generally'.[32]

Such was the pressure in favour of a swivel bridge that the matter was discussed and voted on at a Corporation meeting held on 12 November. The result was twenty-one votes to eighteen in favour of the solid structure. On 14 November the *Cork Examiner*, arguing passionately in favour of the interests upstream of St Patrick's Bridge, declared that this decision could not be, in the opinion of the vast majority of the citizens, 'a more unwise or impolitic decision'. On 30 November the editor continued his campaign against the Corporation decision saying that 'it is not likely' that the decision of the Corporation 'on the question of the bridge will be taken as binding on the citizens and the preliminary steps have already been taken for expostulation and remonstrance … perhaps opposition'.[33]

On Monday 3 December 1855 a huge public meeting took place regarding the issue of whether the replacement St Patrick's Bridge would be a swivel or a fixed structure. The meeting took place in the Court House at two o'clock and was at times acrimonious. When the Mayor Sir John Gordon attempted to direct proceedings in favour of the Corporation's position, John Francis Maguire (a former Mayor himself and founder of the *Cork Examiner*), to cheers from his supporters, proposed that 'this meeting is deeply impressed with the importance of throwing open the navigation of the North Channel by means of a swivel bridge to replace St Patrick's Bridge'. The resolution contained a suggestion that the swivel need only be opened by night, thereby minimising disruption to traffic. The motion was seconded by Michael Cagney. The debate continued, dealing with matters such as the annual maintenance cost of a swivel bridge versus a solid one and whether in fact two swivels should be employed in order to minimise disruption. Mr Edward Scott proposed that the proceedings of the previous Corporation meeting, at which a solid structure was decided upon, be endorsed. This was seconded by Mr Cummins but Mr Fitzgibbon – who was in fact the Mayor-elect – said that 'the people of Cork would not be led away by persons who came there to disturb the great object of their meeting'. He then proposed 'that the meeting is resolved to oppose in Parliament that part of the bill now sought' by the Corporation which 'proposed to destroy the navigation of the upper part of the north branch of the River Lee by erecting a solid bridge to replace St Patrick's Bridge'. Mr Dowden seconded the resolution and following some discussion on the financial aspects of the plan, the resolution was carried.[34] The *Cork Examiner* reported glowingly on the meeting's position, declaring that the Mayor had displayed 'a self-sufficient and rather arrogant tone'.[35]

The early months of 1856 saw a number of final decisions being made prior to the bill for the rebuilding of the bridges being debated in the House of Commons in May. Before all this, however, letters appeared in the press in January, still calling for a swivel bridge.[36] There were also reservations about the methods of finance suggested. When the bill was finalised in May the question of bridge type was finally settled.[37] The Corporation would have its way. The bridge would be a solid structure and although calls against this persisted, the decision was not reversed. Permission was obtained under the bill for monies to be borrowed for the project as well as that of the North Gate Bridge reconstruction. Two further issues now came to the fore. Calls to actually do the job began to appear in the press and, also, a debate began as to what construction material should be used for the bridge, iron or stone.

Following letters to the press in support of the use of stone for the bridge by Thomas Jennings, on 29 March 1858 Alex Crichton wrote to the *Cork Examiner* proposing to 'confute Mr Jennings arguments and to prove by facts that of all the materials generally used in the construction of bridges, wrought iron is the strongest and best suited for that purpose'.[38] In response, on 9 April 1858, a statement was issued by the Society of Stone Cutters in the city. In it, as well as thanking their main supporters, they said that:

we respectfully submit that the Corporation should pause before they decide against us – before they expend a large sum of money amongst strangers instead of in our own city – before they seek materials in another country when better materials are to be had in their own valley and most of them on the very spot (in the remains of the old bridge) and before they choose a flimsy costly ugly iron structure which will not with any amount of tinkering and painting last fifty years when, at very little if any more cost, they can have a permanent inexpensive handsome stone structure which will last for ages.

It was signed by Roger Mathew, president, and Michael Walsh, secretary, and published in the local press.[39]

This statement was followed by a general meeting of masons and builders, held on Monday 19 April in Mary Street in the city. A number of resolutions were passed including 'that the meeting fully agree with the opinions expressed by so many of the enlightened and intelligent burgesses of this city, regarding the greater permanency, desirability and economy of stone in comparison with iron, as a material for the construction of St Patrick's Bridge'.[40] The debate continued throughout the year but eventually John Benson's plans for a three-arch structure were adopted. On Friday 8 and Monday 11 April 1859, the bridge committee met to receive tenders for the project. Five tenders were received: John Edwards at £17,780; William Joyce of Queenstown (Cobh) at £18,250; Joshua Hargrave Jnr at £14,450; Joseph Enright of Dublin at £11,642; and John Moore at £16,350. Enright's being the lowest, it was decided to recommend it to the Corporation and he was awarded the contract. By June, however, problems had arisen. The *Cork Examiner* stated that 'we hear of the contractor [Enright] coming before the committee … with a modest demand to be paid for the work he had already done and to be eased of the burden of his contract'.[41] In July, John Benson was mandated to agree a deal with Joshua Hargrave for the completion of the bridge. By August a Mr Barnard had been appointed Clerk of Works, but this became an issue when, at an Improvement Department meeting in August, Mr Keane wondered why John Benson did not perform the role as well as that of design engineer.[42] The majority of the members, however, approved of the necessity of Barnard in the role and on 10 November 1859, almost six years to the day after the first St Patrick's Bridge was destroyed by a flood,

Left: **Knighting of John Arnott by Lord Lieutenant, the Earl of Carlisle, in November 1859.**
(*London Illustrated News*)

Right: **Crowds celebrate the election of Sir John Arnott as Mayor.**
(*London Illustrated News*)

the foundation stone for the new St Patrick's Bridge was laid by the Earl of Carlisle, Lord Lieutenant of Ireland. Having lowered it into place he proclaimed to the assembled crowds 'I declare the foundation stone of St Patrick's Bridge to be duly and truly laid'.[43] There followed three cheers for the bridge, three cheers for the Earl of Carlisle and a further three cheers for the designer John Benson. The ceremony proceeded with the conferring of a knighthood on the Mayor, John Arnott.[44] (Under the alias Timothy Tightboots, he was well known for his generosity to the poor people of the city.)

On this November day in the 1859, history was repeating itself. The first St Patrick's Bridge had been christened on 29 September 1789 and the ceremony had been performed by the Society of the Ancient and Honourable Freemasons of Cork. So it was on this occasion when members of the Masonic Order again performed the colourful ceremony. Coupled with this was the fact that Sir Gorge Chatterton, Provincial Grand Master of the Freemasons, was wearing a badge that one Lady Aldwoth had worn at the first ceremony seventy years earlier.

The foundation stone that was laid on the occasion of this ceremony was placed at the northeast abutment and into it was placed a glass vase containing a record of the day's events. The scroll read:

The foundation stone for this bridge was laid on the 10th of November 1859, in the 23rd year of the reign of Her Majesty Queen

Victoria, in the year of Masonry 1859, by His Excellency, the Earl of Carlisle. And the Masonic body of the Province of Munster; General Sir George Chatterton, Provincial Grand Master of Munster; George Chatterton Esq. Deputy Provincial Grand Master; William Penrose, Provincial General Secretary.

The vase was placed in a cavity in the huge foundation stone where it remains today.[45] The Lord Lieutenant was then presented with an inscribed silver trowel by John Benson, commemorating his visit to the city for the ceremony. The inscription read:

> Presented to His Excellency the Earl of Carlisle, Lord Lieutenant of Ireland on the occasion of the laying of the foundation stone of St Patrick's Bridge, Cork on the 10th of November 1859; John Arnott, Mayor; Sir John Benson, Engineer; Joseph Hargrave, Contractor; William Barnard, Clerk of Works.[46]

In this inscription lay evidence of yet another piece of historical coincidence: the contractor Joseph Hargrave was none other than the grandson of Michael Hargrave who had helped construct the first St Patrick's Bridge.[47]

Shipwreck

Prior to all this, another shipwreck had taken place at the site, on Wednesday 21 April 1858. This one, however, did no structural damage to the timber bridge which Benson had constructed. It was a Portuguese ship called the *Funchal* under the command of one Captain Rodriguez. With a cargo of 160 tons of salt for delivery to local merchant John Firmo, the ship was piloted upriver from Queenstown. In those days the river dried out very quickly in the late spring and summer periods. Before the ship had been tied off properly, the tide receded and the ship, which was moored opposite the stores of Messrs. Harvey & Co., St Patrick's Quay, listed to starboard until she went over completely and crashed against the quay wall. The entire cargo was destroyed and although an attempt was made to right her the following Friday, with the attachment of ropes and 'three or four relays of men from an early hour' trying to pull her upright, the rope snapped and she again crashed down, this time completely wrecked.[48]

Construction Work and another Temporary Bridge

The task facing the builders of the new bridge was a huge one by any standards. Serious disruption would be caused to the traffic and pedestrian flows due to the works and the machinery that would have to be used. In order to minimise this disruption the Improvement Department ordered that another temporary footbridge be constructed, downstream from Benson's Bridge between Merchant's Quay and St Patrick's Quay, just opposite Hackett's Store. This bridge was described as being 'ten feet in width and although constructed entirely of timber, is light and ornamental in appearance'.[49] Built by Mr Barnard and contractor Mr Edwards, the bridge took only three weeks to complete and was opened to the public on Friday 27 May 1859.[50] (When St Patrick's Bridge was completed, the *Cork Examiner* suggested, the timber footbridge could 'without difficulty be raised and conveyed by barges to the foot of Wyse's Hill where it will be placed and where a foot bridge has long been deemed very necessary'.[51])

This operation completed, the contractors for the main bridge had first to remove the foundations of the old bridge.[52] Divers were used in this operation and the blocks of stone, which were removed, were taken downstream to where the Marina is today to be reshaped for use in the new bridge. Then the foundations for the piers and abutments of the new bridge were sunk into the river bed to a depth of between 10 and 14 feet below the low-water mark.[53] The next process was the laying down of a layer of cement. This was achieved with the use of specially designed boxes, fitted with trapdoors that were released when the correct depth was reached. Each layer was 10 feet wide and cast iron cassions were laid on them. They were then joined together, forming completely enclosed cases around each pier. Further layers of concrete were laid around these and the first levels of masonry work, which consisted of blocks of stone weighing anything up to 3 tons each, were mounted on top of the cassions. When the arches and balustrade on top of the bridge were in place, Cork city boasted the widest bridge in these islands with the exception only of Westminster Bridge in London. The total waterway span was 168 feet, the centre arch being 60 feet with the other two being 54 feet each. The width between the parapets was 60 feet and 6 inches, the roadway being 40 feet. Limestone was used for most of the construction, the material for the foundation blocks coming from Foynes in County Limerick. Only two serious accidents occurred during the course of construction; a workman

Trams on St Patrick's Bridge early in the twentieth century.
(Courtesy Michael Lenihan)

fell into the river when crossing between two barges and was drowned and a man fell 30 feet from a gantry, sustaining serious but not fatal injuries.

On 12 December 1861, the new St Patrick's Bridge was opened to the public for the first time. Rain lashed down and a southwest gale whipped the river into frenzy. One old woman was said to have claimed that if the Mayor tried to open the bridge he would be swept away. Sir John Arnott, however, serving his third successive year as Mayor, was unperturbed. 'I have great pleasure in congratulating the inhabitants of Cork on the completion of this elegant bridge which I now open for public traffic.' The Mayor completed his speech and led the members of the Corporation across the bridge, surveying the workmanship. Before they could return, however, a hackney driver drove his nag across, determined to be recorded in history as the first person to cross the bridge.

Conclusion

Through four centuries, from the eighteenth to the twenty-first, there have been bridges at the northern end of St Patrick's Street. St Patrick's Bridge is today as it was when opened by Arnott, apart from re-strengthening work done in the early 1980s and following which a plaque with his name was placed in the bridge wall. In 1861 the bridge was floodlit by gas lamps. Today, ornamental lamps that stood high over the bridge on that December day are still to be seen. The effigies on the top of each arch were carved by a sculptor from Douglas Street named Scannell; they are of St Patrick, St Bridget, Neptune and three sea goddesses.

4 People of St Patrick's Street

This chapter presents people of St Patrick's Street as they were recorded in a number of ways during the nineteenth and twentieth centuries. It also presents a number of the more famous people associated with the street, two of whom have been identified as 'apostles'. While one is scarcely remembered, the other achieved the status of icon and has a statue in his honour located right at the heart of the city.

Records

Of the forty people listed in the 1787 Lucas directory, only eight were still listed on the street in 1805.[1] Giles Daunt was one of a family of physicians; Sir John Haly, also a physician, was originally a Roman Catholic but conformed to Protestantism in 1771.[2] He died in St Patrick's Street in 1799 having been knighted in 1785 and is remembered for his work on vaccinations.[3] Vezian Pick was a Huguenot wine-merchant and Mayor in

1796 during which year he was knighted for his defence plans for the city in the event of a French assault.[4] Robert Dargaville lived on St Patrick's Street until his death there in 1838.[5] Similarly, John Russell, one of the Society of Friends, died at his house on St Patrick's Street in March 1827.[6] John Thompson, Mayor of the city in 1794, was the father of one of the most notable people associated with the street, socialist thinker William Thompson.

Of the forty listings in the 1787 directory, three, Miss Lloyd (boarding house), Mary Tickells (grocery) and Miss Gardiner (milliner) were women. By 1805–7 this had risen to thirteen. The proportion of women listed in the other directories examined is illustrated in the following table and it can be seen that women were never strongly represented as proprietors on St Patrick's Street. Having reached highs of 17.56 per cent in 1805–7 and 13.21 per cent in 1907, they had reached an all-time low of 2.23 per cent by 1997.[7]

Year	1787	1805/07	1809/10	1820/22	1824	1845	1856	1863	1867
%	7.5	17.56	13.39	8.33	14.07	10.49	8.03	9.85	9.3
No.	3	13	15	9	19	17	11	13	12
Year	1875	1886	1907	1925	1935	1945	1976	1997	
%	11.62	13.12	13.21	10.13	11.82	12.32	4.85	2.23	
No.	15	21	23	16	24	26	5	4	

Figure 8 Women proprietors on St Patrick's Street.

Women feature in the street's history in another way also. As customers they merited their own ledger, separate from that of men, in Dowden's drapery firm. Data from the ledger substantiates the higher class nature of the street.[8] In January 1858, Ladies Benson, Deane, Boyle and Mrs Admiral O'Grady all brought their custom to Dowden's. Mrs Gibbings visited the store three times in February; on one occasion she purchased a shirt for 4s 10d and four plain sheets for 1s 4d. In that month also, Lady Besnard visited the shop and did so again in July. Lady Inchiquin bought six chemises and long-cloth in May and in September purchased another long-cloth and buttons. Long-cloth and buttons sold together were a matter of note in these records. (Today we would call long-cloth dressmaking material.) In February 1858, thirty-six women bought long-cloth and twenty-four bought buttons. Of these, seven bought more than one length of long-cloth and twenty-one bought both long-cloth and buttons. A year later, in February 1859, twenty-one women again bought long-cloth and buttons and five of them bought more than one length. Thirty-six women bought petticoats, among them Lady Bandon who bought four, as well as a length of long-cloth, tape and buttons totalling 14s 6d. In that month thirty-six customers paid by cheque, one was charged to account and seven were marked paid, probably by cash.

Data on men taken from June 1884 demonstrates that it was still the wealthier in society who patronised the establishments on the street.[9] On 2 June Rev. Arthur Sloman ordered the material and making of six Oxford shirts and their washing for £1 14s 6d. Professor Lewis ordered two for 9s 6d while Dr Townsend ordered one for 3s 6d. Richard Allen ordered a cricket shirt. On 23 June, Mr Dorimar, about to depart for India, ordered twelve Oxford shirts to be made. In total to the end of June 1884, the intake from the gentlemen's department was £440 19s 7d rising to £553 9s 5d at the end of July, £984 3s 10d at end November and £1,194 18s 2d at year's end in February 1885. Dowden's continued in business until the middle of the twentieth century.

Another picture of the people of St Patrick's Street is available through examination of census material. In 1911 a total of 340 people were listed as resident on the street, occupying 46 of the 125 premises.[10] These residents ranged from families running a business – sometimes employing live-in domestic servants – to resident apprentices and staff in some of the bigger concerns. The premises of Cash & Co., Nos. 18–21, had twenty residents, nineteen of whom were single and one a widow. They comprised a drapery superintendent aged forty-nine, two drapery assistants aged nineteen

Dowden's in the 1930s.

and thirty-nine, ten apprentices aged between fourteen and twenty, a housekeeper aged sixty and six domestic servants between the ages of twenty and twenty-five. All the drapers were male and all servants female. Every resident was Roman Catholic.

In the Munster Arcade, thirty-six people were listed: fifteen drapers' assistants, thirteen apprentices, one male servant, two dressmakers, one female housekeeper, one cook and three general servants. All the apprentices were male and aged between sixteen and nineteen; of the drapers' assistants, three were male and twelve female, aged between twenty and forty-six. All servants were female. Thirty-four of the group were Roman Catholic while two were Church of Ireland. At No. 101, the 83-year-old widow Mary Foley ran a public house with her three daughters and two sons, aged between thirty and fifty-three. All were Roman Catholic. Next door at No. 102, David Magner, aged seventy, and his wife Ellen, aged sixty, ran a licensed premises. They had three sons and a daughter aged between ten and twenty-one, the eldest being a medical student. Sharing the house with them were two maids aged twenty-two and twenty-three and a servant aged thirty – all female. The entire household was Roman Catholic. Esther Fry (seventy) and her sister Annie (seventy-five) ran a boarding house at No. 113. On the occasion of the census, five females were boarding there. The two sisters were Church of Ireland, as were four of the boarders, the fifth being Unitarian. Resident there also were two Roman Catholic servants, both female.[11]

These brief accounts of St Patrick's Street people serve to illustrate the higher class nature of the street and also provide a snapshot of the residents in a number of premises early in the twentieth century. They also indicate that, valued custom aside, the place of women on the street was inferior to that of the men. Women were the drapers' assistants, not the drapers; men were the drapers' apprentices, not the women. It was women who were the servants, not the men.

Inhabitants

So who were the inhabitants of St Patrick's Street? A wide range of businesses were located there, from apothecaries, haberdashers and milliners to attorneys. In all, some thirty-six businesses are listed on the street for the year 1787, including three wine merchants, and Daniel Dowling operated as a perfumer. A number of city dignitaries are listed to the street: Edmond

Roche the sword bearer; Ed Kinsealagh, the coroner; Thomas Chatterton and James Gregg, public notaries; and three physician/surgeons.[12] All this is further evidence that the clientele visiting the various businesses on the new St Patrick's Street was somewhat affluent in nature.

One business in particular is interesting in attempting to trace the early developments of Cork's new main street: that of Austin Shinkwin, agent to the Dublin Insurance Company. He was one of the earliest businessmen to advertise from his St Patrick's Street premises in the local press of the day, the *Hibernian Chronicle*. On Thursday 26 May 1791 a notice appeared from Mr Shinkwin requesting that those interested in becoming involved in shipping insurance send their names to his offices on St Patrick's Street before the following Wednesday.[13]

Increasing numbers of advertisements and notices in the newspapers from businesses on St Patrick's Street tell the story of the street's development over the following decade. On Monday 25 July 1791, Austin Shinkwin again had an advertisement, this time under the heading of 'Cork Insurance Company'. In the column alongside another advertisement appeared: 'To be let, or the interest sold, of a large house in Patrick's Street. Enquire of Mr Leslie.'[14] Further down the column is an advertisement offering 'Red Port Wine' for sale at Edmond Kenifick's on St Patrick's Street. Four years earlier, in the 1787 directory, he is not shown as operating a wine premises on the street – two Edmond Keneficks are listed, one operating as a merchant at North Abbey and the other as a woollen draper at Shandon Street. It can be speculated, therefore, that this was part of the move by business people to the newly developing areas to the east of the old medieval city walls. Again, an advertisement appears in the paper dated Monday 6 April 1795 offering on behalf of a Mr Mannix, a house and cellar to be let on St Patrick's Street.[15] In September 1805, the former Farming Society House held by Ms M. Sheehan was advertised for letting on a long-term lease.[16]

The newspaper advertisements also give an indication of the nature of the materials being sold in the premises on St Patrick's Street at this time. William Mercer had his shop at No. 3, close to the newly built bridge and an advertisement in November 1795 offered a variety of hosiery for sale, including ladies petticoats, dressing gowns and the new Vandyke cotton stockings.[17] By the time *Holden's Directory* was issued for 1805, William Mercer, still at No. 3, had diversified and is listed as selling hosiery and also toy and fancy goods.[18] Thus it is conceivable that this shop of William

Mercer's was the first toy shop on St Patrick's Street to which children in Cork could visit, carrying undoubtedly a range of dolls, wooden toy soldiers, perhaps rocking horses or spinning tops, a range of board games and all brightly presented, portraying a world of wonder to the eyes of a child.

In 1800, James Long offered for sale quantities of cheap timber and also boxes of Coleraine linens.[19] In 1804, at John and George Newsom's, one could buy 'St Petersburg new hemp, Russian mats and Hogs bristles' among other items.[20] In October of that same year, wine, spirit, grocery and cheese were among the items advertised for McSwiney & Co. who had shops on both St Patrick's Street and French Church Street.[21]

By 1805, the first year in the publication of *Holden's Directory*, many more advertisements were appearing in the press for businesses on St Patrick's Street; three on the front page alone of the *Mercantile Chronicle* for 25 January of that year.[22] The directory itself gives a clear indication of just how much more business was being done on the by now well-established main street of the city. In all, eighty-two businesses are listed on St Patrick's Street in *Holden's Directory*, though seven of these are actually located at St Patrick's Bridge. The nature of business carried on is much more varied than heretofore. As well as the apothecaries, merchants, spirit dealers and attorneys, there are to be found tea shops, grocers, three linen drapers and some woollen drapers. Teresa Devereaux ran a trunk-making establishment while Thomas Hunt's was where you would acquire, or indeed have made, mathematical instruments. Banking too had arrived on the city's new main street with Newenham's and also Sir Thomas Roberts, James Bonwell and John Leslie operating there. Hats were being manufactured by David Shaw while Michael Sheahan was where you went to obtain seeds and plants. Thomas Shinkwin operated looking-glass rooms while Isaac Solomon was possibly the first jeweller and silversmith operating on the street.

Art and Culture

In 1813, the Cork Philosophical and Literary Society was founded, reflecting a changing city wherein it became fashionable for people to patronise the arts.[23] Not long after this a sister Society for the Promoting of the Fine Arts was founded by Richard Alfred Miliken, a native of Castlemartyr and an attorney practising in the city. He was well known as a songwriter, one of his most famous songs being 'The Groves of Blarney' and he was also a member of the Apollo Amateur Dramatic Society, a group that had a building on St Patrick's Street known as the Old Theatre. Here the new arts society held exhibitions, though Miliken himself never lived to see the society flourish, dying in 1815.[24]

It was to this Society for the Promoting of Fine Arts and its building on St Patrick's Street that a series of casts by the famous Roman sculptor Antonia Canova were delivered in 1818, a presentation by the Prince Regent of England, later King George IV. There were over 200 pieces in the set, such as figures of Adonis, Venus de Medici, Young Apollo and many others. The Canova casts remained on exhibition at the Old Theatre, St Patrick's Street, for over a decade. When the society fell on hard times, however, they were taken by the Royal Cork Institution and placed in the old Custom House, the School of Art on Emmet Place today, where they are still to be seen. In time the theatre and exhibition centre that had housed these famous casts would itself become famous as No. 95 St Patrick's Street, the home of the *Cork Examiner*.

The main centre for the literary life of the city, however, was John Bolster's bookshop at No. 7 St Patrick's Street. There, artists such as John Hogan, Daniel Maclise, William Maginn and others met and indeed embarked on their earliest artistic exploits before each in turn moved on to greater acclaim in the artistic world of Europe.[25] Art could also be seen and purchased from Michael Mathews at No.19 while a number of portrait painters resided on the street. R. Gibbs lived and worked there *c.* 1810 and John Corbett had lodgings with a Mr Fanning on the street about this time and advertised that he would take sittings from ten o'clock in the morning until five o'clock each afternoon.

Pigot's Directory, 1824

Pigot's Directory of 1824 not only lists the various businesses operating throughout Cork, but also gives a description of the city in the period leading up to its publication. The city is described as being 'very extensive, and several of the principal streets are well built and airy'. The article also says that the principal street St Patrick's 'is elegant and modern'.[26]

In all, some 139 businesses are listed on the street in *Pigot's Directory*. Also included is the French Consul, Colonel McMahon, who had an interesting experience on St Patrick's Street in December 1816. As he was taking a walk with a lady named Austen from Waterfall, three gentlemen by the names of Isaac Varian, Tom Haines and Jessamy Jemmy Morgan passed by. These gentlemen were engrossed in conversation and just as they passed the happy couple, one was heard to say, as part of their conversation, that he was not even a captain. Miss Austen, thinking they were referring to her suitor, turned and insisted that 'it's a lie Sir, he is a Colonel, a full Colonel'. The event was reported in the *Freeholder* newspaper as 'an awkward affair'.[27]

Two day academies, at Nos. 10 and 88, in the names of Mrs Albey and Mrs Bewley respectively, are also listed on the street and, as well as Bolster's bookshop where much artistic development was encouraged, seven other bookshops traded on St Patrick's Street, all indicating that, for certain sectors of society at least, education was an ever-increasing aspect of life. A circulating library was operated by Thomas Kingsfold at No. 32 while no fewer than three newspaper periodicals were published from the street. These were the *Mercantile Chronicle*, produced from No. 1; the *Cork Mercury & Weekly Advertiser*, owned by Thomas Coldwell at No. 93; and the *Southern Reporter* at No. 130. The Victoria Hotel, constructed in 1810, played host over the following decades to many famous guests such as Charles Dickens and Charles Stewart Parnell. Despite this, the Victoria Hotel does not appear in *Pigot's* listings. The hotels that do appear are Frank Best's at No. 86, the Chamber of Commerce Hotel at No. 104, Mrs Day's at No. 94 and the Rawlinson at No. 90.

What is significant in terms of the street's development is that the trend away from it being a place of merchants continued and there is by this time a much wider range of business types than had been evident in the earlier directories. Also, even within categories that are present, greater competition had developed. Thus thirteen toy shops now operated in the city and four of them were listed on St Patrick's Street: Mary Ann Skillin's at No. 25, Etty Dunne's at No. 45, Nano Coleman's at No. 49, and Ann Connor's at No. 60. Joseph Bowles operated a gunsmith shop at No. 22 while Richard Gillispie sold musical instruments at No. 33. Two opticians, Thomas Bennett and Thomas Hunt (perhaps the same man who had dealt in mathematical instruments in 1805) practised at their premises, Nos. 65 and 80 respectively, while tailors traded at Nos. 101, 102, 129 and 132 – Thomas Tangney, Jeremiah O'Grady, Francis Flanagan and John Evans being the owners. Straw hats could be purchased from Catherine McMullen at No. 118 or Mary Ann Hamilton at No. 124. That great institution of Irish culture, the Spirit and Porter House was also to be found on the city's main street at this time, Daniel Flynn's at No. 92 and Denis O'Leary's at No. 119. Four watch and clockmakers operated from the street, including John Murphy at No. 59 and William Byron at No. 68. The other two clockmakers introduce to us names that create an immediate tie to the lives of Cork people in the twenty-first century: Samuel Haynes at No. 114 and James Mangan at No. 81.

Clockmakers

Samuel Haynes is remembered today on two counts. Firstly, the public clock on the premises that used to be Woodford Bournes' on St Patrick's Street at the Daunt Square end was made by him. He was also the maker of clocks for the termini of the Cork, Bandon and South Coast Railway. These clocks, when the railway began its operations, showed Cork local time. From about 1860 they were readjusted to show Dublin time and in 1912 were adjusted again to show Greenwich Mean Time. In 1821, Samuel Haynes married Jane Brookes and their son, also Samuel, joined his father in the business and together they moved to No. 51 St Patrick's Street. In 1852, Samuel junior married Sarah Cooke of George's Street.[28]

The story of Cork's public clocks is a fascinating one. A tale is told of a Corkman giving a guided tour of the city to some visiting Americans. Upon a tourist remarking that it was not the number of public clocks in Cork that was unusual, but that they all showed different times, the guide responded wisely that if all the public clocks in the city showed the same time, there would be a need for only one. The Cork character is well demonstrated in this story which also brings to mind the clock at Shandon Steeple, known to generations as the Four-Faced Liar. Famous the world over for its bells immortalised by Fr Prout in his song 'The Bells of Shandon', this loveable old north-side tower is the public timepiece of the citizenry, proclaiming to the whole world, north, south, east and west, that in Cork it is now a quarter past such an hour.

Shandon church was built in 1722 and the bells, cast by the Gloucester firm of Abel Rudhall, were installed two years later. The story of the clock at Shandon began in February 1843 when a certain Councillor Delay suggested at a Corporation meeting that a public timepiece should be mounted on the tower. It would, he argued, be visible from all parts of the city and should the bells be used for chiming purposes, the sound could be heard up to five miles away. Councillor Delay told the meeting that 'it

Facing page, main picture: Mangan's Clock, one of the icons of St Patrick's Street. (Courtesy sandraocallaghan.com)

Top right: Samuel Haynes clock on the Woodford Bourne building. (Courtesy sandraocallaghan.com)

Bottom right: Mangan's clock on Shandon Steeple, known as the Four-Faced Liar. (Courtesy sandraocallaghan.com)

would be a working charity for the poor and sick, who, at times, when being ordered medicine, didn't know the proper hour to take it'.[29]

On 23 May 1843, the Corporation made a grant of £250 towards the erection of the clock and the work was performed by James Mangan and his son Richard, two of the city's best known clockmakers. Upon completion the clock was the largest four dial in the world until the construction of Big Ben in London in1854. In building the clock, James Mangan had to take into account the prevailing winds that struck the tower. Without due consideration in the design, these winds could make the hands on the east and west faces move more quickly than those on the north and south.

The clock at Shandon is undoubtedly Cork's most famous public timepiece, but another is more generally associated with the name of Mangan: that which stands outside the Merchant Quay shopping centre on St Patrick's Street, where the premises of James Mangan Ltd stood since its founding in 1817 until the building of the centre. This clock, atop a standard, is well over a century old and was originally slave to a driving mechanism inside the building and which was wound in the cellar. The original face of the clock was damaged during the fight for independence when gunfire left a bullet hole in the dial and the current face dates to that time.[30]

Councillor Delay's comments were significant on two counts as he argued for the installation of a clock on Shandon tower; first his reference to the poor of the city and second that they would be taking medicine. While the development of St Patrick's Street since its beginning in the 1780s and over the subsequent decades can be seen in perhaps a romantic light – the emergence of a new main thoroughfare and the movement of a sector of society into the spacious and luxurious surroundings that it afforded – it nevertheless occurred while continuing poverty and hardship were the daily existence of thousands of others in the city at the time. In 1826, the city was described as a place of rampant 'distress, disease, destitution and death from starvation'.[31] Epidemics of diseases such as typhus in 1818 and cholera in 1832 were not uncommon; prostitution was rife in all parts of the city; filthy lanes and open sewers added to a perpetual existence of misery for the poor of Cork. Poverty and hardship had been the lot of Cork's poor in better times during the eighteenth century when trade had made the city a wealthy place. What chance subsequently of things improving in a declining economic situation?

William Thompson

In 1910, James Connolly referred to William Thompson as 'this earliest Irish apostle of the social revolution', a description that encompassed both the revolutionary ideals that had prevailed since the eighteenth century to that time and the specific revolution that had occurred in France during Thompson's formative years.[32] He was born in 1775, the son of merchant and Mayor, Alderman John Thompson, and from their home at No. 4 St Patrick's Street William would have experienced both the luxury of a wealthy upbringing and also seen the poverty of the masses.[33] 'Behind the paper facade of prosperity, the masses lived in a poverty and squalor which beggared description.'[34] Although only fourteen years old when the French Revolution occurred, he found that later journeys across Europe reinforced his sympathies with the revolution's ideals.[35] Travelling in France and Holland, William encountered the writings of Saint Simon and Sismondi, who believed manufacturing improvements adversely effected the situation of the industrious classes.[36] At home, it was not uncommon at the time for the wealthy to engage in philanthropic endeavours and William's father was chairman of the Society for Bettering the Conditions and Increasing Comforts of the Poor. William himself became a subscriber and adviser to the body.[37] Thus his formative years were lived 'in a period when the ancient ways of life were being shattered by the twin forces of the French and industrial revolution'.[38] Through reading and personal experience William Thompson developed beliefs and ideals that rejected his own Ascendancy heritage and laid the foundation for socialist theories that were advanced later in the nineteenth century by Karl Marx. In this way he was an 'apostle', an advocate for the ideals emanating from France and author of writings from which future socialists such as James Connolly could read the gospel of their movement.

That William began a thought process to discover a social science that would show the wrongness of inequality, a process that led eventually to the publication of his famous socialist writings, reveals two important points about Thompson and Cork society at the time.[39] Firstly, it locates both Thompson himself and Cork society alongside the other European countries where similar situations prevailed. 'In England, France and Germany a crop of social philosophers sprang up, each with his scheme of a perfect social order ... Hence it is not to be wondered that the same period ... produced in Ireland an economist more thoroughly socialist in the modern sense than any of his contemporaries'.[40] Secondly, Thompson was more than a theoretician; he fought for his cause on his native soil. Fundamental to his thinking was the education of those deprived by the societal norms of the day.[41] He argued with the Cork Institution in 1818 on account of its misuse of funding for education.[42] The interests of the privileged, he said, were being given priority over the needs of the workers and unemployed.[43] Thompson also had plans for a juvenile institution where young people would learn arithmetic, reading, writing and natural history. During time in England he encountered the philosophers Bentham and Owen, who reinforced his desire to advance the cooperative movement which he believed was 'the right way to organise society'.[44] For this he used his own lands in west Cork as a location. He also became a champion of women's rights through his publication with Anna Wheeler of *Appeal of one half of the Human Race, Women, Against the Pretensions of the other Half, Men* in 1825. William Thompson died at his family estate in west Cork in 1833. His legacy was one of challenge to the upper echelons of society. To this day, the battles that William Thompson fought against inequality and exploitation and to achieve education and co-operation continue to be waged.

On St Patrick's Street today, the iconic sign of Roches Stores recalls William Roche; Ben Dunne is remembered in Dunnes Stores; James Mangan's clock is testimony to his part in the street's history; Sir John Arnott is commemorated in a plaque on the wall of No. 54; the other 'apostle', Fr Theobald Mathew, is celebrated with his effigy, mounted on a plinth at the most prominent location on the street. William Thompson, however, is all but forgotten. History has been unkind to the Cork philosopher who expounded his ideals, partly at least based on his early life experiences on St Patrick's Street.[45]

The developing consciousness on the part of many people about the social structures of Cork continued and a number of societies were founded to help those who were most badly off. One in particular was founded by a man whose name would in time become synonymous with St Patrick's Street in Cork. The Society of St Joseph was founded in 1820 to help the sick and destitute poor by Fr Theobald Mathew, a Capuchin priest who, although originally from Tipperary, would become as much a part of Cork history as St Patrick's Street itself.

Fr Theobald Mathew and His Times

Fr Theobald Mathew, who lived also in the William Thompson era, was of a wealthy background and dedicated his life to the less well off. He was born on 10 October 1790, the fourth son of James Mathew and Anne Whyte of Thomastown Castle, Cashel, County Tipperary. Ordained a Capuchin priest in Dublin on 17 April 1813, after a brief period in Kilkenny he moved to Cork in 1814 where he was appointed chaplain to the county gaol. Of his commitment to the impoverished of the city, his biographer in 1947 wrote that the 'big hearted apostle was working with a generosity that had never been seen before … The poor he had always with him.'[46] For the benefit of Cork's poor he began a school that in 1824 had 500 pupils; lest the destitute have nowhere to be buried he acquired the old botanical gardens and established St Joseph's Cemetery.[47] Between 1832 and 1850 he oversaw the building of a new Capuchin friary and church at Holy Trinity. 'After twenty-two years of unostentatious labour, his name was a household word.'[48] But far greater fame would soon follow. On 10 April 1838, at the request of a number of people (including the Quaker William Martin) who were concerned with the level of alcohol abuse among the lower classes, Fr Mathew joined and agreed to lead a new temperance movement. Thus began a period of his life that would see him become the Apostle of Temperance.[49] Across the country, thousands flocked to hear him preach and to take the pledge of abstinence from alcohol.[50]

BRONZE STATUE OF FATHER MATHEW, BY J. H. F

Fr Theobald Mathew.
(*Illustrated London News*)

Trade and Temperance Societies

Prior to 1824, it was illegal for any type of unionisation or structural organisation among employees. Following the repeal of the Combination Acts in that year, however, though matters were still very restricted, trade societies such as the coopers, bakers, tailors and printmakers, some of which may have been in existence for decades, could become much more vocal and visible in pursuit of their beliefs and goals.[51] Initially quite inward looking, with the onset of the national movements in pursuit of Catholic Emancipation and the repeal of the Act of Union, a unifying of the trade societies came about. In the processions that passed through St Patrick's Street in subsequent years, thousands marched behind the banners of their respective trade societies proclaiming aloud and unafraid

85

their beliefs, displaying to all who looked, then and now, their place in the history of Cork.

In 1814, Fr Mathew, who had been posted to the friary at Blackamore Lane off Cove Street in the parish of St Finbarr South, as well as his work at the county gaol, immediately threw himself completely into working for the betterment of conditions in the tenements, workshops, factories and hospitals throughout the city. Realising that drunkenness was contributing to the misery of the working classes with many people drinking excessively to escape the conditions in which they found themselves, he agreed to lead the crusade of temperance and from 1838 began to set up societies throughout the city and in time the whole country. One of the first such societies, set up in 1838, was the Barrack Street Total Abstinence Society and Band, the first gathering of the famous Barrack Street Band that still entertains the people of Cork into the twenty-first century.[52] Many other temperance societies also had bands in pre-Famine Cork and it was a common sight to see these bands marching through the city streets, including almost always St Patrick's Street, inviting people to follow them to their meeting rooms and join the ever-expanding temperance association.

Throughout the latter half of the 1830s and the early 1840s, two great preachers enthralled and enticed the people of Ireland, Cork being no exception. Fr Theobald Mathew preached the gospel of temperance while Daniel O'Connell did the same in pursuit of repeal of the Act of Union. On one famous and historic occasion, Easter Monday 1842, the two men met and together made their way through the streets of Cork, marching behind the Barrack Street Band, together with fifty-four other societies from the city and county. Rarely before had Cork's St Patrick's Street seen such an event.

> Every road, street, lane and avenue leading into Cork echoed to the sound of music, as hundreds and thousands poured in from the neighbouring towns and districts of the county, or even from places so far distant as 30 or 40 miles … at the hour of eleven the procession began to move slowly from Corn Market, and on reaching the Country Club House it was met by O'Connell who advanced to join Fr Mathew. Their greeting was warm and affectionate … We could tell of the wild, joyous shouts that rent the very air when the two great men of Ireland, the political and moral emancipation of her people, met together. The eagerness – the exclamations of delight

– the rapture and enthusiasm of the moment, are beyond our power of description … Fr Mathew then walked with the Liberator on one side and the Mayor of Cork on the other. Every window was crowded with brilliant groups of fashionably dressed and elegant-looking females, who waved their handkerchiefs as the splendid array filed before them. Every roof, hall, door, balcony, balustrade, wall and projection was literally covered with a mass of eager and delighted beings, who cheered with all their might as the Liberator and Apostle came in view.[53]

So reported the *Cork Examiner* of the events on that famous day when Ireland's two most famous leaders appeared together on the stage that was the streets of Cork and in particular St Patrick's Street. At the end of Lancaster Quay, Daniel O'Connell, before departing, knelt and received the blessing of Fr Mathew amidst tumultuous cheering of the crowd and the playing of the Barrack Street Band. It was one of the largest abstinence processions that had been held in Ireland to that time.[54]

Historians have debated at length the motives of O'Connell in paying homage to Fr Mathew on that Easter Monday. It certainly increased his esteem among the followers of Fr Mathew. Over the following years Daniel O'Connell returned to Cork on a number of occasions and each time thousands of people congregated in the city centre to give support to the Liberator. Just over a year after the famous procession with Fr Mathew, in May 1843, O'Connell was back in St Patrick's Street. The *Cork Examiner* again carried detailed reports of the proceedings:

The iconic figure of Daniel O'Connell. (Courtesy National Library)

so early as ten o'clock Patrick Street, the Grand Parade and the South Mall began to be occupied by the trades for the purpose of taking their order in the procession according to the programme published in recent numbers of the Journal. The gay flaunting of the banners – the decency and decorum of the tradesmen, each with a white wand in his hand, and marshalled under the proper standard of his craft – the thousands of well-dressed persons who crowded the streets, feasting their delighted eyes on the stirring scene passing in review before them.

A poem was composed:

Grateful ages to come will remember thy fame,
When alike we are free from the serpent and slave:
Children will prattle O'Connell's great name,
And pilgrims of freedom will visit his grave![55]

The crowds marched out to beyond Glanmire where they met Daniel O'Connell and following speeches and the reading of a poem specially written for the occasion, the last verse of which is the above, the assembly returned to Cork and into St Patrick's Street where 'the scene was magnificently grand from end to end of the street, the most extraordinary enthusiasm was displayed, ladies waving handkerchiefs – gentlemen joining in the chorus for old Ireland's independence – the bands playing with increased vigour'. The entire assembly in time made its way to the Victoria Hotel where an address of welcome was made by Mayor Thomas Lyons. Following a response by the Liberator, some 700 people sat down to a sumptuous banquet. A top table for the guests of honour was positioned a few feet higher than the rest and the 'galleries, boxes and seats were lined with green cloth – the pillars supporting them, twined with laurels and roses'.[56]

The food for the banquet was quite spectacular, consisting of:

20 Dishes of Salmon	20 Fillets of Veal
5 Turbots	46 Couples of Roast Chicken
10 Dishes Mock Turtle	15 Roleaus of Veal
20 Rounds of Beef	30 Pieces of Roast Beef
40 Rumps of Beef	50 Ox Tongues
34 Hams with the	30 Couples of Ducks
word REPEAL carved on each	Of glasses there were 1,000
16 Legs of Mutton	Of knives and forks, 150 dozen
20 Shoulders of Mutton	Of blue ware 1,200

Coffee was served to the teetotallers and those who partook of the 'juicy grape' were supplied with it in abundance.[57] Congratulations were extended to Mr McCormack of the Victoria Hotel for the spectacular proceedings which he had orchestrated. All too soon Daniel O'Connell had to leave Leeside once more but he would return on a number of occasions before his death and the death of his repeal movement in 1847.

The *Cork Examiner*

A sumptuous banquet such as that described was of course a far cry from the fare that the majority of the population of Ireland could expect during the 1840s. Many of the thousands of people who marched in support of O'Connell and Fr Mathew in these times were living lives of extreme poverty, destitution and famine. Recognising this, John Francis Maguire, the son of a local businessman, decided that ordinary people needed a voice. He therefore started a newspaper to counteract the influential attitudes articulated in the *Cork Constitution* which served the interests of the landed gentry and southern unionists. The *Cork Examiner*, the newspaper which carried such eloquent reports of proceedings in the city as those quoted above, made its first appearance on the streets of Cork on 30 August 1841. The paper, Maguire declared, would 'live by the honesty with which the columns are devoted, not to private and personal ends, but to the welfare and interests of the whole community'.[58]

Initially operating from rooms on Marlborough Street, the headquarters of the paper were soon established at No. 95 St Patrick's Street, the site of a theatre of old. Initially published as an evening paper three times each week, it cost 4d and since its inception has provided a continuous account of many elements of Cork life. On 25 April 1843, some 500 labourers assembled at Daunt's Square following which they proceeded to march through the city, passing beneath the *Cork Examiner* offices en-route. Their concerns were twofold. Firstly, the high level of unemployment in the city and leading on from that the consequent hunger of themselves and their families. They therefore paraded behind a symbolic loaf of bread affixed to a tall pole.

Famine

Their cries would not be heard, however. Within two years, the Great Famine had begun and the streets of Cork saw scenes far different from parades and processions, scenes of horror unequalled before or since. Starving souls from outside the city began to arrive in the hope of finding food. By September 1846 thousands of homeless were arriving at the doors of the Relief Committee. By November, it was reported that 'more than 5,000 half-starved, wretched beings from the country' were begging in the streets.[59] Amongst those vainly trying to help was Fr Mathew who provided soup from his own 'besieged dwelling'.[60] By 1847 the situation had deteriorated dramatically, with up to 30,000 beggars on the streets. Thousands of others had died. Corpses were found on the streets every morning.

So what of St Patrick's Street at this time? Always a place of relative affluence where an ever-increasing variety of goods could be obtained, did the horrors of the Famine make their way on to St Patrick's Street or did they remain in the narrow lanes and streets of the old city? There are few, if any, detailed contemporary accounts specific to St Patrick's Street during these years. Nevertheless, the newspapers of the day give us some clues as to what was happening on the main street.

Above all else, St Patrick's Street had by now developed into a highly successful commercial street and this characteristic of its existence continued throughout the Famine in spite of the difficult circumstances in which the business people operated. Fewer advertisements than before suggested a downturn in trade. The main advertisements page on the *Cork Examiner* of 27 January 1847 gave an interesting mix of notices. Alongside ones of thanks from a variety of relief districts, such as Donoughmore, for assistance received to help their efforts, were two advertisements for businesses on St Patrick's Street. One was for household furniture to be sold at the auction rooms at No. 81 and it listed items such as easy chairs, feather beds, a piano, ceiling lamps and some china and dinnerware. Being sold as a separate item by private contract was a full-sized billiard table. In the next column Wood & Son of No. 69 advertised for sale 'Short Napped Beaver Hats' of a rich, brilliant and permanent black. The hats, gentlemen were told, combined beauty and durability. Waterproof 'Felt Jerry' hats were also offered in the advertisement.[61]

On the front page of the *Cork Examiner* dated Friday 14 May 1847, George Allder of the Linen Drapery, No. 110 St Patrick's Street, announced to the nobility, gentry and inhabitants of Cork that in consequence of the severe distress experienced in the manufacturing districts of England and the north of Ireland, he had been induced to visit them and made considerable purchases which enabled him to offer the very best goods at the lowest prices. These items consisted of Oregon plaids, fancy ginghams, printed cambrics, rich black silk and many other items. He further advised that he intended to sell off his old stock for very low prices thus affording his customers every advantage in his power.[62]

On the same paper were two interesting items of news. One, headlined 'PEDESTRIANISM', told how:

Four officers of Her Majesty's 54th regiment, fully accoutred in heavy marching order, each carrying sixty rounds of ball cartridge, walked for a wager of £10 from the Kinsale barracks to Cork, a distance of 20 miles, on this morning. The condition on which they were to pocket the wager was that, thus accoutred, they would walk the required distance in six and a half hours. They started from Kinsale at a quarter after four and reached the Victoria hotel on St Patrick's Street at 5 minutes to ten o'clock, thus winning by three quarters of an hour.[63]

One wonders what sights they may have encountered as they made their way to the city. In an editorial on the same page, John Francis Maguire spoke out angrily, as he promised he would in 1841, about the attitude of people in the city towards relief for the poor:

We perceive by the report of the meeting of the local Board of Health held yesterday, that the Mayor expressed his intention of calling a Public Meeting, in compliance with a requisition signed by some of the citizens, to petition against Out-door Relief. We know not the names of those attached to the requisition, nor any more of the matter than what we have seen in the report alluded to; but we have no hesitation in adopting the emphatic denunciation of Dr Lyons against an intended opposition so inhuman and cruel. The Workhouse is filled beyond what prudence would suggest as safe to the health of the inmate, or that of the city. At most it can shelter but a few hundred more – while every lane in the city has its hundreds of starving poor – while every parish in the city swarms with THOUSANDS of destitute men, women and children. What then is to be done? Are the citizens of Cork, who can appear at a public meeting, to protest against giving relief to their fellow-citizens, because they are poor – because they are wasting away – because they are helpless, and at the mercy of the rich? Can it be possible that any man will come forward and oppose the only species of relief that can save thousands from death by starvation? Or; if they oppose Outdoor Relief, what relief are they to substitute for it? What is their plan? Who is to put it forth?[64]

Such was the view emanating from the St Patrick's Street offices of the *Cork Examiner*.

By the autumn, all hope that the situation would improve in the country had disappeared with the failure of the entire potato crop throughout the land. The paper had reported optimistically in the early summer that the crop was looking healthy but soon had to change that viewpoint. On Friday evening, 8 October 1847, the *Cork Examiner* reported 'A RETURN OF DEATHS AND EMIGRATIONS' in west Cork showing deaths of over 7,000 in the Skibbereen area alone. There is no account of the situation in the city but in the previous nine months over 13,000 souls had been buried in St Joseph's Cemetery and the area for free burials was now closed. On the same page of that edition of the *Cork Examiner*, notices pertaining to the other side of life are to be found. Owing to the depressed state of trade in the manufacturing districts of England and the north of Ireland, an immense reduction in prices was to be obtained at Fogarty & Co. Commercial House at No. 91 St Patrick's Street in woollen clothes, plain and fancy doe skins, cloakings and blankets among other items. At the Cork China and Glass House, No. 88 St Patrick's Street, 'M. Norris, having completed his arrangements this day, commenced to sell for cash only … several packages of dinner, dessert and tea china'. And one may speculate that the music business was doing well if Alex Roche's decision to move his Pianoforte and Music Warehouse from the South Mall to No. 29 St Patrick's Street is anything to go by. Pianofortes were advertised for sale or hire in town or country and instruments could also be tuned or repaired.

Despite the editorial quotes above, a letter appeared in the edition dated 11 October from A CITIZEN:

> Gentlemen, will you permit me to ask you if you have consulted the law officers of the Crown, whether the late act for the suppression of street begging is to be rendered a dead letter by the fact of three persons carrying for sale a box of matches. If you have not done so, I say you have been guilty of a most culpable neglect of your duty, in compelling the police to carry out the only boon to the heavy rate-payers. If you have done so, and that we are still, as I cannot think it possible to be, burthened by these beggars, it shows the utter humbug of Irish legislation. If this act is not stringently carried out now, our city will be inundated with beggars from the country, and the same

deplorable consequences as last year will be the result.[65]

Clearly two strata existed in the Cork of the 1840s and both were to be found in the central place wherein was reflected all aspects of Cork society, St Patrick's Street. On the one hand the commercial sector of the city sought to entice those with means to part with their money and purchase a wide range of both necessary and luxury goods. Many succeeded in their endeavours. On the other hand, thousands of destitute poor roamed the streets begging for just enough to sustain them and keep them alive. Many of these failed in their endeavour. If St Patrick's Street was the stage on which was played the various elements and aspects that made up Cork society, then surely this dark period in its history was one of the greatest tragedies played thereon.

As 1848 dawned, from the offices of the *Cork Examiner* on New Year's Eve came words that would echo down the centuries, words of emotion and of heartfelt pain:

> We have passed through a year of horrors, every way. The records of human afflictions have had nothing like it in their mortal archives. It was a year of graves and ghosts; when the whole island smelled of a churchyard, and putridity from rotting humanity filled the tainted air as if from a reeking shambles … Men and women of Ireland, in the name of God – of the poor – of Charity – of Country – in the name of all that is good, and great and holy – determine now, on the threshold of the new year, to do something for the poor that starve, and for the country that mourns.[66]

During the dark years of the Famine, Fr Mathew, along with his temperance work, had lived among the poor, the hungry, sick and dying in the laneways and streets of Cork. By the end of the Famine he had given his all to the poor of the city and it had taken its toll. In April 1848 his health deteriorated when he suffered a stroke and it was decided that he should depart Leeside and indeed the shores of Ireland and go to America.[67] He left in May 1849 and, though much afflicted by the stroke which he had suffered, for the next two and a half years, he continued to preach the twin gospels of temperance and charity, often to people who had heard his voice in Ireland before emigrating. In December 1851 Fr Mathew returned to Cork but his health was now 'shattered beyond all reasonable hope of restoration'.[68]

By 1853, having suffered a second stroke, he could no longer make public appearances and in an effort to restore some degree of good health, in 1854 his loyal and dedicated temperance followers helped send him to Madeira where good weather, it was hoped, would lead to a recovery.[69] It was not to be. He returned and made his home in Cobh where his old friend John Francis Maguire wrote of him:

> a white haired venerable man of countenance noble in outline and sweet in expression might be seen slowly creeping along the sunny places of Queenstown [Cobh], his tottering steps assisted by a young lad on whose shoulder one hand of the invalid rested for support. This was Theobald Mathew.

In November Fr Mathew suffered a third stroke and on 8 December 1856, the Capuchin from Tipperary passed peacefully to his heavenly home. Fr Mathew was no more. His funeral procession was 3 miles long and passed through a silent St Patrick's Street. At St Joseph's Cemetery, 50,000 people gathered for the final prayers.

The Statue

It was only a matter of weeks after the death of Fr Mathew in 1856 when suggestions were made that a memorial should be erected in his honour. Popular opinion supported the idea and a poem by John Fitzgerald called 'The Apostle's Grave' said:

> And all that he had gain'd in the land of his birth
> Was that simple cross and six feet of earth.

Another poem, 'City of Cork Alphabet for 1860', from the same writer had:

> M is for Mathew that's fam'd o'er the earth,
> Though his name seems forgot in the home of his birth.[70]

In the years following Fr Mathew's death, a committee worked to achieve that ambition consisting of, among others, John Francis Maguire, Sir John Benson, Richard and Isaac Varian of St Patrick's Street, Mr W. Dowden and

Mr James Dwyer.[71] Significantly, the Corporation placed at the disposal of the committee any site they wanted within the city and that chosen had the approval of the artist commissioned to do the work.[72] It was 'the most judicious that could be pitched upon. It is St Patrick's Street, principal thoroughfare of the city, within 100 feet of St Patrick's Bridge and fifty of a line drawn from the end houses of the street'.[73] All sections of Cork society had contributed to the fund for the statue.[74] It was the first statue of a private citizen in a public place in Cork.[75] Following the successful campaign, on Monday 10 October 1864, a crowd of 100,000 gathered in the centre of Cork, 40,000 of them on St Patrick's Street between Winthrop Street and the bridge, to witness the unveiling of the statue in honour of Fr Theobald Mathew. The event had been publicised for days in

Fr Mathew Statue on
St Patrick's Street.
(Courtesy Michael Lenihan)

advance, calling for there to be no political dimension to the occasion and calling on employers to close for at least six hours so that workers could participate and for shopkeepers to shut so that assistants and customers could attend.[76] On the day 'the city had a festive appearance' and 'not one shop of any class remained open on St Patrick's Street'.[77] Numerous bands played music as the temperance societies, followed by the trades associations marching behind their banners, processed to St Patrick's Street from the Navigation Wall. 'By 12 o'clock the principal streets were barely passable.'[78]

The procession that would begin proceedings on that October morning was scheduled to leave Marina Park near Victoria Road at twelve o'clock in the afternoon. Then the Corporation and various dignitaries made their way to the park where, in six carriages, they led the procession which began as the twelve bells tolled. Included among the dignitaries were Mr Charles Mathew of Lehenagh, brother of Fr Theobald, and three nephews of the honoured Capuchin. These were then followed by the Temperance and Trade societies along a route of Albert Quay, Anglesea Road, South Terrace, George's Quay, Sullivan's Quay, South Gate Bridge, South and North Main Streets, North Gate Bridge, Pope's Quay, Camden Quay, St Patrick's Bridge, Merchant's Quay, Warren's Place, South Mall, Grand Parade and finally St Patrick's Street, a distance of over 2 miles in total.

> By half past one o'clock the head of the procession had reached the statue … At this moment the scene was particularly striking. The windows on every side were crammed with figures, and from the sea of heads rose up the banners, all ablaze with colour, and fluttering gaily in the wind were the apparently countless streamers from the processionists. In the midst of the multitude rose the statue in its red veil, a white wreath upon the head. Fully an hour passed before a sufficient proportion of the procession could be filed past, it being found quite impossible that the whole of the trades could pass previous to the ceremony.[79]

Never before had Cork seen such a spectacle; never before had St Patrick's Street been the stage for such a display of passion and emotion. As the Mayor rose to speak a silence fell over the crowd.

Citizens of Cork, this is a proud and a happy day for you, for you have assembled here to do public honour to the memory of a great and good man ... where is the name more worthy of honour than the name of Theobald Mathew? where the man more entitled to an enduring mark of public respect than Fr Mathew, the Apostle of Temperance ... remember him in that terrible famine time; and if Theobald Mathew had no claim upon your gratitude previous to that awful hour when the food of a nation lay sitting in the fields, he deserves from you – from his countrymen throughout the length and breadth of this land – a statue not of bronze, but of gold, for his heroic services to his fellow man in those disastrous years.

Think of the time when multitudes of God's creatures – young and old – the strong man and the tender infant, lived upon his charity, would have perished without his daily bounty; and then say, however glorious his fame as the most illustrious reformer of his age, whether he is not dearer to you as the devoted priest of the sanctuary, as the dauntless champion of the poor – as he who fed the hungry, and gave drink to the thirsty, and clothed the naked, and sheltered the stranger and the wanderer and protected the widow and orphan ... He died as a soldier of the Cross with his armour on. He died amidst the tears and benedictions of all men; and upon his sainted grave no hand has flung aught but a flower, and no tongue has coupled his holy name with aught save a blessing or a prayer ... It is now my pleasing duty, in the name of the citizens of Cork to unveil the statue which is to stand henceforth in your city as an enduring memorial of its best and greatest citizen, and to present to the gaze of those whom he loved and served in life the semblance of those features which are so familiar to their memories and so dear to their hearts. Let the statue be now unveiled.[80]

Huge crowds at the unveiling of the Statue in 1864.
(*London Illustrated News*)

At the conclusion of the address a string was touched and the wrappings disappeared. A shout was raised which swelled along the street and was caught up from point to point of the procession until it became a long and continuous roar that lasted fully fifteen minutes.

According to the *Cork Examiner*, printed that very evening:

amongst the people who flocked to take part in the procession, or as mere spectators to gaze at its gay and jubilant features, there was no reservation of feeling.

Every business on St Patrick's Street closed for the day –merchants, manufacturers and shop-keepers alike, many with fond and personal memories of the man whom they gathered to honour … Amongst the surging masses who surrounded the procession from the moment it left the park till its arrival at the spot where the statue is placed, those who were old enough to have a distinct remembrance of the man who brought peace and happiness to the humble home, whose lips were ever breathing kindness and good will, and whose hand was open as day to melting charity … the statue raised to the Apostle of Temperance is also the memorial of the dearly cherished friend of all who needed friendship.[81]

The order for the construction of the statue was in fact placed by the committee some years previously with the distinguished Irish sculptor John Hogan, but his death in March 1858 delayed the execution of the project. In time the commission was given to the eminent sculptor John Henry Foley and was brought to the site a fortnight prior to the unveiling. The *Cork Examiner* again gave a detailed description:

It is of bronze and stands 8 feet high including the plinth. Fr Mathew is supposed to be in the act of blessing the multitude upon whom he has just conferred the temperance pledge. One hand gathers up the folds of the large cloak, which it is no violation of liberal truth to place upon his shoulders. The other, slightly extended, seems as if it were about to be raised in benediction … A temperance medal upon his breast is equally characteristic and significant. But the triumph of artistic effort is in the face. Though Mr Foley we believe never saw Fr Mathew, and had therefore been compelled to depend upon such help as he could get in the way of portraits, he has not only produced a most striking likeness of the mere features, but he has contrived to throw into the lineaments that expression of sweet and beaming benevolence which made the charm of the countenance the people so loved to look upon. The statue has been most successfully cast by Mr Prince of London. The cost has been £1,000. The pedestal, which stands 9 feet 6 inches high has been designed by Mr Atkins, architect.

Its best feature is its suitability. There is no ambitious attempt to outshine or hide the statue.

The article then went on to describe the inscriptions.

> The word MATHEW and APOSTLE OF TEMPERANCE on the frieze. On the block THE TRIBUTE OF A GRATEFUL PEOPLE is inscribed on the front and at the back ERECTED IN THE MAYORALTY OF JOHN FRANCIS MAGUIRE MP, 1864. On the sides towards the footpaths are small marble drinking fountains and the stonework has been executed by Mr Egan of this city.[82]

Henceforth, the centre of Cork, the meeting place of countless generations, the central terminus for all transportation – as much a symbol of Cork as the Bells of Shandon – would be the Statue. In time it became an icon, not just of St Patrick's Street but of Cork. As noted earlier, many buses carried simply the word 'Statue' in their destination windows; the term 'Statue' came to mean among other things a meeting place or a reference point from which much else in the city was described or measured. The iconic status and place of the Fr Mathew Statue in the hearts of Cork people was reinforced in recent times and there was an outcry when it was announced that as part of Beth Gali's plans to revamp the street the Statue would be moved to a new location at the junction of Winthrop Street. The *Evening Echo* newspaper did a poll of Cork people and the result was 85.6 per cent to 14.4 per cent against the move.[83] On Friday 21 July 2000, columnist T. P. O'Mahony wrote that 'whatever is intended for St Patrick's Street, it is a big enough street and wide enough place to accommodate change without messing with one of its features, something that is part of the very texture of the street – the Father Mathew Statue. The message of the people of Cork is clear. Leave the Father Mathew Statue alone.'[84] In November the headline in the *Evening Echo* summed up the outcome: 'You win the day for Father Mathew. He shall not be moved and it's all thanks to people power. The famous Father Mathew is staying put on St Patrick's Street following a public outcry.'[85] The plans were modified and the statue retained its place as the very heart of Cork city.

Other Famous Names

John Arnott is another famous name associated with St Patrick's Street in Cork. Born at Auchtermuchty near Glasgow in Scotland in 1814, he moved to Cork in 1834. After time spent in Belfast and Glasgow, he returned to Cork in the 1840s and opened a large drapery store at Nos. 52–54 St Patrick's Street where he was later joined by Alexander Grant.[86] Successful in business, John Arnott spread his interest into bakery, brewing and flour-milling; was chairman of the Cork and Macroom Railway and chief proprietor of *The Irish Times*.[87] In the world of politics John Arnott had a second association with St Patrick's Street. As Mayor he presided over the laying of the foundation stone for the new St Patrick's Bridge in November 1859, on which occasion he was knighted. Shortly after his tenure as first citizen was completed, he left Cork for Dublin where his business interests on Henry Street developed into the famous Arnotts of Dublin. The St Patrick's Street store became Grant's of Cork.

One of the people who resided as a drapers' apprentice in Cash & Co. on St Patrick's Street, such as those written about earlier, was a young man named William Roche, a native of Kilavulen, County Cork. Of his apprenticeship in the drapery trade he later said that 'tyranny of a heartless type' was his lot for the five years and that 'a good many apprentices died off because of the want of fresh air and cleanliness'.[88]

Following the failure of three early business ventures, he moved to London and in five years made enough money to return to Cork and set

William Roche.

Left: **Roches Stores Building.**
(Courtesy sandraocallaghan.com)

Right: **William Roche.**
(Courtesy Michael Lenihan)

up a small furniture store on Merchant Street, just off St Patrick's Street. Joined by a friend James Keating, together they sold affordable furniture for cash based on an ethos of how they could best serve the customer. 'Our predominant thought was how we could give the customer more for his money. We told the customer the truth at all times.'[89] After twelve years the firm expanded into ladies' fashions and the name Roches Stores was put above the Merchant Street premises. Then, in 1919, the London House at No. 15 on St Patrick's Street came on the market. Roches acquired it in June and, applying the successful principles of customer value, 'for the first round year of our working we did almost exactly five times the trade which they had been doing'.[90] In that year the company officially became Roches Stores Ltd.

In December 1920, Roches Stores was one of the premises destroyed in the 'Burning of Cork', which will be dealt with later in the book. Expanded new premises reopened in 1927 and from then the firm grew, opening stores in Dublin, Limerick and further afield as the century progressed. William Roche died aged sixty-five in February 1939. From an apprenticeship of tyranny to giving the customer good value and honesty, he built a business that became synonymous with St Patrick's Street, its location on the prime retailing street of the city and at the centre of the transport system ensuring that in the dialect of English spoken in Cork, Roches Stores had many meanings; a department store, the city centre, a meeting place and a geographical reference point from which much else was measured. Now its obituary can be written with the takeover by the British firm Debenhams. One suspects, however, that the Roches Stores term and the name of William Roche will live long on St Patrick's Street.

During the 1930s a young man named Ben Dunne joined Roches Stores in Cork as a buyer from Cameron's Drapery Shop in Longford. He had been born in Rostrevor, County Down, in 1908 and served his apprenticeship with Anderson's in Drogheda. During his time with Roches Stores, seeing that William Roche's philosophy of good value to the customer worked, he decided that he could offer 'better value' and in 1944 opened the first Dunnes Stores at No. 44 St Patrick's Street, painting the 'better value' logo on the side of the building. The store opened on 30 March 1944 and after three years Ben Dunne opened a second store on North Main Street. Expansion continued and in 1958 he opened on Henry Street in Dublin.[91] Thus the empire that is Dunnes Stores today was another that began on St Patrick's Street, another begun by a drapers' apprentice whose name ranks among the street's most famous. His career, and those of John Arnott and William Roche, marked a subtle change in the type of businesses to be found on St Patrick's Street with cheaper, more affordable goods being sold on a street that had once been the domain of the wealthy.

The motto that made an empire in Cork and Irish retailing.
(Courtesy sandraocallaghan.com)

Mass Gatherings

Much had changed in the minds of Cork people in the years since Catholic Emancipation in 1829. A developing consciousness regarding their place and rights in society brought another aspect of the history of St Patrick's Street into focus. This wide and spacious main street of the city became the stage on which the people of the city played out their rights claims, their aspirations and their cultural beliefs, over the following decades and centuries. Very often the vehicle through which this was done was the public procession and from early in the nineteenth century these processions, often attended by tens of thousands of people, were commonplace and often these people paraded behind the banners of firstly, trade societies to which they were affiliated and secondly, temperance societies of which they were members. People, other than those resident on the street, made use of the space for a variety of purposes throughout its history. Business, shopping and socialising were among the daily activities. St Patrick's Street was and is also used by the people of the entire city as a location wherein a

Crowds watching a Eucharistic procession in the mid-twentieth century. (Courtesy Michael Lenihan)

variety of statements are made through cultural events such as processions and mass gatherings.

Peter Burke has identified carnivals as huge plays in which 'streets and squares became stages – the city a theatre without walls and its inhabitants the actors and spectators'.[92] This analysis formed part of Gary Owens' work on the mass gatherings of the O'Connell period in Irish history. In processions, he argued, 'crowds metaphorically capture the spaces they occupy'. They were 'elaborate secular rituals' and 'no great event was complete without one'.[93] Furthermore they presented a picture of the society from which they emanated. Peter Jupp and Eoin Magennis identified seven types of crowds: sports, religious, temperance, political, celebratory, protest and entertainment. They also identified two types of crowd activity, participation in an event and onlooking.[94] In each case,

A typical mid-twentieth-century procession on St Patrick's Street. (Courtesy Michael Lenihan)

participation was seen as an assertion of identity. Processions 'were a statement unfurled in the streets through which a community represented itself to itself and to the outside world'.[95] A variety of mass gatherings in Cork, whether funeral processions such as those of Terence MacSwiney or Jack Lynch; celebratory, such as the greeting of an All-Ireland winning team or St Patrick's Day parades; protest, such as anti-war demonstrations or tax marches; political, such as the gatherings of O'Connell and Parnell or more recent election rallies; religious, such as the annual Eucharistic processions, either began, passed through or culminated in St Patrick's Street. Each makes its own primary statement. However, at another level, together they also make a further statement. Through their association with St Patrick's Street they say that the street was and is a central part of the space or theatre within which the various spectacles were performed. Thus, for Cork, St Patrick's Street is that space wherein these experiences are located. There may well be 'people of St Patrick's Street' but in truth St Patrick's Street is of and for all of the people, as manifest in these events. As well as those already met, more of these events will be encountered throughout the remainder of this book, in the eras in which they occurred.

Thousands line St Patrick's Street as the remains of former Taoiseach Jack Lynch are driven through the street.

Conclusion

For nearly two and a half centuries, St Patrick's Street has been central to the lives of Cork people. It has been the place where they come to celebrate and protest, to pray and to praise, to shop and to socialise. It was also the place where they gathered in mass numbers to make a statement about their time. This chapter presents people of St Patrick's Street as they were recorded in a number of ways during the nineteenth and twentieth centuries. From the trade directories it is clear that women fell far short of men in positions of significance on the street. Census data indicates that the role of women resident on the street was that of assistant rather than apprentice; servant rather than mistress. Data from business ledgers still extant for both men and women reinforces the claim that the street primarily served the better off in society. A number of people famously associated with Cork's main street represent different phases and aspects of social development in the city. Sir John Arnott was a pioneer of 'monster house' developments during the nineteenth century and William Roche and Ben Dunne were entrepreneurs of the twentieth century when there were improvements for the less well off in society. Two other famous men associated with the street during the nineteenth century were each identified as apostles, William Thompson and Fr Theobald Mathew. Each sought to improve the circumstances of the poorer people in society. Fr Mathew is today remembered by the iconic statue in his honour that stands at the entrance to the street from the north, unveiled before a crowd of 100,000 people, a statue that is an icon of the street and the city. However, while history has granted to Fr Mathew the status of icon, William Thompson is scarcely remembered by the people of St Patrick's Street.

5 Commerce on the Street

This commercial portrait will illustrate that from early in the nineteenth century the properties on St Patrick's Street were consistently of a higher value than elsewhere in the city and that from this time also St Patrick's became primarily a retailing street. It will also show how, despite changes of ownership, the nature of business transacted in many concerns remained constant for decades, creating traditions of customer loyalty which were then passed on to future generations.

Valuations

In 1809, following the development of a public water supply through the 1760s and 1770s, the Pipe Water Company evaluated properties in the city supplied with water.[1] In the report St Patrick's Street is divided into the south and west sides of the street.[2] Fifty-eight properties are listed for the south side ranging in valuation from £22 15s to £150. On the west side forty-seven premises were listed, the lowest being £45 10s and the highest £120. The average valuation figure for the street was £80 6s and in total twenty-one properties were actually valued at £80. Eighteen properties were valued at £100 or over. By comparison, a sample of twenty-nine properties on the neighbouring Paul Street had an average of just over £32. Thus, from early in its history, St Patrick's Street was a place of higher value properties than those in nearby streets.

Griffith's Valuation of 1851 again divides St Patrick's Street into two, between Holy Trinity and St Paul's parishes.[3] Those in Holy Trinity were

Nos. 1– 65 with the lowest valuation of £6 (the offices and yard of Joseph Harty at No. 5, alongside his house which was valued at £75). Next lowest were the two parts of No. 63, occupied by Tim Finn and Robert Johnson and valued at £14 and £19 respectively. The highest valuation was John Arnott and Co. at Nos. 52–53, valued at £220. The average was £62 14s.[4] On the St Paul's side, the lowest valuation was £1 for a store to the rear of Guy's property at No. 63. Highest was £112 for John Perry's house and store at No. 89. On this side the average was £63 10s. By comparison with these figures, two samples on South Main Street, Nos. 1–40 and 70–101, indicate highs of £125 and £30 respectively and lows of £3 and £11. The average between Nos. 1–40 was £20 and between Nos. 79–101 £18 14s. On North Main Street, between Nos. 1–56, the lowest valuation was £8 10s and the highest £120 (St Peter's Market) with an average valuation of £21 5s 4d. Thus it is again clear that St Patrick's Street retained its higher-value status over other streets.

The averages in *Griffith's Valuations* are lower than the Pipe Water Commissioners. However, the latter was only a limited local evaluation while *Griffith's* was a national one. As such it allows a comparison between Cork's main street and Dublin's Sackville Street, for example. Sackville Street was divided into two parts, Upper and Lower. Lower, including the General Post Office valued at £1,500, had an average valuation of just over £126 while Upper had an average of £109. The St Patrick's Street average value, therefore, was just over half that of Dublin's main street. By the end of the twentieth century St Patrick's Street's position and status remained unchanged within Cork. A sample of eighty-seven commercial rateable valuations, accessed through the valuation office website and dating to between 1993 and 2005, yielded an average of €537·14[5] From the same source the North Main Street averaged €151·60 (seventy-nine listings) and the South Main Street €86·79 (seventy-eight listings).[6]

Development into Retail

The economic historians of Cork are agreed that the period between the early eighteenth and early nineteenth centuries was one of prosperity for the city, based largely on the developing provisions trade and 'the buoyant regional economy'.[7] Dickson has said that as a consequence of victualling (providing food and provisions) for the British forces, 'every episode of war from the mid-1740s through to 1815 turned out to be good for the Cork

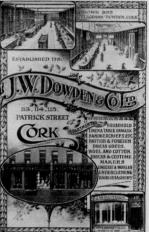

(Courtesy of Local Studies Deptartment, Cork City Library)

region' and that in many parts 'wartime prosperity had left a legacy in stone and brick'.[8] The provisions industry declined after 1815 with a consequent downturn in much of the Cork economy.[9] Nevertheless, developments, particularly in the commercial area, that occurred throughout Ireland during the nineteenth century were also manifest in Cork. St Patrick's Street illustrates well the changing nature of society in that period.

In an interview for the RTÉ programme *Secret Sights: the Long Nineteenth Century*, historian Gabriel Doherty gave an overview of the changes occurring in Ireland during that century. He highlighted the establishment of a cash economy: 'there was money, more of it and you could do more with it', and summarised that while at the bottom of the scale people's sole concern was survival, the upper elements of society became commercialised.[10] This was facilitated by the development of shops, which the manufacturing and professional classes all availed of. Cormac Ó Gráda, meanwhile, argued that 'increasing urbanisation brought greater commercialisation' and that 'the impressive rises in tobacco, tea, and sugar consumption were largely due to higher incomes'.[11]

The directory of 1787 provides the first snapshot of St Patrick's Street since its commencement four years earlier.[12] There were forty listings for the street in the directory and these can be divided into a number of categories. For the purpose of this portrait, five categories are employed in examining a number of directories between 1787 and 1997.[13] Professional were those involved in the services industry such as the law or medicine; merchants were those who imported, warehoused and sold a range of goods; retailers were those involved in the developing shops; artisans were the skilled craftworkers; and manufacturers were those directly involved in the manufacture of goods. Inevitably there was crossover between the categories requiring decisions as to where to locate certain businesses. These decisions are based on factors such as the precise title used in the directory.[14] Over time certain categories disappeared, being subsumed into others. Tracing these categories through a range of directories reveals the nature of commercialisation of the street and how it evolved.[15]

In the 1787 directory the largest category was that of 'Merchants' with fifteen listings: eight merchants, four wine merchants, two spirit and porter and one stationer and medical warehouse. The next category was 'Professionals' with thirteen, including seven attorneys, three physician/surgeons and one each boarding school, insurance and an alderman. Six 'Artisans' were listed, four in ironwork, one plumber/glazier and one cooper.

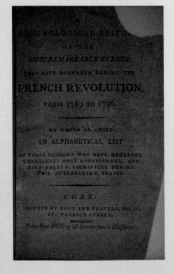

Tract on the French Revolution published by Daly and Travers of No. 16 St Patrick's Street in 1797.
(Courtesy Michael Lenihan)

In 'Manufacture' there was a candle and soap-maker and a cabinet-maker. Finally, in 'Retail' there was just a haberdasher, a perfumer, a milliner and a grocer. Thus the 'Merchants' comprised 37.5 per cent, 'Professional' 32.5 per cent, 'Artisans' 15 per cent, 'Retail' 10 per cent and 'Manufacture' 5 per cent of the street.

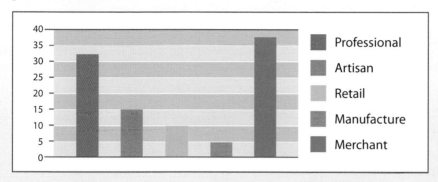

Figure 1: 1787: Percentage of each category on St Patrick's Street.

Twenty years later, with the publication of *Holden's Directory* for 1805–7, of seventy-four listings for St Patrick's Street, the 'Retail' group had become the largest with twenty-four (32.43 per cent), followed by the 'Merchants' at seventeen (22.97 per cent), 'Professionals' at fifteen (20.29 per cent), 'Manufacture' at seven (9.46 per cent) and 'Artisans' at four (5.4 per cent).[16] Attorneys at eight, followed by merchants at seven and haberdashers and grocers at six each were the three highest single categories. The 'Retail' group rose by 10 per cent and the 'Manufacture' group by 5 per cent, while the others all dropped. In this period a toy and fancy goods shop appeared on the street for the first time and during this period also a charity shop opened on the street in 1800. It was short-lived, however, closing again in 1803.[17]

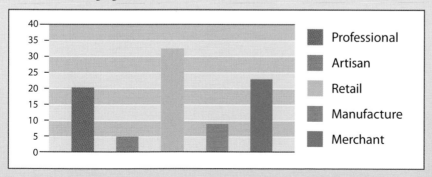

Figure 2: 1805–7: Percentage of each category on St Patrick's Street.

In the 1809–10 directory, of 112 listings, the 'Retail' group retained its prime position with thirty-nine premises (34.8 per cent), followed by the 'Professionals' at twenty-four (21.42 per cent), the 'Manufacture' and 'Artisans' at fourteen each (12.5 per cent) and the 'Merchants' who had fallen to twelve (10.7 per cent). The attorneys, merchants and grocers as well as printers/booksellers were the top four individual categories.[18]

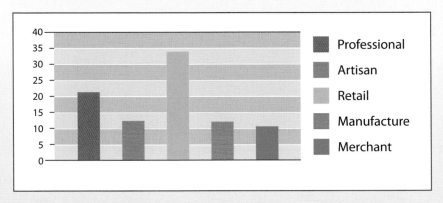

Figure 3: 1809–10: Percentage of each category on St Patrick's Street.

The 1820–22 directory confirms the trends already under way – an increasing 'Retail' group and a reduction in the numbers of 'Merchants'. From a total of 108 entries, 'Retail' numbered forty-five (41.66 per cent), 'Artisans' twenty-five (23.15 per cent), 'Professionals' eighteen (16.66 per cent), 'Manufacture' fourteen (12.96 per cent) and 'Merchants' five (4.62 per cent).[19] Grocers at nine moved to the top of the individual table but a point to note is that the combined number involved in drapery within the 'Retail' group was twelve, more than a quarter.

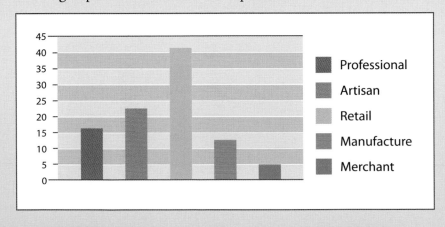

Figure 4: 1820–22: Percentage of each category on St Patrick's Street.

Pigot's Directory of 1824 had 135 listings for St Patrick's Street, sixty-two (45.5 per cent) in 'Retail', thirty-three (24.2 per cent) in 'Professionals', twenty-four (17.7 per cent) in 'Artisans', ten (7.4 per cent) in 'Manufacture' and seven (5.18 per cent) in 'Merchants'.[20]

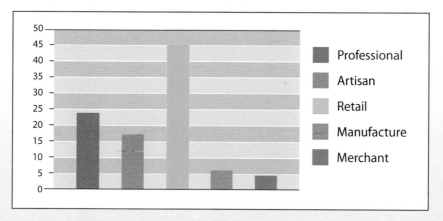

Figure 5: 1824 Percentage of each category on St Patrick's Street.

Thus, in the first forty years of its existence, St Patrick's Street was already developing into a primarily retailing street. The merchants were moving out and while grocery (sometimes along with wine and spirits) had become the most common type of shop on the street, it was closely followed by books, china and glass, perfume and straw hats, along with draperies. This indicates that the profile of goods available was that of higher status luxury items.[21]

With the street developing in this way, the question arose of where basic food necessities could be obtained from, by those patronising the new commercial sector to the east of the old city. A number of markets existed in different places, such as one for milk at the Old Market Place off Blarney Road and a fish market at Hanover Street to the south of the old town. Meat markets, or shambles, were to be found at Barrack Street to the south, at the Coal Quay where Corn Market Street is today and another near Shandon, but these largely catered for the poorer sections of the populace. Coinciding with the development of St Patrick's Street, from about 1788, a covered market was established at the heart of the newly developed commercial centre within a few yards of the new main street. In time this came to be known as the English Market and the choice of location indicates the intention of the Corporation that it cater for the better off, among whom were also the patrons of St Patrick's Street. Today

(Courtesy of Local Studies Deptartment, Cork City Library)

the English Market is not just at the heart of the city, but also at the heart of Cork culture.

Few directories for Cork are extant relating to the following four decades. *Aldwell's Directory* (1844–5) and *Slater's* (1856) confirm the continuation of the trend whereby St Patrick's Street was becoming a retailing street.[22] In 1844–5, the 'Retail' group had increased to 90 out of 162 listings, (55.55 per cent). Grocery accounted for sixteen of these businesses while twenty-six were involved in the drapery trade. In 1856, 'Retail' moved to 62.04 per cent (85 of 137).[23] Eleven years later in 1867, 'Retail' was at 79.84 per cent, the highest it would achieve during the century. Thereafter, it declined to 68.76 per cent and 73.12 per cent respectively in 1875–6 and 1886. In 1886, across all categories, forty-five listings were associated with the drapery trade.

An examination of directories for the twentieth century reveals a downward trend in retailing between the 1930s and the 1970s, from 65.8 per cent in 1925 to 63.5 per cent, 60.18 per cent and 55.3 per cent in 1935, 1945 and 1976 respectively. During this period also, the 'Artisans', 'Merchants' and 'Manufacture' groups disappear from the street, being subsumed into larger business operations.[24] With the economic upturn of the 1990s the two remaining groups, 'Retail' and 'Professional' were 80 per cent and 19.2 per cent respectively in 1997 with the drapery trade alone accounting for 26.8 per cent of the retail businesses. So the street remained primarily one of retailing. Furthermore the product sold there was of a luxury nature. A brief examination of advertisements further emphasises this point. For this purpose the two main Cork newspapers of 18 or 19 December every ten years from 1830 to 1900 were examined. The following tables give the figures of advertisements from businesses on St Patrick's Street as a percentage of total advertisements in each paper on the day.

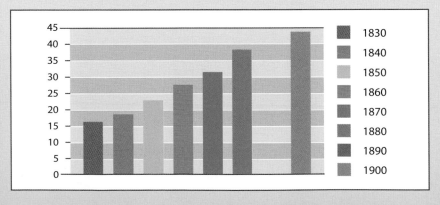

Figure 3: St Patrick's Street advertisements as a percentage of total advertisements in the edition of 18 or 19 December in each of the years. *(Constitution or Cork Advertiser)*

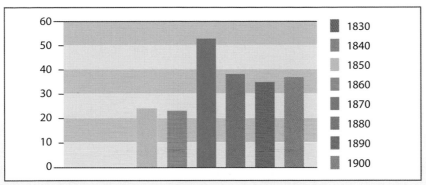

Figure 15: St Patrick's Street advertisements as a percentage of total advertisements in the edition of 18 or 19 December in each of the years. (*Cork Examiner*)

No definite pattern emerges but a trend can be noted that as the century progressed, between one-third and a half of all revenue expended on advertising in the newspapers came from St Patrick's Street. A sample of product being offered consisted in 1840 of woollens and linens, cheapest at 3s 6d to most expensive at 19s; tea at 5s to 5s 4d per pound; Malabar coffee; and beaver bonnets.[25] In 1850 tea was 4s per pound and was offered to 'the nobility and gentry' along with German fruits, Hertfordshire roses and candles at 6½d per pound.[26] 1860 offered foreign birds, tea at 3s 8d to 4s 4d and pianofortes.[27] In 1870 a chainless watch could be obtained on the street for £3 10s and Danish gloves from 1s 6½d.[28] Gloves in 1880 ranged from 2s 6d to 29s 6d while in 1890 blankets were 17s 9d a pair.[29] Better prices for the less well off were beginning to appear, however. Thompson's offered cakes from 1s to 10s and apple tarts for 6d. Guys offered Christmas cards from 6d a packet. In 1900 tea was now only 1s 6d to 3s a pound.[30] A striking comparison can be made between these prices and the daily wage rates in Cork city between 1800 and 1900 as tabulated by Maura Cronin.[31] Here, general labourers earned 1s 4d to 2s per day in 1850 and 2s 6d to 2s 8d in 1900. In 1850 a labourer would have spent two or three days' wages to buy a pound of tea on St Patrick's Street. Beaver bonnets, Danish gloves or Hertfordshire roses would have concerned him little in his battle for survival.

Tradition

Maura Murphy, in her work on nineteenth-century Cork society, concluded that 'the vast majority of businesses survived less than twenty years' and that 'relatively few businesses passed on from father to son'.[32] Her analysis was based on smaller concerns throughout the city. In this examination of St Patrick's Street, however, a different element of legacy

Top: Tim Keane, grandson of Tom Keane outside Michel jewellers in November 2007.

Bottom: Advertisement from the *Cork Constitution* announcing the intention of Arnott & Co. to take on the competition in the Cork retailing market of the 1840s.

is seen to have been passed on through the generations, that of tradition. Data extracted from the directories between 1824 and 1997 indicates that although premises may have changed hands on many occasions, 30 of the 125 premises on the street retained their core business for more than 99 years. A further 59 premises kept their business for between 50 and 99 years while only 37 did so for less than 50 years. Thus multiple generations of Cork people went to No. 6 on the street for their cigarettes and tobacco. In 1844 it was in the hands of Chambers & Lambkin; from 1856 William Clarke, whose son joined him in 1875, ran the business; from the 1920s to 1945, Santry's sold tobacco there – a total of over 100 years.

This is not the only example. Next door at No. 7, from George Purcell Atkins in 1856 to Blair's in 1976, apothecary was the business within. Further up the street, Brown Thomas of today continues the department store tradition of Cash & Co, dating back to the 1840s. Egan's catered for jewellery, ecclesiastical and liturgical requirements in the city for over a century. It also added to tradition in another way. John Joe O'Callaghan, Tom Keane and Mickey Roche left Egan's *c.* 1918 and continued their trade further up the street in No. 61. John Joe's son Denis went into the clockmaking business and today Tom Keane's grandson Tim continues the jewellery trade at Michel's, No. 116 on St Patrick's Street. At the western end, seven different listings, all involved in drapery, are found for No. 60 including Barnardo & Son, Dennehy & Son, Birmingham & Talty and Con Murphy, the latter still operating today. Many of the street's premises became associated with a range of activities by the populace. Shops such as Roches Stores, Grant's, Cudmore's and others were visited by generations of families who learned, almost as if it were received wisdom, that for First Communion or Confirmation clothes, for example, Mannix or Fitzgerald's was where 'we always went'; for novelty goods 'we always went' to Woolworth's; for wedding presents 'we always went' to Roches Stores; the real Santa was always found in Grant's.

After nearly half a century of grocery and tea being sold by Beale & Co. at No. 14 that premises became the Atkins London House, selling a wide range of luxury goods until it was in turn taken over by Roches Stores.[33] This example is of considerable significance. The advent of the Atkins London House was a manifestation of a cultural change, the mid-nineteenth-century development of the department store, also seen in Arnotts, Cash & Co. and the Munster Arcade. Cormac Ó Gráda has described how 'there was a protracted struggle between specialised retail

Brown Thomas, formerly Cash's, one of the major department stores on St Patrick's Street. (Courtesy sandraocallaghan.com)

outlets and all-purpose department stores' at this time.[34] The development of such stores as the precursors to Clerys in Dublin and Roches Stores in Cork illustrate that the department store had come to stay. The iconic Roches Stores has now departed from St Patrick's Street, replaced by Debenhams.[35] As happened in the past, on the one hand the department store tradition will continue while on the other hand the change is a clear manifestation of external forces shaping the cultures and traditions that will pass on to future generations. Thus the main street is one conduit through which future generations receive their heritage from those who have gone before them; a legacy, not just in stone and brick, but also in culture, tradition and memory.

Condition of St Patrick's Street during & after the Famine

If one looks at Cork and in particular St Patrick's Street in the years between 1840 and 1865, an apparent contradiction arises. Could it be that the shops that happily closed their doors in honour of Fr Mathew on 10 October 1864 were the same ones that advertised cheap goods available owing to the poor circumstances of suppliers while thousands starved and died during the Famine? Indeed they were in many cases and the explanation for this lies not just in the respect and love in which Fr Mathew was held by all, but also in the complexity of Cork society of this time.

As we have seen, St Patrick's Street was the place of the merchant middle class and their patrons. Though the lower classes frequented the street, they would not have been in pursuit of goods to purchase. Rather perhaps it was to beg of people better off than themselves, to talk with others in the hope of hearing news of an improving national situation or to make their way to the quaysides in pursuit of relief from afar. These and many others were the reasons why the poor made their way along St Patrick's Street and it was not always that they passed on their way quietly. In 1846 a report of 'WANTON OUTRAGE' appeared in the local press:

> We record with feelings of disgust and shame, the disgraceful fact that, on Monday evening, at an early hour, a stone was flung at the handsome shop window of Mr Henry O'Hara, by which a beautiful pane of glass, value £10, was smashed. As yet, we understand, there is no trace of the perpetrator of this wanton and infamous act; but we sincerely hope that the police who are so uncommonly active in matters of less moment, will be enabled to discover the guilty party, and bring him or her to punishment ... If there be no redress for acts of such wanton wickedness, there must, naturally, be an end to all improvement and embellishment.[36]

In January 1849 the street was described as 'filthy and its conditions would disgrace a Kaffir village'.[37]

The merchants themselves sought merely to survive the extraordinary difficulties of the time and they too suffered, though in no way as severely as the poorer classes. Mainly it was as a result of disease epidemics that people of the middle and upper classes died. In August 1849 John Maguire, father of John Francis Maguire, contracted cholera and died. John Francis Maguire himself also contracted the disease but he was successfully treated. As a result of the Famine, and with the city's population growing due to a continuing influx of people from the countryside and also England, the middle and upper classes became an even more closed sector of society, described by John O'Brien as 'a small minority surrounded by a broad mass in various stages of deprivation'.[38] Furthermore, these merchants and professionals now sought to distance themselves from the poor and move to suburban Cork, away from the confines of the city centre. Nevertheless, they also wanted the centre to be improved and so as time passed and the Famine years slipped into memory, thoughts and actions turned to making the city and especially St Patrick's Street a better place.

John Francis Maguire was to the fore in the campaign. During the

1850s he strongly advocated stamping out Sunday begging – whereby beggars congregated outside the city churches – and he also sought to reduce the numbers of prostitutes in the city. As Mayor he ordered that prostitutes could not gather in the streets after eight o'clock in the evening. Progress was slow, however. All streets including St Patrick's Street remained filthy and indeed the smell from the sewer running beneath the city's main street was particularly foul. In no time at all the wags had made an observation that would eventually become the basis of a famous couplet in a well-known Cork song.

> The smell from Patrick's bridge is wicked
> How does Fr Mathew stick it.

A certain amount of improvement did occur, but still the prostitutes gathered, one of their more popular locations being the corner of Marlborough Street and St Patrick's Street.[39] Such was their behaviour in the city centre that a resident of the Victoria Hotel complained of disruption. At midnight:

> there began a series of noises consisting of cries, curses, howlings and screams the most appalling, accompanied with language the most abominable that human lips can utter or human ears listen to, all rapidly increasing in violence and intensity as the night wears on until about 3 in the morning.[40]

McCormick's Victoria Hotel on St Patrick's Street was one of the most popular in the city at the time with a range of visitors from near and far. Arriving at the hotel in November 1862 were A. Newson, Dublin; Rev. J. Byro, Newfoundland; R. Forsyth, Aberdeen; Councillor Devitt, Limerick; Rev. Dr Quin, Dublin; J. J. Hill, Carbery, 14th regiment; M. G. Visity, France; Rev. John Curly, Dublin; J. McMaster, Manchester; Dower and Lady Lenton, Dungarvan; and many others.

Popular Businesses

St Patrick's Street was by now almost eighty years old and although it held within the grip of its hand much at which criticism could be levelled, nevertheless it was continually improving and changing. Some names

(Courtesy of Local Studies Deptartment, Cork City Library)

had survived the dramatic years just passed. Many were relatively new and just beginning an existence that would last even to this day. Just a few were there almost from the very beginning. In *Guy's Directory* of 1875, William Harrington & Son are listed as operating as druggists at No. 80. Seventy years earlier William Harrington operated as a druggist at No. 17 and was listed in *Holden's Directory*. Also in 1805, Florence McAuliffe ran a Fruit and Grocery Store on the newly built main street. Seventy years later H & S McAuliffe were fruit merchants at No. 50. It is most likely that these were family businesses that had stood the test of time.

Changing business but with the same name, Henry Franks in 1805 was a linen draper while Henry Franks in 1875 had a Grocery and Wine Store at No. 76. Relocating to the street perhaps was Massey's. In 1805 they had a bookshop on Castle Street and in 1875 N. Massey was a leading bookstore at No. 84 St Patrick's Street. J. Haughton was a grocer on Devonshire Street in 1805 while John B. Haughton was similarly a grocer at No. 104 St Patrick's Street in the later directory. The Varian brothers, next door at No. 105 making brushes, were also the family of the Varians making brushes at Broad Lane earlier in the century.

Virtually every name operating on St Patrick's Street in the 1870s can be found in earlier directories but whether or not they were direct descendents or even related is another matter. The likelihood, however, must be that many of them were. The family name Atkins appears in all accounts with three operating in the city in 1787. So also were there three McAuliffes (all grocers) in 1787. One further name in all the directories and operating at No. 46 in 1875 was that of Wood & Son, hat-makers.

Wood & Son

This business had begun almost 200 years before the 1875 directory when Daniel Wood of London joined the forces of William of Orange. Posted to Ireland, when the fighting was over he resumed the trade in which he had served his apprenticeship – hat-making – and based himself at Youghal.[41] The business was extremely successful and in time he moved to Blackrock where his sons carried on the manufacture of Beaver hats on a large scale. Later again the business moved into the North Main Street and it is there that the business is found listed in the 1787 and 1805 directories. By the time *Pigot's Directory* of 1824 was published, Wood & Son had moved to St Patrick's Street where, from the 1870s up to the end of the nineteenth century, it was run by Mr Samuel Wood and his son Richard Ponsonby Wood. Now no longer dealing in Beaver hats, their elite clientele could obtain silk hats for gentlemen, silk hunting hats, livery hats, ladies' riding hats, soft alpine, torquay, theresa and park patterns as well as soft and hard felts. The Woods also dealt in leather cases, hat brushes, hat guards, cockades, mourning bands, helmets and other accessories. There were those who believed at the time that Wood & Son was the oldest merchant trading house in Ireland.

Egan's

Another name, relatively new to St Patrick's Street, but of long standing in the city, was that of Egan's. In the 1780s John Egan operated as a jeweller on Castle Street. By 1805 he had moved to Fishamble Lane. Over the following decades the business moved to a number of locations including Nile Street until in the 1870s the premises at No. 32 St Patrick's Street became vacant. Egan's moved into this location and also that of Fitzpatrick & Sons, tailors, next door at No. 33 and developed high-class jewellery, gold and silversmith workshops.[42] Watchmaking too was engaged in and they also developed a considerable trade in ecclesiastical furnishing, vestment manufacture, embroidery and sacred vessels such as ciboria and chalices. The ordinary person also had reason to visit Egan's where old silver teapots and an assortment of other items could be restored to former glory. Egan's in fact became renowned in the art of silver creative work and one

Vero Moda of today, formerly Egan's, No. 31, centre building.
(Courtesy sandraocallaghan.com)

famous piece crafted by them was a silver model of the church and tower at Shandon for the Cork exhibition of 1883. They also crafted a silver and gold brooch for each of the members of the church choir at St Vincent's, Sunday's Well in the 1970s, on the occasion of the 120th anniversary of the church. The firm was also renowned for the stock of valuable diamonds held at the premises and contemporary accounts tell that no other store in the islands of Great Britain and Ireland held such a variety. Egan's of St Patrick's Street would operate well into the twentieth century to face and indeed survive troubles of a dramatic kind, as we shall see later in the story of Cork's famous main street.

Fitzgerald's

Another firm, operating in drapery, is Fitzgerald's at No. 24. It originally opened at No. 119 in 1860 and moved to No. 44 before changing to its present location. The manager of the shop today is Eddie Mullins, but the former manager, Hugh Burke, reminisced with this writer about his fifty years in the firm, starting at £1 a week in the 1940s when 'carriage trade' was still a term used when referring to the exclusive side of trade. This, he said, referred back to when carriages brought wealthy women to the street and rather than have them leave the carriages, employees brought material and other items out to them from which they selected their purchases. The credit trade which developed during his time, he said,

John Fitzgerald Kennedy passing Fitzgerald's Men's Shop on the occasion of his visit in 1963.
(Courtesy Fitzgerald's)

was interesting on two accounts. It gave women independence on the one hand in that they did not need money, but on the other hand it denied them the independence of having money. The outstanding customers in Hugh Burke's memory were not locals but celebrities such as Fred Astaire, Alec Guinness and Burl Ives to whom he sold a hat.[43]

Other Businesses

A number of other businesses operating on St Patrick's Street in the latter half of the nineteenth century had been in existence for a considerable period. Purcell & Co. at No. 124 was a firm of stationers and printers operating since 1797. For half a century they were the compilers of a directory of city businesses and did much of the printing work for a wide range of clients from their printing rooms at the back of the premises, which were accessed from Lavitt's Quay.[44]

Towards the end of the nineteenth century, William Hartland was a seed merchant and florist operating at No. 24, where Fitzgerald's is today, a business which had been started by his grandfather Richard Hartland almost 125 years earlier.[45] A notable feature of this business was that it had one of the city's earliest telephones, putting it in direct contact with nursery lands it had at Blackrock. As a seeds man and florist, William Hartland had a considerable reputation but was best known for the range and quality of daffodils that he grew. The company issued a full catalogue of all its products and was especially well known for the production of a book entitled *Floral Album of Daffodils* which was beautifully illustrated by Gertrude Hartland, described as an artist of much ability. Such was William's ability that he was a member of one of the committees of the Royal Horticultural Society.

Another famous business name on St Patrick's Street and indeed one that is still to be seen there today (though merely as an architectural element of its former premises) is that of Woodford Bourne & Co.[46] This firm was one of the leading grocery, wine and spirit traders in the south of Ireland and had its foundation as far back as 1750. It began in Falconer's Lane (solely in the wine trade) in the name of Maziere & Sainthill. In 1824 the senior partner Mr Maziere died and Mr Sainthill took control of the business. Nearby a grocery business in the name of Woodford & Co. operated at premises previously occupied by Morley & Co. During the Famine John Woodford devoted much time and energy to the poor

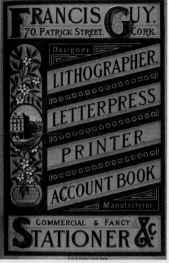

(Courtesy of Local Studies Deptartment, Cork City Library)

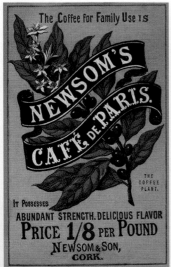

WOODFORD, BOURNE & CO. Ltd., 64 & 65, PATRICK STREET, CORK.
An Old Established House noted now over a Century for the Choice Quality of their supplies.

Left: **Advertisements for Newsom's**
(Courtesy of Local Studies
Deptartment, Cork City Library)

Right: **Nineteenth-century
advertisement for Woodford
Bourne & Co.**
(Courtesy of Local Studies
Deptartment, Cork City Library)

and sick to such an extent that he contracted fever and died. In 1850, his widow married the manager of their firm, a man named Bourne. So what then was the connection between the firms owned by Sainthill and Woodford Bourne? It was described in *Slater's* review of businesses in the city, published in 1892, as one of 'the most cordial relation'. Thus, when Mr Sainthill died, his death wish was for this business to be transferred to his friends the Woodford Bournes and this indeed occurred in 1869. They expanded the premises at the Daunt Square end of St Patrick's Street to the designs of William Hill and carried a large stock, including vintage port, sherry, madeira, claret, hock, champagne, French brandies and a rare stock of Scotch whisky. They also stocked a wide range of teas and were well known as a firm that would send 6 or 10 lb parcels of tea, post free, to any part of the United Kingdom. They developed cellars at Sheares Street and by the 1890s had well over a million bottles of wine stored there. By the end of the century, Woodford Bourne & Co. was importing so much wine that it necessitated the presence of a full-time customs officer at the business. The nineteenth century had seen much change to this most famous of firms on St Patrick's Street. The twentieth would bring even more change to this old Cork business.

Quaker John Newsom, son of Samuel and Sarah Newsom, began a tea business at No. 109 St Patrick's Street in 1816 and over the following decades dealt in a wide range of items such as Jamaica coffee, Berkley cheeses, fine salad oils, Italian liquorice and Zante currants. Other Quakers who had businesses on St Patrick's Street were William and George Wright who operated at No. 35 and the Silkes, also tea specialists, at No. 27. In 1858 the Wrights moved to a bigger location at No. 16 on the street.

James Hackett at No. 42 was the owner of a watchmaker, jeweller and silversmith business founded in 1820 by his grandfather, also James. Over thirty people were employed at the premises, cutting stones, manufacturing jewellery and operating a highly successful repair department.

William Todd & Co. began a drapery business at Nos. 18–19 and in the 1830s Mr John Carmichael acquired a controlling interest in the business. The Carmichaels were connected through marriage to the McOstrichs and over the following twenty years they became partners in the business. In 1868 the firm came solely into the possession of John Carmichael 2nd and Alexander McOstrich, having expanded to take in Nos. 20–21 along with the original two premises. The owners decided to expand still further and so formed a limited company in which they were the principal shareholders along with a certain John Arnott. The company name was then changed: C for Carmichael, A for Arnott and SH for McOstrich, perhaps spelling what they were they were in pursuit of – Cash & Co. John Arnott later sold his share in the company back to the other investors. John Carmichael was senior director until his death in 1907 when Alexander McOstrich took over the roll until his death in 1914, just six years before the traumatic events that occurred on St Patrick's Street in December 1920.[47]

Day's of St Patrick's Street

In 1831 Robert Day founded a business that would become synonymous with St Patrick's Street. Starting out as a saddle and harness-making firm, over the next half century it became a considerable employer and expanded the stock that it offered to its customers.[48] Single, double, tandem and four-horse harnesses in silver and brass; military and hunting saddles of any weight; trunks, hat cases, hide travelling bags and horse clothing were all offered. The firm also catered for all outfits necessary to rugby and association teams, lawn tennis racquets, balls, poles, nets and all essential equipment of that game. The large staff made their way to the workshops via an entrance on Bowling Green Street, while the frontage at No. 103 St Patrick's Street had large double plate glass windows.

Day's became one of St Patrick's Street's most remembered shops during the twentieth century, not least because of the window display put

Advertisement for Robert Day & Son, Ltd. (Courtesy of Local Studies Deptartment, Cork City Library)

Robert Day & Son at No. 103 on
the street.
(Courtesy Amy and Chris Ramsden,
The Day Collection)

on at Christmas time every year. The business had expanded considerably
and by the 1930s boasted a marvellous toy section that drew generations
of children to the store, particularly as the season of Christmas drew near.
For the boys and girls, one fascination was the huge model railway with
trains chugging under tunnels and stopping at a variety of meticulously
crafted stations where figurines of animals and people waited. For girls an
incredible selection of dolls, many of them handcrafted on the premises,
were beautifully arranged in the window, often in nursery rhyme settings.
Inside and up the stairs and down a darkened passageway with lighted
alcoves along the way were more dolls and toy animals and worlds of
things that only the child can imagine, before reaching the most magical
cavern in Cork … Ireland … the world – and there he sat, Santa Claus,
as real now in the memories of those who were privileged to visit him as
he is when he visits the children of the world on Christmas Eve. This was
Robert Day's of Cork: this was St Patrick's Street, Cork.

Monster Houses

The 'expanding industrial production of Britain and Europe was creating
the goods for trading in, on which the growth of shops in department
stores could be based'.[49] From the mid-nineteenth century onwards,
notices began to appear in the local press advertising goods at greatly

reduced prices being imported from manufacturers outside Ireland.[50] Maura Cronin identified the 'general goods stores, the Monster Houses' as 'main offenders' in the undercutting and displacement of local product.[51]

During the troubled years of the 1840s a number of businesses started on St Patrick's Street, two of which in particular would fit into this category and become very famous names associated with the centre of Cork. In 1842 Sir John Arnott – a man described as a pioneer in the monster warehouse system of trading – began a monster warehouse business at Nos. 52–54 St Patrick's Street. The nature of this type of business was promoted as being of considerable benefit to all sections of the public. Some years later Sir John was joined by a junior partner, Alexander Grant, and when in time the senior partner retired from the business (moving to Dublin where he was the founder of the famous Arnotts of Dublin), sole ownership became vested in Alex Grant. The next step in the business development was the amalgamation with two other firms, Lyons' Warehouses and the Queen's Old Castle Co. The latter of these had been the second of the 1840s monster businesses on the main thoroughfare. Included on the board of directors were William Thomas Barrett, Thomas Hayes, Francis Lyons, John Kelleher, managing director and Thomas Mulcahy, secretary.[52]

The window frontage of Grant & Co. was 65 feet in length and the business dealt in a wide variety of luxury goods from silks, velvets, ties, scarves and ribbons to art furnishings, tapestries, curtains and carpets, to hats and caps and fashionable wools and tweeds, all efficiently managed by Mr Moynihan. In time Grant's became famous for one very special event that happened each and every December: the arrival of Santa Claus. He would make his way on to the balcony that stood above the main entrance and wave to the crowds on the street below. For many years in the twentieth century, such was the popularity of this event that hundreds and indeed thousands would gather to wave and cheer as one in this welcome from the people of Cork to Father Christmas. Then the children would queue for a personal meeting with the 'real' Santa because only the 'real' one came to Grant's. Parcels wrapped in pink and blue were eagerly accepted with exuberant childhood excitement and quickly unwrapped to reveal perhaps a colouring book, a small doll or a bugle or toy gun, treasured items that in time became treasured memories.

Alexander Grant & Co. also had part of their premises fronting on to the Grand Parade where the Capitol Cinema stood for many years. It was there that in the spring of 1942 an inferno of proportions rarely seen

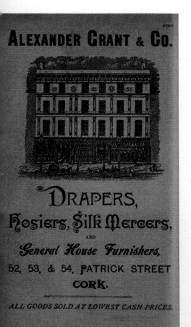

ALEXANDER GRANT & CO.

DRAPERS,
Hosiers, Silk Mercers,
AND
General House Furnishers,
52, 53, & 54, PATRICK STREET
CORK.

ALL GOODS SOLD AT LOWEST CASH PRICES.

Advertisement for Grant's
(Courtesy Cork City Library)

in the city erupted. The premises were completely gutted and although the St Patrick's Street element of the business continued until the 1960s the end was nigh. The institution that was Grant's disappeared from the Cork scene completely. St. Patrick's Street had lost one of its most famous businesses.

The Queen's Old Castle Co., although not strictly on St Patrick's Street, nevertheless can be considered as part of the main thoroughfare given that, as one heads westwards from the Statue, having rounded the curve at the Pavilion cinema, the elegant frontage of this business location faces the traveller. Dealing in upholstery, furnishings, drapery, carpets, silks, and many other items, the firm was founded in 1842 by a gentleman who for a number of years had been Mayor of Cork, the honourable William Fitzgibbon.[53] The location was one of the most historic in the city, having at one time served as a court house and civic office of old medieval Cork. Following the amalgamation with Grant's and Lyons' in 1873, upwards of 100 people were employed in the various departments of the Queen's Old Castle and this firm too, just like Grant's, lived on well into the twentieth century before succumbing to commercial factors. The premises for many years then became a modern shopping centre with a variety of businesses located there from Ted Twomey's photography shop to fabric shops and the famous Noddy's toy shop, a delight for the children of the city. Today it houses a media outlet and Argos.

Another St Patrick's Street firm to open in the 1840s was that of Daniel Sheehan who ran a china, glass and lamp warehouse at Nos. 109–110.[54] It was started by Dan senior in 1848 and steadily built up a clientele from among the elite of Cork society. Cut glass tumblers and decanters, Royal Vienna, Crown, Derby, Capo di Monti and a range of other potteries were available at the store and such was the standard of service that Daniel Sheehan in the 1890s held a special appointment to the Prince of Wales as a royal glass and china merchant.

Two businesses which began trading on St Patrick's Street in 1857 were Haynes Fishing Tackle Manufacturer at No. 63 and the Munster Woollen Warehouse owned by T. D. O'Brien at No. 37.[55] William Haynes was famous not only throughout Ireland and Britain but he also had a sizeable client base as far away as India for his fishing tackle. Packages would regularly be dispatched to there from his premises on St Patrick's Street. Specialising in Irish tweeds, T. D. O'Brien was one of the city's most successful retailers within a very short period of opening his premises.[56] He established warehouses at Faulkner's Lane and was also a senior partner in another business on St Patrick's Street, the drapery firm known as the Munster Warehouse located at Nos. 27–28.

It can be seen yet again that many of the businesses developing on St Patrick's Street dealt primarily in luxury items and indeed the street was a place where the very best wares to be found anywhere in the world could be obtained. Nevertheless, commodities of a more basic nature were also to be found there. Newsom's had sold tea on the street since 1816 and from 1866 a grocery, tea and wine merchant business operated at No. 119, one of a number on the street. Ownership of this firm was obtained in 1890 by Fred Russell who immediately introduced some innovative business practices. A prompt system of van deliveries to anywhere in the city was introduced and it was indeed attractive to have his range of products available to be so delivered.[57] Guinness stout was sold at 1s 9d per dozen; light dinner claret at 12s per dozen. Rare six-year-old Cork whiskey could be bought and all varieties of coffee were roasted and ground on the premises daily. All were of course essential items for the family grocery basket and there was one more item which no one could possibly leave out: Olden's Horse Application, a cure for horse and cow ailments, invented by the famous Cork surgeon Robert Olden.

Humorous as this is to the modern shopper, it was an important factor in the history of Cork's main street. Although growing in sophistication and glamour, the street nevertheless still served and was patronised by both city residents – very many of whom possessed livestock of one type or another – and people from the rural hinterland. All expected that the businesses operating in the centre of their cultural world would provide them with all their requirements and needs, both for themselves and their livestock.

Another very famous St Patrick's Street firm opened its doors in 1866, Messrs. Robertson, Ledlie, Ferguson & Co., better known to generations of Cork people as the Munster Arcade.[58] It originally began in Waterford in 1848 under the control of William Robertson and James Crawford Ledlie. In 1853 a branch was opened in Belfast and Robert Ferguson and Henry Hawkes joined the firm. Finally in 1866 the Cork branch was opened. It was an instant success and in 1880 was reconstituted as a limited liability company under the chairmanship of Mr Robertson and the managing of the Cork branch was put in the hands of two sons of Mr Ledlie. A wide range of goods was available to the clients including ladies' dress goods,

Two clocks and a flag. The white clock was made by Egan's and is today on the premises of Penney's, previously the Munster Arcade.

(Courtesy sandraocallaghan.com)

bonnets, fur coats, calicoes, Irish linens, curtains, carpets, a full range of gents' clothing, bespoke tailoring, furniture for all rooms of the house and a wide assortment of other goods. Over 200 people were employed at the premises and for their relaxation a library of over 1,000 books and a billiard room were provided. A commercial report from 1892 describes how the Munster Arcade was 'daily visited by throngs of purchasers, whose support and confidence have been secured by the uniform standard of exceptionally high quality'.[59] The twentieth century, as with so many businesses on St Patrick's Street, would bring enormous change and ultimately see the end of the Munster Arcade – but not without its having developed a special place in the hearts of Cork people. Indeed, as the twenty-first century advances, very many people still refer to the premises now occupied by Penney's as the Munster Arcade.

Throughout the decades of the nineteenth century various businesses had come and gone on St Patrick's Street, giving to each generation of Cork people their own special set of memories, their own special history that will forever remain unrecorded and thus can only be imagined by those who seek to know and understand the past of their own place. Egan's at Nos. 32–33 took the premises that Daniel Corbett, a dentist at No. 32 and Richard Gillispie, a music shop owner at No. 33 had occupied in the 1820s. Fred Russell's store was once the place of Denis O'Leary, a vintner and Robert Day's was where John Hare, an oil-and-colour-man had operated from. The various premises of Cash's at Nos. 18–21 had been occupied by Michael Bennett, a tinplate merchant, Richard Barrett a fruit merchant and the Misses Curry who dealt in toys. Dan Meagher's, where a distillery shop had been at No. 52 early in the century, was subsumed into Grant's. No. 43 was where George Cooke had sold shoes and in the latter end of the century it was taken over by Miss Kate McCarthy who operated a fruit, flower and vegetable shop there.

As the nineteenth century moved into its last quarter, the process continued. During the 1870s over a half a dozen new firms opened on the street.[60] James Atkins, one of three firms of that name to appear on the street by the end of the century, opened a pianoforte warehouse at No. 111 where earlier Francis Hodder had operated a wool drapery store. James Atkins was well thought of throughout the country for his technical understanding of the mechanics of the piano. At the double-fronted shop he carried a wide range of musical instruments with the piano being his own forte.

Gentlemen's outfitters Allan & Holden at No. 44 specialised in shirt tailoring. This business began in 1872 at the location where for many years John Hoare had operated as a fruit merchant. With the death of Mr Holden in 1875, the business came fully into the possession of Peter Allan and for a period was also operating next door at No. 45. One of their best-known brands was the 'Success' shirt, especially tailored for each individual who purchased. Numbered among the firm's clients were many military and naval officers as well as clergy and medical professionals.

John Gilbert began as an optician at No. 120, also in the year 1872. As well as the range of eyeglasses and spectacles sold there, the business sold a variety of prints and frames, and an artist's colour-man and illuminator was also based at the shop. A well-known artist and draughtsman in his own right, John Gilbert received many accolades from the people of the city, particularly for the sympathetic way in which he treated the poorer members of society. No. 120 had seen a number of businesses located there over the decades. Most recently before the arrival of John Gilbert, Timmy McCarthy had operated as a brush manufacturer. Earlier in the 1820s and

1830s Michael Doyle had sold a variety of perfumes to the discerning ladies of Cork.

At No. 49, J. V. O'Connell operated a linen warehouse, which he started in 1874. Like Peter Allan's, this business was well known for shirt manufacturing, with unusually a number of the staff residing on the premises. A report in *Strattens'* commercial directory of the 1890s describes that at times sale prices impossible to compete with were offered with reductions of as much as 42¾ per cent. Roche Brothers & Co., hardware merchants, had been at the premises since the 1850s and, before the troubled years of the 1830s and the Famine, Nano Coleman had operated her toy store there.

Like their namesakes at No. 111, T. & J. Atkins at No. 117 were also involved in the music business, being a pianoforte and organ warehouse. Here until the 1860s James Finn had operated a large grocery store and the spacious interior was now occupied with a variety of instruments the most famous of which were the Chappell & Co. pianos from London which were valuable and much sought-after instruments.

Yet another tailoring firm operated at No. 82 St Patrick's Street where James McCarthy, a specialist naval and military tailor, had begun operating in 1875 in the premises where previously Tobin's woollen drapery had been located. Prior to that, Minton's silk merchants were operating there and before that again James Byrne had his attorney practice there and Thomas Coleman operated as an insurance agent. Such was the excellence of the workmanship that James McCarthy was the only recipient of a prize medal at the Cork exhibition of 1883 for military uniforms.

In 1878 John O'Brien began the Cork Woollen and Hat Warehouse at No. 58 St Patrick's Street, dealing in a range of Irish tweed products, coach-makers' trimmings, upholstery materials, tailors trimmings and an extensive selection of hats and caps. John O'Brien was politically very active and not alone did he become an Alderman on the Corporation, but he also served as Mayor. He was a firm supporter of the nationalist movement and was twice imprisoned, the first time as a suspect during a government clampdown on nationalist activities in 1886. The second of these occasions arose when, as Mayor, he was presiding over a public meeting that got out of hand. Ever the responsible one, he rushed at the police … seeking to protect them from the angry mob. The police however did not quite see it in the same way and accused him of assault. Found guilty, he was imprisoned for a period in 1887. Like so many other premises, No. 58 too had seen a variety of businesses operate there throughout the century. Up to the 1860s Chabrel silk hat manufacturers had been there and earlier in the century James Hodnett had had a paper warehouse at the site.

Thomas Tangney was a well-known tailor operating at No. 101 prior to the Famine. Later, during the 1860s, the premises were operating as a baby linen warehouse in the name of Mrs. M. Gibson.[61] It changed again in the 1880s when Miss Foley began her Stationery and Bookselling Shop there and business grew steadily through the latter 1880s and early 1890s according to the commercial reports of the day. Many tourists are said to have visited the shop where they could obtain locally made jewellery, bog oak, Connemara marble and a variety of framed photographs of Irish scenery.

Tailoring was undoubtedly one of the most lucrative businesses operating in the city through the latter years of the nineteenth century, if the number of establishments offering this service is anything to go by. As well as the above mentioned, George Walker had his business at No. 98 where a staff of twenty tailored to a very high standard. His namesake Frank Walker began his establishment at No. 59 in 1887 – Joe Murphy had operated a watchmaking business at the premises in the 1820s and after the Famine it had been the home to Barnardo & Co., furriers, drapers and fancy goods suppliers. Frank Walker had started his business at No. 28 Grand Parade before moving to London's Regent Street. Specialising in Scottish, English and Irish tweeds, he mainly dealt in bespoke tailoring, particularly hunting and shooting outfits.

Conclusion

Commercially the street's development from early in its history was identified with the better classes in society. The premises were of a higher valuation than elsewhere and the goods sold on the street were priced beyond what the lower classes could possibly afford. St Patrick's Street had also become a place where all strata of society could meet and greet; where symbols of the character and culture of nineteenth-century Cork were on display. It was there that people would outwardly exhibit their beliefs and their aspirations – and at times this could lead to confrontation and violence, as we will see in the next chapter.

6 Violence on the Street

The trades associations of the 1820s and 1830s had found great unity and solidarity with one another through the pursuit of national goals such as Catholic Emancipation and the repeal of the Act of Union.[1] Their support for the temperance movement had further strengthened that bond. However, the Famine years and the huge numbers who either died or emigrated left the associations very much weakened. Nevertheless, as the 1860s dawned, the lot of the working artisans and craftsmen was again becoming an issue among that class in society.

The 1860s was also the decade of Fenianism and as word of rebellion reached the city from the county in 1867 (the year of the abortive Fenian Rising), the fears of the population were aroused and suspicions grew that certain groups in the city were actively supporting the rebels. On Friday 8 March 1867, the *Cork Examiner* reported that there was excitement in the city and that trade was generally at a standstill. All the public houses closed at six o'clock in the evening and there were 'hundreds of startling rumours floating around the city'.[2] However, in regard to actual rebellion, the press of the next day reported that 'the utmost quiet continues to prevail in the city'.[3] A week later, under a heading of 'Drapers Assistants and Fenianism', it was reported that 'the most absurd exaggeration has prevailed with regard to the numbers of this respectable class who went to join the Fenian outbreaks. We have, on enquiry, come to the conclusion that not half a dozen out of the whole number of large houses in Cork associated themselves with the mad enterprise.' A letter to the local newspaper read as follows:

Sir,

A report having been extensively circulated that a number of employees in the drapery establishments in this city had joined the Fenian movement, we consider it but right, in justice to those in our employment, to state that not a single individual has been absent from business, either before or after the 5th instant.

We are your obedient servants,

A. Grant & Co.

St Patrick's Street.

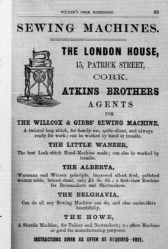

Top: Advertisement for sewing machines for sale in Atkin's London House. Sewing machines were a source of difficulties for the tailors in 1870s Cork. (Courtesy Cork City Library)

Bottom: Atkins London House, where sewing machines were available in the 1870s. (Courtesy Amy and Chris Ramsden, The Day Collection)

Such contemporary accounts do not, however, reveal the full picture. The Fenian movement gave a renewed impetus and energy to the trade associations who saw that action would be needed to achieve better conditions for the workers. The 1860s had been a decade of falling wages, contracting employment and increasing social unrest.[4] Certain numbers of the working class had indeed become affiliated with the Fenians. Maura Murphy says, regarding groups that had an influence on city politics, that 'the clerks and shop assistants in the city's draperies, groceries and pawn-broking establishments' were one such group. 'Their main importance was their role in the Fenian movement in which they formed over ten percent of the membership and twenty-three percent of the leadership.'[5]

With the failure of the 1867 rebellion some militants redirected their attention to the ongoing and unresolved labour issues and there was a revival of interest in organisation; the trade parades through the centre of the city, including St Patrick's Street, were revived in 1868; a strongly pro-Fenian Cork Grocers and Wine Merchants Working Men's Society was founded in 1869. By 1870 over 4,000 registered tradesmen from sixty-seven trades and twenty-five trade societies had combined in spirit. To each other they indicated support for their fellow worker. One of the most important groups in the development of this labour movement was the Tailors Society which numbered over 400 in its membership.[6]

The issues which concerned the tailors were falling wages and the introduction of sewing machines, which they saw as a major threat. Many master tailors agreed to increases in wages but, with the use of the machines, were in a position to reduce the number of hours their employees worked, thereby negating the increases. By May 1870, nearly every tailoring establishment was affected and strikes began to occur. By

June the situation had become critical for the businesses and in an attempt to meet customers' demands, some made a move that would lead to enormous unrest and ultimately serious rioting on St Patrick's Street. Four German tailors were brought in to break a strike and on the afternoon of Monday 20 June they made their way to the premises of Edward Arnold on Winthrop Street. This incensed the tailors who increased the level of picketing on the various tailoring establishments throughout the city. Two days later, on Wednesday 22 June, four men were picketing the premises of Lee's Tailoring shop on St Patrick's Street:

> Mr Lily, foreman cutter to Mr Lee, Patrick Street, accompanied by a friend, was walking on the footway and was in the act of turning into the establishment when they were encountered by a group of two or three of the journeymen on strike, one of whom, it appears, first jostled and then struck Mr Lily's friend. Mr Lily interposed, whereupon the man turned upon him, when he instantly drew a revolver and presented it at the head of his assailant, who, upon seeing the weapon ran off, and up to the hour of going to press had not been arrested.[7]

It took very little time for word to spread throughout the city that a gun had been drawn on one of the striking workers and within an hour crowds gathered on St Patrick's Street exhibiting, according to the *Cork Examiner*, 'symptoms of dangerous excitement'.[8] Throughout the afternoon the crowds continued to grow and word spread among the assembly that the Germans were now operating in two separate tailoring establishments on Winthrop Street.

Despite calls to come out and join them, the Germans stayed within. One man however did venture out from his premises, perhaps not realising the mood of the crowd. William Lee was soon seen and an angry mob chased him up St Patrick's Street. At Cook Street they cornered him but, fortunately for Mr Lee, some policemen were nearby and rescued him before any serious harm was done. However, the crowd, thwarted in their anger, now grew ever more aggressive and turned their attentions to the police, attacking them with stones and bottles. In response the police drew their swords and the crowd realised they were no match for the cold steel that faced them. They grew increasingly frustrated. A serious and angry situation had developed on St Patrick's Street.

Carmichael Credit Token showing a sewing machine (top and centre). Credit tokens were used for a variety of reasons such as when coinage was in short supply or as a credit note or form of gift token.

(Courtesy Michael Lenihan)

It was inevitable that the anger of the crowd would be vented somewhere and in a short time attentions were turned to No. 15 St Patrick's Street, better known as the London House, owned by the Atkins brothers and where sewing machines could be purchased. Stones were thrown at the windows as the staff attempted to put up shutters. For some reason one man from within made his way on to the roof of the premises and began to retaliate, throwing 'jugs, bottles and a variety of other household articles'. A battle ensued until the arrival of a large force of police who formed a defensive line in front of the building. The street was now thronged and when Mayor William Hegarty ordered the police to disperse the crowd, the outcome was inevitable. Disturbances spread to all parts of the street. At ten o'clock in the evening the constabulary charged for the first time and the crowd fell back. A barrage of bottles and stones was hurled at the advancing police who sustained at least five serious injuries. By eleven o'clock, the crowd was again gathering and its attention was once more directed towards property. Lee's shop was attacked by:

> a number of lads who boldly collected in front of the house and commenced a terrible and sustained discharge of stones upon it ... The crashing of the plate glass as it fell in heavy masses at every volley, and the battering of the shutters and window frames was quite appalling. The wreckers pursued their work of destruction uninterrupted 'til the handsome front was entirely demolished and presented a pitiful spectacle.[9]

In yet another attempt to regain control of the situation, mounted police arrived at the scene and the police fixed bayonets before commencing a new charge. The numbers of injured rose considerably, though none was serious. By midnight the police had regained the street, but not before three other premises had been seriously damaged: the London House, Arnold's on Winthrop Street and Fitzpatrick & Co.

On Thursday morning crowds gathered on the main street where the riots of the previous evening had been acted out. Disbelief would scarcely describe the general feeling that such an event should have happened on the street over which Fr Mathew presided. Little did they know that a long week was only beginning. Three men were brought before the courts and convicted on charges of malicious damage and rioting. They were Robert Nunan, David Tierney and George Hosford. Each was sentenced to hard labour for a period. The afternoon came and went and as evening fell the crowds gathered on St Patrick's Street once again.

The German tailors were spotted being escorted from the street and violence was again directed at the tailoring establishments. Within an hour St Patrick's Street was a battlefield for the second night running. Immediately, mounted police and ground troops with fixed bayonets charged, determined to stamp out the violence at the outset. A squadron of dragoons with sabres drawn rode into the street from the barracks. They were followed by two companies of the 63rd infantry regiment and they spread themselves in front of the buildings, from Winthrop Street to St Patrick's Bridge, as well as further along the street. Tensions fell – but only for a short period. The instigators of the assaults had seen the authorities' tactics and regrouped at the western end of the street where they attacked Woodford Bourne which in a very short while suffered severe damage. Once again the police had to engage the crowd which dispersed through the lanes off the North and South Main Streets. There were fewer casualties than the previous night. Four police were admitted to hospital.

On Friday morning the alarm was raised early when a procession of men, women and children made their way through the main streets as they marched to Wandesford's Quay. There was no trouble, however – it was a body of striking timber workers and their families converging on Richie's timber yard to force a shutdown. On St Patrick's Street, one Mary Sullivan, having consumed a sizeable quantity of alcohol, spied a gentleman entering the premises of Fitzpatrick's tailor shop and verbally assaulted him with threats of murder. He called the police and she was arrested. The situation on St Patrick's Street grew tenser by the hour.

As on the previous two nights the crowds gathered before eight o'clock in the evening and the violence began at about nine o'clock. Yet again the London House was attacked and as before the dragoons and the infantry were called into action. This time, however, as they began their charge, they discovered that ropes had been laid across the street, which were pulled taut by people located at either side. Crowds had been strategically located in all the side streets and as the advancing troops were brought to a halt by the ropes they were caught in the crossfire of bottles, bricks, paving stones and iron bolts. Then, at an appointed signal, all the lights in the street were quenched and in the darkness many of the police were severely beaten. It took some time before the police regained control but by then most of the crowd had again dispersed and gone home.

On Saturday the police and dragoons were deployed early and charged the main street before even the crowds had gathered. They did not stop there either, but continued into the North and South Main Streets and the laneways, attempting to intimidate people into staying at home. They did not succeed. By one o'clock in the morning, a huge and angry crowd had gathered in St Patrick's Street, again using ropes to stop the mounted advances. Pitched battles continued until dawn, but as the dawn approached people dispersed to change into their Sunday best for Mass.

Throughout the city there were calls for peace from the pulpits. The authorities, however, were neither prepared to see if such calls would prove effective, nor were they willing any longer to tolerate the violence of the previous four nights. As night fell and the rioters gathered, a heavy hand was taken by the police. Anyone suspicious was severely beaten and by two o'clock in the morning of Monday 27 June the last of the riots had ended. It had been a week like none other before in the history of St Patrick's Street; damage in today's money would be counted in millions. On the stage that was Cork city's main street, a proclamation had been made, the voice of the working class had spoken aloud – treat of us better, give us our daily bread.

Although the rioting had ended, the battle for better conditions continued, with strike action widespread throughout the city. In July large groups of workers gathered at prearranged points, including the Fr Mathew Statue, and marched through the city. The Women and Juvenile Factory Hands marched on St Patrick's Street in early July and proceeded from there to all premises wherein women worked; calling on them to join the protest, which they duly did, increasing the numbers of this particular action. In some cases conditions did improve for the workers. Shop porters and foundry workers, among others, received some increases in the weekly wage packet. For the owners of the premises damaged during the riots, compensation was granted amounting to £594 in total. William Lee received £110, Woodford Bourne £75, Fitzpatrick & Son £75 and Richard Allen £67. All agreed that the amounts granted in no way compensated for the damage sustained.

One further group of workers that struck in pursuit of higher wages was the city's jarvies, seeking an increase from 8s per week to 10s. In most cases it was granted, but change of a degree far greater than such an increase was about to be visited upon them. Transport in Cork city and St Patrick's Street in particular was about to undergo a dramatic change.

Following pages: **Looking westwards towards Woodford Bourne & Co. on St Patrick's Street in the 1890s.** (Courtesy Michael Lenihan)

PATRICK ST. CORK 2608. W.L.

7 St Patrick's Street and the March of a Nation

We have already seen in Chapter 2 how transport contributed to the physical profile of St Patrick's Street. This chapter takes a more detailed look at transport and how it changed on the city's main street in the latter half of the nineteenth century. This period was also one in which major cultural shifts occurred in Ireland with the development of a political nationalist movement led by the MP (Member of Parliament) who represented Cork at Westminster and also the growth of the greatest sporting organisation the country had ever seen. St Patrick's Street played an integral part in all these developments. The continued availability of luxury commodities on the street is also examined.

Tramways, Bicycles and Umbrellas

Throughout much of the nineteenth century the poorer people of Cork still resided for the most part in the lanes and alleyways that formed the old medieval city and lived their lives without ever travelling very far from their own locality. Many of the more affluent people, however, now resided in the ever-expanding suburbs. Transport to and from the city centre was thus of concern to many people. For those who could afford such a luxury it mainly took the form of horse and carriage but there also operated within the city a gingle service, effectively an early form of horse-drawn covered cab, run by the gingle-men who made a fine livelihood from their operations.

Transport developments that were occurring elsewhere in the world, however, inevitably made their way to Cork, in particular through the endeavours of one George Francis Train, described by Walter McGrath as 'an eccentric American' and a supporter of the Fenian cause.[1] As early as 1860 he visited Cork and along with the son of a local man, Henry Hugh Roche, surveyed the city for the installation of street tramways – coach and wagon transport hauled by horses through the streets on rails. The gingle-men strenuously objected to this proposed development, seeing it as a major threat to their livelihood. Eventually, however, the system was put in place and opened for public use on 12 September 1872.

Initially it was greeted with some enthusiasm, with local wags – as always – making their own statements about the development.

>As I was going down Patrick Street
>I heard a lady say;
>Oh it's jolly to be riding
>On the new tramway.

The tramway was built by a company called the Cork Tramways Company Ltd at a cost of £10,000 and its primary purpose was to join the termini of the main railways operating in the city (the Great Southern and Western, the Cork and Passage, and the Cork and Bandon Railways) while serving the principal streets also. The central point of the tramway, as with everything else in Cork by this time, was the Statue. The length of the line was just over 2 miles, stretching from Victoria Road at the southeastern end of the city, via Albert Road, Anglesea Bridge, South Mall, Grand Parade, St Patrick's Street, St Patrick's Bridge, Bridge Street, King Street (now MacCurtain Street), to Alfred Street and finishing near the present-day railway station. There was also a short-cut line from Anglesea Bridge to St Patrick's Bridge via Warren's Place and Merchants Quay.

The tramway itself was laid by Nelson & Roberts to the engineering specifications of Matthias O'Keefe and Sir John Benson and the tramcars were built by Starbuck & Co. from Birkenhead near Liverpool. The opening was another great occasion in the annals of Cork history. Great entertainment was had by all when, on the inaugural journey, at the Berwick fountain, one of the carriages ran off the line – 'The sweeping curve into Patrick Street was rounded in great fashion. Opposite SS Peter and Paul's Church, the same carriage again went off the track.' On the return journey 'the carriages ran on to the wrong track several times'. All else went well and by day's end Cork city boasted a horse-drawn tramway comparable with any to be found throughout the civilised world.

It was not long, however, before the citizens grew frustrated with the system, finding it too slow a means of crossing from one side of the city to the other. Furthermore, although the company had expansion plans, in particular to service suburban Cork, the Corporation opposed the plans, not least because the tracks had begun to protrude above the surface of the streets and become a nuisance. In 1875 the entire enterprise was sold for the princely sum of £510 following a decision in October of that year to break up the lines. The last trams drew to a halt at the Statue and early in 1876 the tracks were removed. St Patrick's Street returned to what it had been a mere four years previously. Two decades would pass before trams were again seen on the main street – but then they would last somewhat longer.

In the meantime those who had to make their way to and from St Patrick's Street continued to do so using private carriages, hackney gingles or simply walking. For a short period the gingle-men had their monopoly restored but another form of technological development was soon to bring unrest to their world.

In the early 1800s the German Baron Von Drais modified a wooden toy horse with a fixed front wheel into a machine that would assist him to get around the extensive royal gardens more quickly. It consisted of two wheels, one steerable, mounted on a wooden frame and the device was propelled by straddling the frame and pushing the feet against the ground. Known as the Draisienne or hobby horse it never gained popularity as it was impractical to use outside the level pathways in the German royal gardens. In 1839 Kirkpatrick McMillan, a Scottish blacksmith, added pedals to the device and by the 1860s the engineering had further advanced, based on the belief that a bigger front wheel would allow further travel for each pedal rotation. This wonderful piece of transportation engineering had by now become commonly known as the bicycle. By the early 1880s it began to appear on city streets everywhere and Cork was no exception. With the addition of the pneumatic tyre (which had been invented by a young Belfast doctor named Dunlop) to each of the wheels, a much more comfortable ride than heretofore could be achieved.

The arrival of the bicycle on the main streets of Cork in no way pleased the hackney drivers but there was little they could do to stem the tide. Hundreds of bicycles were soon in use and by 1884 a bicycle club had been established, gathering at regular intervals – often on Sundays and at the Statue – before heading off on a 'spin' to some exotic seafront destination such as Crosshaven.[2] Such was the proliferation of the bicycle that a complaint was made to the police by one William Harrington. He was reported as commenting on the practice of riding bicycles in the city's main streets:

> He did not know what the law was, or whether there was any law in reference to those machines having bells … he wished to bring it forward there to see if there were any redress for the danger that the public were exposed to by those machines.

Nevertheless the advance of the bicycle was not to be stopped. A Lieutenant in the Royal Irish Fusiliers complained that a hackney driver had attempted to run him over. One Dr D. J. O'Connor was injured while riding his bicycle and a Mrs Yourdi was injured through negligent bicycle driving on the South Mall. In 1885 the cycle club sought permission to ride on the Mardyke and Marina walks.[3] But as ever it was St Patrick's Street that was central to the display in Cork society of this new element of culture. It became fashionable to ride a bicycle through the street and very soon one of the earliest cycle shops in Cork opened at No. 118, run by the McTaggarts, in the premises where until recently Abraham Harty had operated a bakery.

From the outset the bicycle was by no means a luxury item in society. Many other commodities of a luxurious nature, some of them only recently developed, were to be obtained from premises on St Patrick's Street. In the Munster Arcade, both fur- and silk-lined cloaks as well as fur-trimmed jackets could be purchased. Willow-patterned brooches were exclusively available from James Hackett. Egan's sold a variety of watches ranging in price from £2 for a silver horizontal up to £10 for a gold case watch. Only available at Purcell & Co. was the Stylographic Pen, an 'air tight ink pencil, with which common writing ink can be used and holding sufficient quantity for several days' general writing; can be carried in the pocket; always ready for use. It will write at a single filling from 15,000 to 20,000 words.'[4]

Sewing machines, only a decade previously the cause of such destruction and trouble on the street, could be purchased from the warehouse at No. 92 with no reasonable offer being refused, while another 'device' which displeased the hackney drivers and to some extent affected transport could be purchased from Richard Allan at No. 69. This was an item that had been used in ancient times by the Egyptians and the Romans and in more recent times was to be seen on fashionable streets throughout the British empire ... but strictly only used by the ladies. No self-respecting gentleman would be seen carrying 'an umbrella'. Its popularity increased, however, from early in the nineteenth century and by the 1880s it was quite the fashion accessory – best obtained from Richard Allan, of course.

Each year, as Christmas approached, the list of items advertised for sale on St Patrick's Street (and other streets) increased. Seal bags from the Munster Arcade; real seal gloves, as well as silk handkerchiefs from Allan & Holden; Parisian novelties from Sheehan's China and Glass Emporium; real wax candles from Edward Ryan's Soap, Candle and Oil Warehouse at No. 114. On the last Saturday before Christmas 1880, the front page of the *Cork Examiner* carried no fewer than twenty advertisements from businesses on St Patrick's Street. By contrast, in as much as the North and South Main Streets represented areas of lesser affluence, not one advertisement appeared for shops on those streets. The nearest was an announcement from James O'Connor of No. 4 Castle Street that cheap potatoes for Christmas were to be obtained at his premises, price 6d per weight.

Another smaller advert on that same front page was arguably of greater significance in terms of Irish society at the time. From Henry O'Shea, photographer, of Limerick, could be obtained 'the only correct portrait of Charles Stewart Parnell'. Three sizes were available; Imperial at 3s 6d, Cabinet 1s 6d and Card at 1s. The popularity of 'the uncrowned king' was rapidly rising at this time and nowhere more so than in Cork city, the constituency that he represented at Westminster. He visited the city on a number of occasions and always the events were reminiscent of and indeed compared with the great occasions of the past such as the visits of O'Connell and the temperance processions.

Charles Stewart Parnell

National issues were very much to the fore in the last quarter of the nineteenth century with the land question and the Home Rule movement dominating every sphere of life. At this time, a man who had no family, business or political affiliation with Cork was elected to represent the city in the election of April 1880. Charles Stewart Parnell came in second with 1,505 votes, after local businessman John Daly, who was first past the post with 1,923 votes, and ahead of the other two candidates, William Goulding with 1,337 and Nicholas D. Murphy with 999.[5] Throughout the land the popularity of Parnell was rivalled in history only by that of Daniel O'Connell and everywhere he visited, thousands gathered to hear him speak and to declare their loyalty to him, his cause, and to Ireland. When, in October of 1880, he paid a long-awaited visit to Cork city, an expectant crowd of thousands from near and far gathered to hear his word – that independence in the form of Home Rule was imminent. According to the *Cork Examiner* 'the oldest inhabitant, who usually had something better to cite from the days of O'Connell, readily acknowledged that yesterday's demonstration for its proportions and the magnificence of the display, entirely excelled the most enthusiastic efforts of the former days'.[6]

Early in the day, representatives of the local branch of the Land League gathered, among them Mr Farrell, Mr Timothy Harrington, and several others, ready to go and meet the great man at the train station at Blarney from whence he would proceed to the city. As they made their way to the village, people gathered at the roadsides, seeking the best possible vantage point. Commercialism had arrived for the occasion with 'perfectly fabulous sums' being asked for 'even the most ramshackle turn out' by the livery men.[7] The sense of disappointment was palpable when Parnell's train did not arrive on time. It finally pulled into the station at ten minutes past one o'clock in the afternoon and huge excitement grew. Huge cheers greeted the leader of the Irish Parliamentary Party as he alighted from the train and was welcomed by the Land League representatives. The procession, as it left Blarney 'began to assume immense proportions', and proceeded to the city via Faggot Hill, Clogheen Cross, Shanakiel Road, Sunday's Well

Above: **Charles Stewart Parnell addressing crowds during an election rally.**
(*London Illustrated News*)

Road and Wellington Bridge where the Mayor of the city formally welcomed him to Cork.[8]

The Western Road was thronged and many more joined from the county at this point. Local bands struck up 'The Wearing of the Green' and 'Let Erin Remember' as the procession made its way up the North Main Street, across the North Gate Bridge, Pope's Quay, St Patrick's Bridge and then to St Patrick's Street where the majority of the crowds who had not journeyed out to meet Parnell had gathered. Here, in the main street, almost 60,000 people were waving and cheering as flags and banners proclaimed the message that Parnell would indeed free Ireland. From every window and housetop people waved. Even the Fr Mathew Statue was used by some to achieve a better vantage point by climbing on its shoulders, as they sought to greet Parnell. All shops were closed for the occasion and as in days of old the trade societies were prominent, none more so than the tailors' society. Led by John Barry, Timothy Sheehan, William Collins and William Brown, behind the SS Peter and Paul's fife-and-drum band, the Liberty Street Boys Association carried a large banner inscribed with the words:

He will rescue the soil
Which was given by God
From the hold of the cold-hearted stranger.

Other trade societies that processed on the day were the stonecutters, the typographical society, the carpenters, the millers, the painters and many others. In the annals of Cork's St Patrick's Street, Saturday 4 October 1880 ranks as another of the great days when the people of Cork came to the main street and showed a belief that their land and their culture was to the fore in their hearts and minds and St Patrick's Street was where this was displayed to a watching empire.

Over the following years, Charles Stewart Parnell returned to Cork on a number of occasions, each time receiving the adulation of huge crowds.

St Patrick Street pre-1898, before the electric trams appeared on the street. This would have been the street that Charles Stewart Parnell was familiar with.

(Courtesy Michael Lenihan)

His name became a part of Cork life. On 18 November 1882 a new bridge was opened at the site of the former Anglesea Bridge between Warren's Place and Sleigh's Marsh. It was named Parnell Bridge and Warren's Place became Parnell Place. Charles Stewart Parnell represented Cork at Westminster until his death in 1891. It was yet again to the assembled crowds in the city that, on 21 January 1885, he made one of his most famous statements:

> No man has a right to fix the boundary to the march of a nation. No man has the right to say to his country, 'thus far shalt thou go and no farther', and we never attempted to fix the *ne plus ultra* to the progress of Ireland's nationhood, and we never shall.

Parnell was buried in Glasnevin Cemetery on 11 October 1891, and his funeral was attended by over 200,000 people, many having travelled from his constituency of Cork city.

GAA

On 27 December 1884 an event occurred in the Victoria Hotel, St Patrick's Street, which was of great significance in the cultural revival of Ireland and with which Parnell was associated. This was the second meeting of the Gaelic Association for the Preservation and Cultivation of National Pastimes, the founding meeting of which had been held some time previously at Hayes Hotel in Thurles, County Tipperary. The name was considered too long and was soon shortened to the more familiar Gaelic Athletic Association.

The meeting at the hotel on St Patrick's Street was attended by the Mayor-elect Alderman Madden as well as Maurice Davin, president of the association, Michael Cusack, the secretary, A. O'Driscoll of the Cork Athletic Club and others from Dublin, Templemore and Cloyne.[9] The first item of business was the happy announcement that the patronage of three important personages had been secured and confirmed. These were the Archbishop of Cashel, Michael Davitt and Charles Stewart Parnell. This having been achieved, Cusack said, the ideals proposed at the Thurles meeting could now proceed with the association firmly established throughout the land.

The meeting then adopted two resolutions. Firstly, and proposed by John O'Connor, that 'the officers of the Association already elected and the organising committee of the National League together with two representatives from every recognised athletic club in Ireland be elected as the Central Committee to carry out the work of the Association'.

An advertisement, a luggage label and headed notepaper with branded envelope for the Victoria Hotel on St Patrick's Street.
(Courtesy Michael Lenihan)

Seconded by Mr D. Horgan, the resolution was adopted and the stage was set for forming the first central council. Mr Bracken then proposed that 'the President Mr Maurice Davin and the Hon. Secs. Cusack, Power and McKay are requested to draft the rules under which the work of the Association would be conducted'. Mr Joseph Kennedy seconded this resolution which was again agreed by all. This crucial second meeting of the Gaelic Athletic Association then finished. Central Council would be formed; the rules would be written. Those present secured their place in history and although it will forever be recorded that the GAA was founded on a November day in Hayes Hotel in Thurles in 1884, nevertheless the Victoria Hotel on St Patrick's Street in the rebel city played just as important a part, with the hosting of the crucially important second formative meeting when, in the words of Secretary Cusack, the ideas of Thurles could finally be implemented.

Did the gingle-man in the right of the picture realise that the tram coming up behind him would overtake him in more ways than one?
(Courtesy Michael Lenihan)

Following pages: A superb colour view of St Patrick's Street with, unusually, no trams at the Statue. Note, however, the variety of head attire, which often was a mark of class.
(Courtesy Michael Lenihan)

8 A Changing Streetscape

As the new century dawned, perhaps the thirteenth since the followers of Finbarr made the hills and valley of Corcach Mór Mumhan their own place, a renewed ownership and pride in all the elements of Irish heritage and culture was under way. Many famous names were associated with this development and in Cork, Tomás MacCurtain, Terence MacSwiney and Dómhnall Óg Ó Ceallacháin would become famous in the Republican movement. On the literary front Daniel Corkery was a founder member of the Cork Celtic Literary Society and two students of his, Seán Ó Faoláin and Frank O'Connor, became famous throughout the world for their writings; and the writings sometimes reflected the deeply held sentiments that resided in their hearts and also painted a picture of the place that was the city of Cork.

Last night I was in Cork: the climate was Italian; I lay on the steps of the square in Patrick Street … and Pigott's front was just two immense doors from roof to pavement in black and gold lacquer, and Egan's the jewellers had a hallway of great size surrounded by walls covered by life size brass repousse goddesses and gods and warriors designed by Harry Clark … Suddenly Jack Hendrick and Kitty O'Leary appeared. Jack wore a lieutenant's uniform, Irish army … and then, lo, and how exquisitely beautiful it was, he flung himself down beside me, threw down the army cap, and Kitty curled up too … and my god how he laughed and how Kitty laughed, and we were all young again and full of joy and to-hell-with-the-world feelings, and life was our oyster, and Ireland was the world the way it used to be. What woke me up was crying because in my heart I knew it was only a dream I was dreaming.[1]

This was one memory of Ó Faoláin, the man who described Cork as 'a notoriously wet and windy place' and the era, (referring to the Palace theatre), as one of 'hobble skirts, harem skirts, Phul Nana scents, hats two feet wide, violets in furs, pipe clay belts, brass buttons and puttees, barouches, muddy streets, crossing sweepers, trailing skirts held up to show buttoned shoes … this oriental bazaar called Cork'.[2]

St Patrick's Day Parade

The renewal of cultural spirit now coming to the fore had its roots in the actions of great Irish leaders, O'Connell, O'Donovan Rossa and the Fenians, Davitt and Parnell. All things Irish were to be celebrated, none more so than the feast day of the national saint, 17 March, St Patrick's Day. For nearly a decade people had gathered at various locations to honour the patron saint but not in any official manner. Elsewhere in the world the day was celebrated with great fervour. In the United States a parade in honour of Patrick had first been held in 1737, organised by the Irish Charitable Society of Boston and the first parade held in New York was when Irish soldiers serving in the British forces there marched on 17 March 1762. Now was the time that the tradition would become part of life throughout Ireland.[3]

In 1900 a contemporary news reports tell us that:

The city was crowded on Saturday as it usually is on Patrick's day when many country people take holiday. There was an air of great animation visible everywhere and the day was celebrated with heartiness and unanimity not usual in the country.

The shamrock was almost universally worn. Ladies displayed great bouquets of green favour and the national emblem. Every class in the community favoured the pretty trefoil. Flags floated from a number of public buildings and shipping on the river were gay with bunting. Verily a change seemed to have come over the town.[4]

The reports further tell that the Mayor left to attend a ceremony of commemoration of St Patrick in Dublin, while on the eve of the feast, under the auspices of the Cork Young Ireland Society a crowd of people gathered near the Courthouse and at about nine o'clock started to march through the city accompanied by several bands.

The following year the matter became official – in so far as the Corporation members and the Lord Mayor attended the parade in their robes. (Only the nationalist Corporation members attended, however.) On a day when the weather was not favourable, the officials made their way to the Cathedral in carriages to attend twelve o'clock Mass. Then they proceeded to the city to participate in the parade. It was scheduled to begin at one o'clock but such was the turnout that it did not get under way until an hour later. As on so many occasions in the past, the trades associations were prominent, as were a number of the city's bands: the Workingmen's, Butter Exchange, Fr Mathew's, Carpenters', Blackpool, St Coleman's, Barrack Street, Greenmount Industrial School, Quarry Lane and Douglas.

Having started at Great George's Street, the parade made its way through the South and North Main Streets, Pope's Quay and across the bridge into St Patrick's Street. Great emotion was felt by the many thousands participating when the parade commemorating the national saint made its way through the street named in his honour. The procession continued through Grand Parade, South Mall, Parliament Street and George's Quay to the Cornmarket where City Hall is today. There, the President of the Young Ireland Society, Mr Crowley, congratulated the people of Cork for reviving the St Patrick's Day celebrations and Mr J. Horgan of the Cork United Trades Association proposed that:

> this vast public meeting of Irish nationalists, trades bodies and Friendly Societies held on this festival day of our patron saint, resolve that steps be taken towards making St Patrick's day on all future anniversaries an Irish national holiday and for that purpose pledge ourselves to seek the sympathies and co-operation of all sections of citizens for effecting this object.

An old tradition had been recreated, and year by year (continued annually today) parades in honour of the national saint make their way through the main street of the city, named in his honour, on 17 March, his feast day

– yet another pageant associated with the traditions of Cork and Ireland played out of St Patrick's Street.

Horseless Trams

We have seen previously the horse-drawn tram system of the 1870s as well as the other transport developments that occurred in the latter half of the nineteenth century. Shortly before the century ended another development of major significance occurred. This was the advent of an electric tram system, which began in December 1898 and lasted until 1931. Not alone were tram tracks and cars again a feature on St Patrick's Street, but now poles carrying the electric cables upon which the trams depended for motive power ran the length of the street in the centre.[5] 'Tram stops dotted St Patrick's Street.'[6] The owners of the system were the Cork Electric Tramways and Lighting Company Ltd and the fleet consisted of thirty-five cars. These were the first horseless carriages operating on St Patrick's Street and the existence of the system meant that Cork was now on a par with other great cities and even three years ahead of London.[7] As with the horse-drawn trams of a quarter of a century earlier, the Fr Mathew Statue at the north end of St Patrick's Street was the hub of the service.[8] These

Electric trams on St Patrick's Street.
(Courtesy Michael Lenihan)

Above: Another view of Trams on St Patrick's Street.
(Courtesy Michael Lenihan)

Right: Postcard map of Cork showing the Electric Tram routes.
(Courtesy Michael Lenihan)

trams differed from the earlier horse-drawn ones, however, in that they were soon beloved of all the people. A mere three years after their arrival on the streets they were stretched to capacity when carrying thousands to and from an event of international significance on Leeside.

The International Exhibition: 1902

The Cork Mayor who visited Dublin for the 1900 St Patrick's Day commemoration was Daniel J. Hegarty. Shortly thereafter, having delivered an address of welcome to the visiting Queen Victoria on behalf of the citizens of Cork, he became the first Lord Mayor of Cork when she honoured the city by elevating the status of First Citizen to the same as that of a select number of other cities such as London, Belfast and Dublin.[9] The next person to hold the office of Lord Mayor was Edward Fitzgerald – later Sir Edward – and he was instrumental in organising in Cork the major international exhibition that took place in 1902 and which brought huge crowds to the city streets, particularly for the opening procession which, in a humorous way, could be said to have taken about six months from start to finish.

The idea for the exhibition was first mooted at a Corporation meeting held in February 1901 and was taken up with great enthusiasm. Mr H. A. Cutler was appointed honorary architect and Mr R. A. Atkins the honorary secretary. After nearly eighteen months of exhaustive preparations, the opening took place on 1 May 1902 and thousands of people gathered in the city for the occasion. Special excursion trains brought visitors from all over the country and St Patrick's Street was again thronged. The anticipated commercial benefits from the event were obvious from the outset. Trams on the main street were full to capacity and carriages could not be obtained. Many people chose to process to the grounds of the exhibition, joining the officials, the trade societies and the bands as they made their way from the municipal buildings via St Patrick's Street to the grounds at the Mardyke and the banks of the River Lee. The Lord Mayor was joined by the Lord Mayor of Dublin and the Mayors of Derry, Drogheda and Waterford on the occasion. Among those performing in the procession, to the great cheers of the watching crowds, was a wagon with girls in Irish costumes dancing, singing and playing Irish airs behind the banner of the Irish Pipers Club. All the city bands marched and, in keeping with the nature of the exhibition, the Shop Assistants carried a banner in support of home produce. Leaving St Patrick's Street behind, the assembly crossed St Patrick's Bridge and proceeded to the exhibition grounds via Pope's Quay, the North and South Main Streets, Western Road and the Mardyke, arriving to the strains of the 500-strong orchestra and chorus specially gathered for the occasion.

A number of St Patrick's Street businesses were exhibitors at the event, such as Cash & Co., Atkins' of No. 117 and William Dennehy & Sons, purveyors of silk, felt and straw hats and caps at Nos. 60–62. Egan's had a considerable display of their ecclesiastical wares while Fitzgerald & Sons displayed the most modern fashions in gentlemen's shirts. Grant's, Guy's, and John Gilbert of No. 120 were also present. Lambkin's tobacco merchants, Mangan's clocks and Joseph Mayne's china and glass all had impressive displays. Newsom's gave samples of their teas; Perry & Sons showed the craftsmanship of their fireplaces; Purcell & Co. displayed their lithography; and the London House was a popular stand with foreign visitors. Two other firms that would become synonymous with St Patrick's Street during the twentieth century also exhibited: F. H. Thompson & Son of Nos. 71–72 and J. W. Elvery & Co. of No. 78.

The exhibition continued until the end of October 1902. On 1 November, the procession which began on 1 May was completed when dignitaries and officials, followed by large numbers of ordinary people processed back to the Municipal Buildings via St Patrick's Street and declared the event closed. It was deemed such a success that it was agreed to hold it again the following year and on that occasion the city and exhibition was honoured with a royal presence.

The Visit of Edward VII

An era had ended. Queen Victoria, for so long on the throne of England, had died and the empire was overseen by a new king, Edward VII. In July and August 1903, alongside Queen Alexandra and their daughter Princess Victoria, he visited Ireland and came to Cork on Saturday 1 August. The royal yacht, the *Victoria and Albert*, arrived in Queenstown just after nine o'clock in the morning, accompanied by four first class cruisers, the *Good Hope*, the *Sutlej*, the *Dido* and the *Hogue*. As the *Victoria and Albert* gently moved into docking position, the King was on deck to see the town and the magnificent Cathedral that lay before him. Addresses of welcome were made and then the royal party transferred to the *Vivid* under the command of Captain Nathaniel Sutton and made the remainder of the journey to Cork where they arrived just after noon. As they passed upstream from Queenstown, a royal salute was fired by the Royal Cork Yacht Club.[10]

Royal procession of King Edward VII and Queen Alexandra through St Patrick's Street in 1903. (Courtesy Amy and Chris Ramsden, The Day Collection)

Three views of King Edward and Queen Alexandra about to depart from Cork following the 1903 visit. (Source unknown)

From early in the day people had gathered to see the visitors. Before nine o'clock crowds were making their way through St Patrick's Street, across the bridge and down the quays to the landing stage. The weather was magnificent and at just before half past twelve in the afternoon guns boomed from the Marina to announce the arrival of the party. As they disembarked from the *Vivid* the naval band played 'God Save the King' and then the King, Queen and Princess were officially welcomed to Cork by the Lord Lieutenant and the Lord Mayor. King Edward was dressed in the uniform of a Field Marshall and wore the ribbon of St Patrick as well as the Star and Garter (he had become a Knight in the 1860s). The youngest daughter of the Lord Mayor then presented a bouquet of flowers to the Queen.[11]

First on the King's itinerary was the presentation of new colours to the 2nd Battalion Royal Irish Regiment and also the 2nd Battalion Royal Munster Fusiliers. Then the royal party processed to the exhibition grounds where they stayed, visiting the various stands, until about four o'clock. Lunch was provided by the Tivoli Restaurant of No. 5 St Patrick's Street and owner Henry O'Shea, a future Lord Mayor of the city, placed advertisements in the newspapers over the following months alluding to this fact as a recommendation of his eating establishment.

It was on the return journey that the King and his family made their way through the city centre and St Patrick's Street. Under the direction of Mr James McMullen, the contractor to provide decoration of the streets for the occasion, a magnificent display had been engineered and according to the press reports of the day, these were so attractive that in themselves they drew huge crowds. The London & Newcastle Tea Company hung flags from their premises and archways of flowers were placed at intervals along the route to the railway station from where King Edward, Queen

Alexandra and Princess Victoria departed. The streets were lined with military personnel and many of the city population gathered to wave farewell to a monarch whom they believed had an appreciation for the Irish political perspective and who would be kindly disposed to the Home Rule argument. In an editorial published on Monday 3 August, the *Cork Examiner* said that:

> the people are thoroughly pleased with the whole course of this memorable visit, and good reason they have to be satisfied. They have secured the sympathy of a broad-minded and capable ruler, who has grasped the leading facts of our social and political state with marvellous precision and firmness. King Edward has manifested rare courtesy and extraordinary good-will towards the Irish people, has evinced a keen interest in all that pertains to our commercial and industrial progress, and has effectively dissociated himself from the ancient and narrow prejudices which were hitherto the peculiar appendage of Royalty.[12]

Not everybody agreed that the British royalty should visit Cork or indeed Ireland. Nevertheless the visit to Leeside went off successfully and without incident, a fact much lauded in the press over the following weeks. As the King's train headed northwards towards Mallow and beyond on that August evening, the people of Cork returned to their homes. The decorations were removed from St Patrick's Street and after the weekend was over, all returned to normal.

New Businesses

As the nineteenth century passed into history and the twentieth century dawned, much change occurred on St Patrick's Street. Between 1891 and 1907, forty premises changed hands on the street and in the following three years another fifteen did so. In some cases businesses moved to another location on the street. However, in the majority of cases, names which had been a part of the streetscape disappeared for good to be replaced by new businesses and some of these became much loved by the people of Cork.

Among the famous names to disappear was Wood & Son, hatters at No. 46, replaced by H. Johnson, umbrella and stick manufacturer. The Lee Library at No. 61 became part of William Dennehy's tailoring shop, and

McAuliffe's fruit merchant shop at No. 50 became Sutton's watchmakers. No. 33 was vacant in 1891 but in the following year it was taken over by Egan's Ecclesiastical Shop. Further up the street, on the other side, Punch grocery at No. 78 was no longer extant. The shop now had a large model of an elephant located above the doorway and the name of Elvery's had become a part of Cork's main street.

 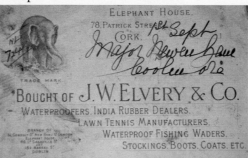 

Left: **The Elephant symbol of Elvery's Shop at no. 78.** (Courtesy Amy and Chris Ramsden, The Day Collection)

Centre and right: **Elvery's and Thompson's headed paper.** (Courtesy Michael Lenihan)

Elvery's was a Dublin firm, located at 45 Lower O'Connell Street. It started out in an area of Dublin known as 'the Lotts', where people had allotments in earlier times. In the latter part of the nineteenth century a market operated there, which took in the corner of Upper Abbey Street and Middle Street. In the market, a shop dealt in tea, imported from among other places Ceylon, and which had as its symbol an elephant, proudly displayed above the doorway. The place became known as the Elephant House and when it closed its business doors and was taken over by Elvery's they also assumed the symbol associated with the premises. They then registered their business as Elvery's Elephant House of Dublin, Belfast and London and when they came to Cork in 1892, the Ceylon elephant made its way to St Patrick's Street. John Larkin of Elvery's in Dublin recalls with amusement that when he would come to the Cork shop in the middle decades of the twentieth century, Cork people would always have a wry comment on 'their' elephant. He had much pleasure in recounting that the elephant of St Patrick's Street was in fact a gift from Dublin.[13]

The elephant atop Elvery's door was but one of many landmarks on St Patrick's Street used by the Cork people as a meeting place and undoubtedly very many people have fond memories of early romantic liaisons when they met beneath 'the elephant'. Another meeting place, whether it was shoppers meeting friends, workers popping out for a tea break or a romantic liaison, was Thompson's, a restaurant and bakery where the most delicious cakes would be served from silver cake-stands and tea and coffee tasted better than anywhere else … at least in the memory

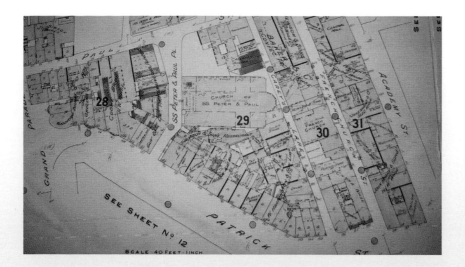

A section from the Goad Maps showing Thompson's and other premises on St Patrick's Street. (Courtesy Cork City Library)

of old romantics. Thompson's was founded as far back as 1826 at No. 2 Clarke's Bridge, by Christina Thompson. Her forebears were Huguenot on the one side and English on the other. The French branch of her family was Malenoir, members of which arrived in Cork, possibly on the *Grafton*, in 1761. They first settled in Fermoy where the young Christina Malenoir met and married a man named Thompson. They then moved to Cork where Christina set up the bakery at Clarke's Bridge.

During the nineteenth century the business moved to 8 Bridge Street, where it was taken over by her son Francis Hanan Thompson. Another son, Samuel, was a bookbinder, but after that business was lost in a fire he joined his brother in the bakery business and adapted his home at Princess Street as second premises. Tensions arose between the brothers and it was only the intervention of their mother, Christina, that brought them back together again with agreement that Samuel would pursue the business on the south side of the city and Frank the north side. When the next generation of Thompson's took over the respective premises, tension still existed between the branches. By arrangement, however, they did still exchange two loaves of bread from Bridge Street for a barmbrack from Princess Street at least once a year. It was Frank's successors who took over the premises of Russell Martin, bakers, at No. 71 St Patrick's Street in the latter years of the 1880s and the brothers reconciled their differences as they both reached old age. Brown's Mills in MacCurtain Street was acquired and became the headquarters of the firm from where a huge range of bakery products, many of which were local Cork recipes, were dispatched throughout Munster and beyond.[14]

A receipt, dated January 1891, from Thomas Lester's of no. 107 St Patrick's Street.

(Courtesy Michael Lenihan)

Generations of Cork people each have their own memories of Thompson's, whether the tea and cakes in the restaurants, where friends met and chatted; the bread or cake for the table at home; or the workplace, where lifelong friendships existed, not just a relationship of workmates. Thompson's of St Patrick's Street, Princess Street and MacCurtain Street was indeed a Cork institution, and a beloved one at that.

Another famous Cork business was that of Thomas Lester, located at No. 106–107 St Patrick's Street, described by *Strattens'* directory of 1892 as unquestionably the largest and 'most handsome drug emporium in Cork'.[15] The premises had undergone a series of refurbishments by the end of the century with no expense spared, and dealt not only in prescription drugs but also in surgical instruments and all that the practising medic would require. Listed as being available at the shop were 'bandages of every description, air cushions, lints, gauzes, arm slings … crutches, elastic bandages … inhalers, invalid apparatus', and a host of other medical items. Like Thompson's, Elvery's and many other St Patrick's Street establishments, Lester's Pharmacy played a large part in the lives of Cork people until the latter years of the twentieth century.

The Goad Plans

Since the middle years of the eighteenth century, the shape of Cork had been recorded on a variety of maps, showing the evolution of a water channel of the River Lee into a street that now played a central role in the lives of the people of Cork. But two-dimensional representations of direction and location could never give an illustration of the pulse of the place. That would only come in the nineteenth century with the advent of photography. The images then and subsequently taken showed the clothes that were worn by the people, the transport that was in use, certain architectural dimension of the various premises in the frames being photographed. In 1897 yet another source in the pursuit of an overall picture of Cork was developed. This was the drawing of the Goad Maps, sketches of streets in the city showing every premises and their architectural features and these were updated at intervals over the following fifty or so years. Not all the premises were named but they were numbered and cross-referencing with trade directories such as the *Guy's* directories, coupled with photographs, gives a much improved picture of the place that was the city of Cork and St Patrick's Street was no exception.

Thus it can be seen that in 1897, the business of Thompson & Sons at Nos. 71–72 St Patrick's Street stretched back and behind a number of other premises on the street, alongside the southern wall of St Peter and Paul's Church. Furthermore, a dressmaking business was carried on above Thompson's at No. 72. Reference to *Guy's* directory of the period tells us that this in fact was owned by a Mrs O'Callaghan.

With the development of business on the street and in particular with the departure of merchants from actually residing in their premises during the 1800s, it had become quite common for ventures to be carried on above the street-level businesses and more of these were recorded as the years went by. Thus, in 1910, above Simcox Grocery at No. 10 were the Misses Hill, dressmakers and Mr E. G. Andrews, a teeth specialist. Dressmaking was quite a common 'overhead' business with Miss Smith above Hartland's at No. 33 (as was the American Photo Studio), Miss Gillman above Baker's at No. 39, Miss Kelly above Hackett's Jewellers at No. 55, Miss Moynihan and also Moynihan & Sons Tailors above Mark's Penny Bazaar at No. 57, Miss Cashman above the English Grocery at No. 76, Mrs McEnery above Twomey's Wines at No. 93, Miss Murphy above Smith's Grocery at No. 99 and Miss S. McDonald above Taylor's at No.123.

Another teeth specialist operated at No. 25 (Cole & Co.) whilst dentist R. S. Criger operated upstairs at No. 12. Hairdressing, French and other language classes, millinery and a number of photographers were all upstairs businesses on the street. Mrs O'Connell operated a high-class luncheon room at No. 112 while at No. 125, right on the corner of Lavitt's Quay, was the Cork Pig Buyer's Association.

Tensions

The early years of the twentieth century saw the consolidation of the Irish literary and cultural revival. For many, however, this was not enough. Nationhood meant more than having one's own culture. As long as decisions of government were made by the foreign occupying country of England, Ireland should never be at peace, was their view, and they aspired to more than Home Rule. They wanted independence. On Easter Monday morning, 1916, Padraig Pearse stood before the General Post Office in the centre of Dublin's Sackville Street (O'Connell Street) – arguably the street that symbolically was the stage for Ireland as much as St Patrick's Street was for Cork – and proclaimed to the people of Ireland that:

A slice of relaxed Cork life at the turn of the century before tensions visited the street.
(Courtesy Michael Lenihan)

in the name of God and the dead generations from which she receives her old tradition of nationhood, Ireland, through us, summons her children to her flag and strikes for her freedom.

In Cork, those charged with leading local battalions of the Volunteers had been in readiness but, owing to a series of contradictory instructions from headquarters in Dublin, the most recent of which had indicated that the rising would not take place, they, as at almost all other locations in the country outside Dublin, did not engage in hostilities. Indeed, historian Peter Hart described them as 'paralysed' and that they spent the week 'anxiously huddled in their homes and club rooms'.[16] When, after a week, Pearse surrendered to the British, the Cork contingents also gave up their weapons in an agreement brokered by the Bishop and Lord Mayor Butterfield. Tomás MacCurtain and Terence MacSwiney were among those arrested. The *Cork Examiner* of Saturday 29 April carried an update saying that 'The situation in the South of Ireland command is good. Reports received today from the garrisons of Galway, Cork, Wexford, Tralee, Limerick, Clonmel, Waterford and other stations in the South of Ireland state that these towns are now and have been up to the present, perfectly quiet.'[17] Another report in the same edition says that the editor had been 'officially informed by the General commanding at Queenstown that absolutely normal conditions prevail in Cork. It is not considered that there is any reason to fear any disturbance whatever, or that it will be necessary to impose any restrictions upon the citizens.'[18]

The inaction of the Cork rebels in 1916 may have been the catalyst that spurred the city and county to such dedicated and intense involvement later in the independence campaign. Tension filled the city streets almost immediately after the rebellion, though much of it was not on display on the city's main thoroughfare; it was largely expressed in the narrow streets and laneways off the main streets. 'Freedom fighters' first appeared on the streets of the city in 1917, men determined to rekindle the spirit of the previous year and this time to take action. At the outset they held marches and demonstrations at which they attacked the police with stones and hurleys. Before long these gave way to guns and bullets. As a consequence of this, the authorities became suspicious of anywhere that arms could be obtained and, among other places, raided Murray's of St Patrick's Street in 1919.

A visiting English journalist, Harold Ashton, reported that:

> the city is in a jumpy mood ... Sinn Féiners were out in platoons roving the streets in a spirit of high bravado. Explosions like revolver shots sent the crowd skipping and the girls screaming, and for an hour or so the warm night was very lively with detonations, explosions, and alarms, but the tall quiet-eyed men of the RIC, moving always in couples among the press, cleverly broke up the demonstration and never allowed any massed formation.

To the hilarity of the locals, it was realised that the events being reported were the post-match celebrations of a local derby between Presentation Brothers and Christian Brothers schools.[19]

Despite this humorous situation tensions continued and grew in the city with street fighting, rioting and assaults on the authorities becoming a regular occurrence. It was inevitable that a climax would be reached and this indeed happened in the final month of 1920. Before that climax was reached, however, the changes that had been ongoing throughout the street's existence continued, with some businesses departing the street and being replaced by others, a number of which achieved the status of institution. Unquestionably that mantle can be applied to two in particular that opened their doors on the street in the early years of the twentieth century. These were Roches Stores and Woolworths, the latter lasting for some sixty-five years and the former for over a century, arguably the most famous store ever to open on St Patrick's Street.

Top: James Keating, William Roche's business partner.
(Courtesy Michael Lenihan)

Bottom: Front page of a 1905 catalogue for William Roche and James Keating's Cork Furniture Store on Merchant Street.
(Courtesy Michael Lenihan)

William Roche was an ambitious man and following his apprenticeship in Cash's, decided to go it alone. Three early ventures, however, did not bring him success. He therefore went to London to try his luck and returned after eighteen months with £225 in his pocket, capital with which to start a business at home in Cork. While in Cash's, most of his experience had been in the furniture department and so in 1901 he opened the small Cork Furniture Store on Merchant Street. His sales policy was one of offering the best value to the customer, telling him or her the truth at all times, displaying his products in an attractive way with the price clearly marked and offering his wares to all classes and creeds. After a year he was joined by James Keating and together they opened a second store and operated quite successfully for the next twelve years. Content that they now had a solid customer base that trusted them, they decided to enlarge the business and establish a new department in costumes, coats and millinery for ladies. Many thought that they could not possibly succeed but business boomed and for the first time a sign proclaiming 'Roches Stores' appeared in Cork.

After a few more years, with the firm having changed considerably – it now operated from Allman's of Winthrop Street which later would become the Lee Cinema – and an ever-increasing customer base, William Roche thought the time right to expand still further and in June 1919 took the decision to acquire the London House on the main thoroughfare of St Patrick's Street. In September of the same year the firm's name was changed by resolution to that of Roches Stores Ltd. Despite the tensions developing in the city, tensions which saw a bomb being thrown just outside the shop, sending shrapnel flying through the front of the premises, the business thrived even more in its main street location. It rapidly became a place synonymous with the street – perhaps even as much as Fr Mathew who stood not far from its doorway.

Further up the street, the other institution of Woolworth's also opened its doors on St Patrick's Street in 1919. Frank Winfield Woolworth was born in 1852 in Rodman, Upper New York State. Like William Roche he was from a farming background and he too left home for the bright lights of the city. He also became a trainee retailer where he soon found that his gift for displaying product drew customers and his belief that selling for the best possible value would keep their custom proved right. He developed the 5 cent store concept and after five years in business the company he had formed had a turnover of $1 million. His enterprise spread throughout the

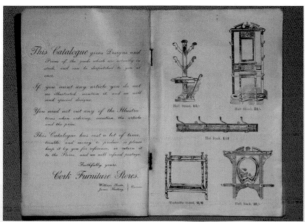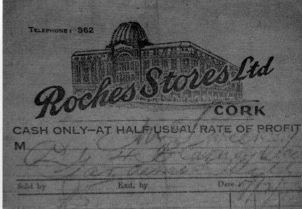

United States and into Canada, following his marriage to Canadian Jennie Creighton, and within two decades reached a turnover of $10 million. By the end of the First World War it had grown to the astonishing figure of $100 million with over 1,000 Woolworth's stores throughout the North American continent.

Europe was by this time familiar to all Americans, not least because of their involvement in the First World War. Woolworth therefore decided to expand his empire to Europe and began this development in Great Britain. Ireland being part thereof, it came to pass that Cork acquired a store filled with magic: with sweets and toys, make-up and clothes, three stairwells to the upper floor and a lift; a place where everything was colourful and bright and where every Cork child, when asked if they wanted to go to town would reply 'oh yes and Woolworth's too!' Located at Nos. 40–41 where Newsom & Son had sold teas and groceries for over a century, for sixty-five years until its closure in July 1984 Woolworth's was indeed a Cork institution.

Left: Part of 1905 catalogue for the Cork Furniture Store.
(Courtesy Michael Lenihan)

Right: Invoice for Roches Stores. Note the telephone number 362.
(Courtesy Michael Lenihan)

9 Destruction and Reconstruction

In St Patrick's Street's history, on a number of occasions, the street suffered physical damage as a consequence of social tensions resulting in violence. One such case which we have seen was in the summer of 1870 when riots occurred on the street during a tailors' strike.[1] Another was the destruction by fire of large sections of the street on the night of 11 December 1920 in an incident known as the 'Burning of Cork'. This chapter outlines briefly the circumstances leading to the burning and then discusses the street's subsequent reconstruction.

The Burning of Cork

The tensions in Cork society leading to the events of 11 December 1920 were associated with the struggle for independence. While nationally Sinn Féin was moving towards dominance on the political front, those wanting to pursue a revolutionary agenda and engage in a war for separation took to the streets. Between 1917 and 1923, over 700 people were killed and nearly 900 injured making Cork the most violent county in the country. Of those killed over one third were civilian victims, 'neither soldiers, policemen nor guerrillas.' Of those actively involved in the action nearly 200 Volunteers and 300 security forces personnel lost their lives. Beyond this 'a vast everyday traffic in terror and destruction; beatings, raids, kidnappings, torture, arson, robbery and vandalism left few families or communities untouched'.[2] As early as 1917, 'freedom fighters' were active on the streets of Cork and in that year three RIC constables were shot

during disturbances in the city.[3] By Christmas 1918, 8,000 men and women were active in the Irish Volunteer movement in Cork. In April 1919, Volunteer Harry Varian shot and killed Constable John Hayes.

In the nine months prior to Christmas 1920 there was a considerable upsurge in violence 'as attacks by the Volunteers on Crown forces were met in turn by the imposition of a curfew during hours of darkness and savage unofficial reprisals in the form of shootings and arson attacks'.[4] At eleven o'clock on the night of 19 March, RIC Constable Joseph Murtagh was killed on Pope's Quay as he walked home to Sunday's Well. Two hours later Lord Mayor Tomás MacCurtain was shot and killed at his home in Blackpool by members of the Royal Irish Constabulary. (A verdict of wilful murder was returned by the Coroner's Jury). The arrival of the Black and Tans in March and the Auxiliaries in July (both auxiliary police forces brought in from Britain) increased tension in the city still further.

They closed life in on us tighter and tighter every month through a varied, incessant and inventive terrorism, constant and often pointless raids and arrests, humiliating and brutal beatings-up in city streets, casual murders on country roads, reprisals both official and unofficial – which usually meant the burning down in public of a sympathisers home and business.[5]

In August Lord Mayor Terence MacSwiney was arrested and sent to Brixton Prison. On 3 October a group of Black and Tans were fired on from Blackthorn House on St Patrick's Street and Constable Clarence Victor Chave was killed. Six days later an attempt to set the City Hall on fire resulted in serious damage. On the 25 October, Terence MacSwiney died on hunger strike, bringing the struggle for independence to international attention. In November the situation escalated still further. A new company of Auxiliaries – K Company – was formed under the command of Colonel Owen William Latymer. On 23 November, three Volunteers were killed in an explosion on St Patrick's Street. Over the course of the following days a number of notices were posted throughout the city threatening retaliation for 'policemen and soldiers being murdered every day'. One was signed B and T, another Black and Tans. On the night of Saturday 27 November, three buildings on St Patrick's Street – Cahill & Co., Blackthorn House and the American Shoe Co. – were set ablaze with the former two being destroyed.[6] On Sunday 28 an ambush took place at Kilmichael in west Cork in which a heavy defeat was inflicted on the Auxiliaries by Tom Barry and his Flying Column.[7] Both sides were now willing to respond with equal ferocity. The destruction of the buildings on St Patrick's Street was a clear message that retaliatory action would be brought to the heart of the community. St Patrick's Street was clearly at risk. On 10 December martial law was declared. The next night a party of Volunteers ambushed the Auxiliaries as they left Victoria Barracks at Dillon's Cross, killing one and wounding eleven others. The British response was swift and severe.

The ambush at Dillon's Cross began shortly after eight o'clock on the evening of 11 December 1920. Within an hour witnesses described increased Black and Tan activity, including discharging of firearms, in the vicinity of St Patrick's Street.[8] At about ten o'clock, a tram from King Street was stopped and 'they broke all the glass in the tram. The tram then went on and at the other side of the bridge near the Statue, it was set on fire.'[9] In his official report to the Lord Mayor subsequent to the events, Captain

Hutson, Superintendent of the City of Cork Fire Brigade, said that 'at 10.30 p.m. I received a call to Messrs A. Grant and Co. in St Patrick Street, whose extensive premises were on fire'.[10] Over the following hours, despite the efforts of the fire services, the blocks of St Patrick's Street between Merchant Street, Winthrop Street and Cook Street were set ablaze.[11] On a radio documentary many years later, memories were still vivid:

> I remember or saw cans of petrol and hand torches in the dark underneath us – laying out the petrol on the floor prior to the fire. Next thing we were – our door was broken in at the front. Then they came around the side and the senior superintendent opened the door – they came upstairs and ordered us out onto the street.

> The tans had heavy sledge hammers and pinch bars – iron bars about four feet long that you would prise a door up and they smashed any place they wanted to get into – they told us to get out of the way and they fired shots, not to hit us but to frighten us.[12]

Such was the intensity of the fire that the heat blistered paintwork on the other side of the street.[13] In total fifty-seven premises throughout the city were destroyed, twenty of them on St Patrick's Street.[14] As dawn broke on Sunday morning, crowds gathered to witness a ruined St Patrick's Street. William Roche of Roches Stores, with some of his employees, tried to salvage material from the ruins. 'We worked until about one o'clock at the

Uniformed man on top of St Patrick's Street ruins after the burning.

(Courtesy Michael Lenihan)

salvaging. This work was done at some risk, as walls were suddenly falling in, in many places.'[15]

The destruction of large sections of St Patrick's Street impacted on the people in a number of ways. Not alone had many of the physical structures that shaped the main street been lost, but so also had thousands of jobs, many peoples' homes, the centre of retail and commerce and, for many people, the social centre of the city. In its reporting of the events the *Cork Examiner* declared that 'thousands were rendered idle' by the destruction.[16] At a symbolic level, much of the form that gave the street its identity was gone. The places and premises that created memories in the hearts and minds of Corkonians were destroyed; history, not least in the form of records, was also gone. Since its founding almost 150 years earlier, the night of 11 December 1920 was St Patrick's Street's darkest hour, a night when much of the street perished forever. It would be more than six years before the newly reconstructed street fully emerged from the ashes.

An examination of newspaper reports in the days immediately following the destruction reveals six different reactions in the city. Firstly, the Corporation held a meeting in the Corn Exchange on Monday 13 December and 'Mr Egan moved and it was seconded by Mr Good that an unemployment committee be formed to take steps to relieve the unemployment necessarily caused by the destruction in the centre portion of the city'.[17] The membership of the committee was agreed and then the Corporation resolved that the new Lord Mayor would send telegrams to the Pope and representatives of the European nations and America regarding the state, in particular, of Cork city. Members then went on to angrily express criticism of the Catholic Bishop Coholan. Lord Mayor Domhnall Ó Ceallacháin said 'it was terrible to think that when the people woke up to find part of their city in ruins at the termination of a week of unbridled ruffianism, there was no word of condemnation from the Bishop'. However, he then went on to say that the Bishop's views, including a threat of excommunication a week earlier against those involved in crimes including murder, were not a matter to be dealt with by Corporation resolution.[18]

A pastoral letter from Bishop Coholan, read to all congregations in the diocese on Sunday 19 December, gave the Catholic Church's reaction to the events. In it the Bishop notified again his decree of excommunication against those guilty of murder. As examples he cited the killing of Constable Murtagh in March, the reprisal killing of Lord Mayor Tomás MacCurtain

and the ambushes at Kilmichael and Dillon's Cross and said that it was for the protection of men and boys and the public at large against ongoing reprisals that he took his action. He also answered criticisms of certain councillors saying that:

One of the timber huts placed among the ruins on St Patrick's Street in order for business to continue.
(Courtesy Michael Lenihan)

> some would like … to divert public attention from … the consequences of false teachings of persons who should know better … that Irishmen have authority to kill English forces and to burn English property in Ireland. Patrick Street is an ugly and to these teachers disquieting consequence of their false and immoral teaching.[19]

This conflict between civic and ecclesiastical leaders in the city was the public expression of deeply held tenets by the participants but was of little benefit to the ordinary folk who were affected by the destruction of St Patrick's Street, whose reaction to the burnings was one of shock and disbelief.

The fourth reaction was expressed in practical terms to the early meetings of the relief committee by representatives of the workers directly affected by the events of 11 December. In a letter to the inaugural meeting held on 16 December, the Drapers' Assistants Association said 400 of its members were unemployed. The meeting categorised the needy into the very poor needing immediate relief; unemployed but not too needy and those whose premises were destroyed.[20] The meeting held on 20 December heard that 100 members of the Amalgamated Society of Tailors were out of employment.[21] An appeal was issued for funds and at the meetings held on 21 and 23 December it was noted that £90 had already been paid out and that 'the next disbursement would be considerably more'.[22]

On behalf of the owners of the destroyed properties and those who had lost their businesses, on Monday 20 December a total of 263 claims for compensation were listed as having been lodged with the town clerk Mr F. W. McCarthy, amounting to 'roughly £2,500,000', indicating the extent of the damage.[23] In an editorial on 29 December the *Cork Examiner* commented that 'to rebuild will take a long time', that 'the hands of the clock of local progress had been set back considerably'.[24] The sixth reaction was the engineering response and also illustrated the extent of the destruction of St Patrick's Street. The city engineer, J. F. Delaney, reported to the Corporation immediately following the burning that the total frontage of St Patrick's Street destroyed amounted to 744 feet or 248 yards in which 'some twenty of the principal establishments in the city, a number of them being the largest of the kind in the province', were destroyed.[25] For the purpose of the survey, he divided the destroyed area into seven zones of which numbers 1–4 and 6 included parts of St Patrick's Street; 1 – from Merchant Street to Maylor Street; 2 – from Maylor Street to Winthrop Street; 3 – from Winthrop Street to Robert Street; 4 – from Robert Street to Cook Street; and 6 – the premises of Grant's and Haynes & Son.[26]

Not unnaturally, in the political climate of the day, the question of responsibility came quickly to the fore. A military enquiry was held by the British and what became known as the Strickland Report was eagerly awaited, particularly by those who wished to see a public exposé of what the British had done. As the weeks passed, however, it became apparent that the report would be suppressed and eventually, on 15 February 1921, Prime Minister Lloyd George told the new session of the British Parliament that 'he would make no promise that the Strickland report would be published'.[27] In a five-page statement issued by him subsequently, he outlined the reasons why it had been a military enquiry and said that:

> it is a matter of regret that the opportunity thus afforded was not more widely taken advantage of by members of the civil community.

He then outlined how:

> Certain members – few in number and up to the present unidentified – of the Auxiliary Company known as K Company, becoming detached from the main body, unfortunately broke their bonds of discipline and, incensed by the recent ambush following as it did close upon the horrible massacre at Macroom, committed either alone or with other persons not members of the Crown forces, acts which resulted in the destruction of a considerable amount of property.

The statement went on:

> The K Company has been drastically reorganised since the date of the occurrences. The commanding officer has been suspended from duty; seven men adversely reported have been dismissed; and a further number have been transferred to other units on disciplinary grounds.

The report concluded that compensation would not be paid by the government; it was 'chargeable upon the locality'.[28]

The clearing of the debris on St Patrick's Street began almost immediately.[29] By Thursday 16 December 1920, the street was passable and the various business concerns set about reorganising themselves.[30] Recalling events a decade later, William Roche said that 'We still had some old premises in Merchant Street. No electric light, no gas as all mains were destroyed. We got twenty or thirty of our staff in at once, who worked all hours and in this confusion and falling walls we started a sale.'[31] An associate of William Roche, Pat Fitzgerald, said that 'even while the premises were still burning, Mr Roche was formulating plans for the carrying on of the business at Merchant Street'.[32] By mid-January 1921, 'substantial progress' had been made in clearing the debris and a number of businesses were in the process of erecting temporary wooden huts from which they would continue to trade. Carpenters were at work on the sites of the Munster Arcade, Cash's, Grant's and Egan's.[33] A report in the *Constitution* newspaper noted that there was a marvellous recovery from the recent fires.[34]

1921

The permanent rebuilding of St Patrick's Street was first and foremost a matter of finance. For the owners there were two possible sources of funding. The first was insurance; however 'the ordinary insurance which we had on stock and premises was useless; we had taken out a policy for riot and civil commotion on stock only, not on buildings'.[35] Secondly, it was a matter of the claims for compensation which were lodged with the town clerk within a week of the burning. Lloyd George in his statement to Parliament had made it clear the British government would not pay compensation, that it was the local authority's responsibility. Believing the British to be responsible, however, the local authority, while willing to award compensation amounts had neither the money nor the inclination to pay such awards. Thus finance was problematic from the outset in the rebuilding of St Patrick's Street. Nevertheless, in February 1921 three significant events occurred. In the first week assessors for Lloyd's insurance brokers visited the destroyed premises.[36] Then the claims hearings began on 16 February, the first session of which saw the Munster Arcade being granted £213,647 and Grant's £107,813.[37] With at least the possibility of building commencing following the awards, at a Corporation meeting held on 26 February a reconstruction committee was formed to operate in consultation with the city engineer as to the plans for the new buildings and the use of Irish materials.[38]

Over the spring and summer of 1921, the reconstruction committee met on six occasions, paid a number of visits to sites of destroyed premises and met with the owners, architects and builders involved in the reconstruction. The main work undertaken was the settlement of building lines as they applied to the frontages in zones 1, 2, 3, 4 and 6. In August a full report was given to the Corporation which included a map illustrating the agreed lines. With the full support of the reconstruction committee, the city engineer wrote that 'the coming new feature in the city should be impressive and monumental, and no owner will be justified in causing disfigurement by the introduction of ill-designed or meanly constructed premises'.[39]

As the first anniversary of the burning approached, for many of the affected businesses, limited trade was again under way in a series of temporary wooden structures. A reconstruction committee and the city engineer had laid out their views on how the reconstruction should proceed and awards of compensation had been pronounced but the only monies received by some owners was insurance on stock. Only one firm, O'Regan's of No. 26, had made progress in rebuilding and reopened for business on Saturday 26 November.[40]

1922

1922 was a year in which a number of initiatives and circumstances coincided such that little progress was achieved in the reconstruction of St Patrick's Street. On 23 February a delegation from Cork consisting of representatives of the Corporation, the Chamber of Commerce, the Trade and Labour Council, the premises owners and the reconstruction committee met with Diarmuid Fawsitt of the Ministry of Economic Affairs, J. J. Walsh, Postmaster General (and a deputy for Cork) and Michael Collins, who was at that time Minister for Finance in the new Irish government.[41] Their request was simple – that the government 'expedite the financial arrangements necessary to enable the work of building to be begun at an early date'.[42] The request was listened to sympathetically and two days later, on 25 February, Mr Barry Egan told the Corporation that the Provisional Government had asked the Corporation to act as trustees for monies they were prepared to make available and that Michael Collins had asked how much per month would be needed.[43]

Lord Mayor Domhnall Ó Ceallacháin welcomed the initiative but also mentioned that some of the decrees of compensation might be subject to review. Here he was referring to the first of the circumstances that would delay rebuilding. On the day of the Corporation meeting, it was announced in the *Cork Examiner* that by agreement between the British and the Irish Provisional Government, a commission was to be set up which would have power to hear all claims in respect of criminal injuries to property and to make awards which would then be paid by the British. It would also have power to review the awards made in undefended claims cases.[44] Nevertheless the funding initiative on the part of the Provisional Government proceeded and in early March the Corporation agreed to be trustees of the fund subject to number of conditions.[45] It was agreed that a subcommittee known as the Reconstruction Finance Committee would be set up. Diarmuid Fawsitt visited the city later in the month and outlined the plans to the Corporation. The subcommittee would oversee the funds; it would be provided with £10,000 immediately and monies monthly thereafter; all work would have to be approved; building works in the same block should coincide as far as possible; a maximum of three-fifths of each decree would be advanced and there would be no more temporary structures allowed. However, more than a month passed without anything happening.

Following the ratification of the Anglo-Irish Treaty in January 1922, the process of British disengagement with Ireland got under way. As tensions increased between those in favour of and those against the Treaty 'the distraction of the political situation meant he [Michael Collins] devoted less time to finance and more to military duties'.[46] These tensions were illustrated when J. J. Walsh in a letter suggested that Lord Mayor Ó Ceallacháin was more concerned with the destruction of the Provisional Government, 'so it would be horribly inconsistent to approach them for money'. He pointed out that the non-participation of Domhnall Ó Ceallacháin in the delegation that travelled to Dublin in February was deliberate and he suggested that communications had been sent not to the Provisional Government but to the department of Local Government of the Dáil (the Irish Parliament) which had nothing to do with the rebuilding programme and that the Lord Mayor knew this.[47] In these tense circumstances delays were inevitable.

On 26 and 27 April respectively, two letters were sent by Diarmuid Fawsitt on behalf of the Ministry of Economic Affairs. The first was to the city treasurer stating that an imprest in the sum of £10,000 was being forwarded to him 'to facilitate and expedite the reconstruction of destroyed properties in Cork city'. The second was to nine nominees of the Corporation expressing the Provisional Government's approval that they serve on the committee to administer the initiative.[48] On Tuesday 2 May the first meeting of the committee took place. The Lord Mayor was elected to the chair but as he had to leave, Councillor Barry Egan chaired the rest of the proceedings. The meeting agreed to advertise in the local press that owners should now submit applications for funding and that the next meeting would be held on 9 May. This meeting was again chaired by Barry Egan but four days later a confidential letter was received by the town clerk from Diarmuid Fawsitt instructing him to take steps to insure that any claimant or beneficiary would not chair future meetings. The letter was marked private and not for publication.[49] This was evidence of further tensions and that the Provisional Government was keeping a careful watch on proceedings in Cork.

On 9 May also, the composition of the compensation commission was announced in the local press. Lord Shaw of Dunfermline was to be the chairman; the Irish representative was Mr James C. Dowdall, a member of the Chamber of Commerce and the Cork Harbour Commissioners, and Mr C. J. Howell Thomas was the British representative.[50] Their first meeting was held on Friday 19 May and on 31 May they sat in Cork to deal with the Cork claims.[51] The first before them was the claim of Egan's and on Thursday 1 June they announced an award of £34,608, substantially lower than the £54,394 awarded by the recorder in the earlier hearing.[52] The claim of another owner, named Sunner, went unchanged; however, in an article in the *Cork Examiner* on 8 June, it was suggested that reductions of between 40 and 70 per cent were to fit in with former Chief Secretary for Ireland, Sir Hamar Greenwood's desire that all Irish claims be reduced by 50 per cent. The compensation commission returned to Dublin in the third week of June to continue deliberations, by which time those who had believed they would receive the recorder's full awards could no longer be certain that they would receive as much as they had thought.

The reconstruction of St Patrick's Street received two further blows over the summer months of 1922. The early months of the year had seen tensions between the pro- and anti-Treaty factions rising considerably. While many in society sought to avoid a conflict – on 24 April a nationwide strike agitating for a peaceful resolution to differences was organised by the Labour movement – fighting erupted on 28 June when Free State troops opened fire on an anti-Treaty garrison occupying the Four Courts in Dublin.[53] The ensuing Civil War impacted on all aspect of life throughout the country. In Cork, while the civic administration of the city continued, it was nevertheless affected in many ways. Due to the seizure of certain instruments, an agenda for the 19 August meeting of the Public Works Committee of the Corporation could not be issued in the ordinary way.[54] On 22 August it was reported that, with Michael Collins in the city, 'a number of deputations were yesterday endeavouring to secure brief interviews, but these could not be received as General Collins visit is solely in connection with military affairs'.[55] Thus national and local affairs could not continue in the ordinary way owing to the conflict.

As a condition of the original Provisional Government's funding initiative for the reconstruction of St Patrick's Street, plans submitted had to be approved by an engineer and architect appointed by the Provisional Government.[56] On 28 July the Lord Mayor reported to the Corporation that 'owing to the conditions prevailing for some time past there had been no communication with these architects; they had not come down to Cork and it was impossible to get in communication with them'.[57] Thus the circumstances of the Civil War presented the first blow: communications difficulties resulting in plans not being approved.[58] A second blow came in the form of a letter, sent on 4 August, to the secretary of the reconstruction committee from Diarmuid Fawsitt, instructing that 'no future advances under the Cork reconstruction scheme should be made in any of the cases which have been the subject of awards by the compensation commission'. The names of Egan, Sikes, Sunner and Anthony Higgins were listed.[59]

In October, William T. Cosgrave, Collins' successor as Chairman of the Provisional Government, stated in the Dáil that 'the arrangements whereby firms could be advanced three-fifths of the monies awarded had not been availed of'.[60] This was at least partially confirmed when, in a statement to the Reconstruction Finance Committee on 1 December 1922, the city treasurer said that 'payments to date amounted to £13,749 13s 4d.[61] As the second anniversary of the burnings approached, little had been achieved by way of reconstruction.

1923

By the start of 1923, the tide of war had turned in favour of the Free State army. In Cork 'republicans had been driven into the mountains and more than 5,000 Free State troops were in command of the city'.[62] Fewer incidents were reported in the local press and these reflected the dominance of the Free State army. On 4 January Michael Murphy and Jeremiah Harrington, both 'irregulars', were arrested in the city.[63] On 23 January, Con Walsh, Richard Mahony and P. J. Lynch were arrested. 'Elaborate plans for an attack on Cork Power House were found on Lynch.'[64] Peace talks between the factions were held during April and in May the anti-Treaty forces dumped their arms.[65] As a greater degree of normality returned, the business of nation-building could get under way.

As early as January another deputation from Cork had visited W. T. Cosgrave, now first President of the Executive Council of the Irish Free State, in Dublin about the reconstruction programme, but no official report was issued from the meeting. On 13 January it was reported to the Corporation that Cosgrave had outlined the grievous financial situation in the country at large. Sir John Scott declared that the delegation had been up against 'a stone wall'.[66] The Corporation meeting also heard that more than 6,000 people remained unemployed as a result of the fires over two years earlier. A disagreement then arose which set the tone for the rest of the year. It was reported that Cosgrave had said that £443,000 had been paid to Cork for use in reconstruction. Alderman O'Sullivan claimed that the money was now 'lodged in the banks and landlords and owners were drawing interest on it while people were absolutely starving'.[67] It was agreed to seek clarification from the compensation commission as to exactly what monies had been paid and in February the commission said that the monies paid were for stock and other items; monies for building would only be paid once the owners began work on the rebuilding.[68]

As the year progressed Labour and workers' representatives repeated Alderman O'Sullivan's claims and sought to have interest payments stopped on monies held in banks and also objected to the renewal of permits for the temporary premises in use by a number of firms. Barry Egan vehemently denied the accusations and said that the reduced awards of the Shaw commission had left owners worse off than in 1920.[69] This commission clarification in February, however, was a turning point in the reconstruction story. Henceforth there would be more emphasis on the plans and materials used in the rebuilding programme.

In early March a letter was received by the reconstruction committee from Burton's saying they would agree to the planning conditions imposed on their block provided they could have Sicilian marble fascias in place of limestone, which they said looked cheap and dull. They also sought to have pilasters of Norwegian granite. It was argued by some committee members that it would be unsightly to have a mix of granite and limestone in the block and furthermore, that the trades would not allow the importation of granite.[70] A week later when the matter was discussed at a Workers' Council meeting it was reported that 'workers would see to it that it didn't happen'.[71] Within a week Burton's again wrote saying that they were willing to forego the granite if they could have the Sicilian marble and the committee agreed to consider this following the submission of new plans.

On 23 May President Cosgrave visited Cork where a major issue put before him was the rebuilding of the railway bridge at Mallow for the benefit of the regional economy. The *Cork Examiner* reported that in the city, 'President Cosgrave and his colleagues must have been impressed with the sight presented by the destroyed buildings, a legacy of the regime of the Black and Tans', which, it was hoped, he would do his utmost to expedite the reconstruction of.[72] In June, however, the reconstruction committee was told that no further plans from any of the owners had been submitted since March and it was agreed to write to them seeking an explanation as to why work had not begun. A deputation of owners came to the Corporation meeting held on 3 June and sought to have the valuations of any new buildings held at the pre-burning values for a period of twelve years. This, they argued, was what had occurred in Dublin post-1916. The chairman said that the Corporation 'could not do anything on the matter that night, but if anyone handed in a notice of motion, it could be discussed at the proper time'.[73] A number of companies wrote to the Corporation stating that plans and drawings were under way and they hoped to begin work soon.[74]

Nevertheless, a statement was made at a Corporation meeting held on 24 November 1923 that 'the condition of St Patrick's Street was a disgrace to their city. The principal thoroughfare was like a graveyard.'[75] This statement came at the end of yet another frustrating year in which little was achieved. While on the one hand the Corporation members were being critical of the owners for lack of progress, a letter on behalf of Burton's outlined a series of reasons as to why it was trades and labour disputes that had held up reconstruction.[76] As Christmas approached Grant's awarded the contract for rebuilding to John Delaney & Co. and it was believed work would begin early in the New Year.

1924

1924 was the year in which progress finally began to be made in the reconstruction of St Patrick's Street. Although the Labour and workers' representatives continued to agitate against lack of progress in the reconstruction, claiming in March that only twenty-five members of the building trades and eighty in the shops were working on the street, by mid-April a report from building inspector John Ryan said that in zone 3 Cudmore's had steel to first floor level and timber joists in place. Elsewhere, in Cahill's, joinery shelving, fitting and polishing were under way; Grant's had taken over the site of Hayne's & Son; the American Shoe Company front wall was almost to full height and work was progressing, while at Egan's the stonework was going ahead.[77] Despite this, a number of issues that had arisen in 1923 remained unresolved. On the question of Irish limestone versus Sicilian marble, Mr O'Reilly of the Cork Industrial

Development Association, following investigations, told the Corporation as early as 16 February that a variety of marbles were available in Ireland from Kilkenny, Galway and Letterfrack.[78] Two weeks later he outlined seven advantages of Irish limestone over Sicilian marble including lifespan and potential for staining.[79] Mr McMullen, architect for Grant's, looked for permission to use metal instead of timber for window frames and sashes. The trades objected to this as the work would be done abroad and following a series of meetings, Mr McMullen agreed to the use of timber. Councillor McCarthy asked at the 2 March meeting what plans were in place for the heating of buildings and Mr Barry said that although it was

St Patrick's Street begins to rise again.

(Courtesy Michael Lenihan)

usually an English contractor who did this work, there was no reason why someone from Cork could not do it. Thus the issue of Irish material and labour continued to be a matter of debate into the early months of 1924.

Rate relief for the owners also continued to be an issue. In June a delegation of the Progressive Association travelled to Dublin to meet W. T. Cosgrave where it was agreed that legislation would be necessary for the granting of relief.[80] J. J. Walsh suggested the government would support a proposal that the 1914 rates would apply for a period of five years and thereafter until Cork was revalued. However, the bill would have to be introduced by the four Cork representatives.[81] In the autumn, however, the Cork Reconstruction Emergency Provisions Bill was withdrawn as J. J. Walsh could not support it. He promised it would in due course be reintroduced, but by then the Corporation would no longer be in place. On 30 October, because 'the duties of the council of the county borough of Cork are not being duly and effectively discharged by them' the Corporation was dissolved by ministerial order.[82] The Corporation and its committees were no more. Henceforth the administration of all matters was in the hands of Philip Monahan, the appointed commissioner.

1925

The issue of the rateable valuation of the destroyed properties was finally resolved early in 1925 when the terms of a bill were agreed such that the valuation of each building destroyed would be the same as it was at the date of destruction until 1930. 'The owners for their part have undertaken to start work immediately and the undertaking is faithfully being carried out.'[83] On 24 October Egan's reopened and just over a month later, on Thursday 10 December, the fifth anniversary of the burnings, Grants announced to the Cork public that, phoenix-like, it had risen from the ashes. In the cases of both Roches Stores and Cash & Co., the two remaining projects as yet not started, architect Henry Hill and builders John Sisk & Sons undertook the Cash's project while Chillingworth and Levie, architects and Murphy Brothers Builders were contracted to Roches Stores. In this latter case, Pat Fitzgerald, associate to William Roche, said that:

> Mr Roche was slow to begin operations on the new building. Other property owners were also for their own reasons, slow in starting. Pressure and intimidation were being brought to bear for the purpose

A superb illustration of the new blocks on the southern side of the street following reconstruction, in contrast to the older buildings on the northern side. Note also the cars lined along the street.
(Courtesy Michael Lenihan)

of having the work begun. Mr Roche however, point blank defied the intimidators and we heard no more of the urgent need for starting the work and began when it suited ourselves.[84]

Before starting, all the premises in zone 1 had been acquired by the firm and so the separate shops of Scully, Connell & Co., Lee Boot Co., the old London House and Mrs Wolfe's would be no more. As the work on zones 1 and 2 got under way, zone 3 was nearing completion.[85] In January of 1926 it was stated at the annual meeting of the Cork Incorporated Chamber of Commerce and Shipping that 'at the rate of progress now being made, all trace of the wicked destruction done in December 1920 will have disappeared by this time next year'.[86]

Completion

Aspects of the advancement of the Roches Stores project during 1925–6 showed that another area of contention over the previous four years was no longer preventing progress. Where once there had been a definite policy on the part of the trades and supported by a majority in the Corporation that only local material and labour be used, this was no longer the case. In the new Roches Stores, in February 1926, the first floor heating system was installed by J. J. Nolan & Son of Dublin, which at least was Irish; in the offices, the counter incorporated white Flemish glass, installed in April 1926; the lavatories were by the Northern Art Pavement Co. Ltd. of Manchester and London and many of the window frames were from Humphrey Jackson & Amber Ltd. of Manchester.[87] Under a headline of 'Roches Stores, New Premises', the *Cork Examiner* announced the reopening of Roches Stores in January 1927.[88] The cost of the new building was £26,474 16s 10d.[89]

Conclusion

The reconstruction of St Patrick's Street had taken over six years to complete. Six blocks of the street were completely reconstructed and it now presented a different appearance to that prior to the burning in December 1920. In 1926 the Cork Town Planning Association, which had been founded in 1922 under the chairmanship of A. F. Sharman Crawford, produced a book entitled *Cork: A Civic Survey* in which they evaluated the project.[90] 'The principal shopping street is St Patrick's Street, which before the destruction of a large part of it towards the close of 1920, contained buildings of greatly varying merit, some of them shabby, though on the whole not unpicturesque. Now, in its rebuilding, it has received more adequate treatment, though more uniformity would have enhanced the effect.'[91]

The story of the rebuilding of St Patrick's Street suggests that events in Cork at the time can be viewed in a number of different ways. As with Dublin's Sackville Street in 1916, the destruction of St Patrick's Street was part of the fight for independence. The reconstruction of the destroyed premises was part of a broader national context in which funding through decree awards and compensation became part of the negotiated process of British disengagement from the Free State; the Civil War delayed progress; the owners of the destroyed premises cited what had happened in Dublin post-1916 as precedent in their pursuit of rates relief; the project was part of the nation-building process occurring at the time – a 'plan in which there are various suggestions as to the reconstruction of the city' was published by the columnist Periscope in June 1922 and shows clear similarities to a proposed reconstruction of Dublin at the same time.[92] One of the main advisers to the Cork Town Planning Committee, whose work was published in 1926, was Patrick Abercrombie, one of the authors of *Dublin of the Future*.[93]

The events clearly impacted on all parties involved. Many thousands were affected through unemployment; although the Strickland Report was never published, Lloyd George was forced to admit publicly that Crown forces were responsible and subjected to disciplinary measures; the destruction was brought to the attention of the wider world by the Corporation and served as a propaganda tool for nationalists.

The destruction and reconstruction of St Patrick's Street also exposed divisions in Cork society at the time. An ecclesiastical/political divide was evident during this tense period of time and was demonstrated through criticism by councillors of Bishop Coholan for his non-condemnation of the burning, responded to in the writings and pronouncements of the Bishop in churches throughout the diocese. In politics, the reluctance on the part of Lord Mayor Domhnall Ó Ceallacháin to recognise the Provisional Government, as pointed out by J. J. Walsh, was evidence of the Civil War divide having a bearing on Cork's development. Representatives of the workers and unemployed continually criticised the owners, claiming that they were making interest on award monies while waiting for labour costs to fall before beginning reconstruction, as a result of which people were starving. The owners for their part vehemently denied this.

The 'Burning of Cork' had a unifying effect in a society that had been collectively damaged by the event. Throughout the nineteenth century St Patrick's Street was one manifestation of the emerging middle class in Cork society; its patrons were those who could afford the luxury products sold there; the carriage trade was common on the street for many years.[94] As the twentieth century dawned, however, this was changing as more people could afford items on the street due to a combination of increased disposable income and reducing prices. The advent of Roches Stores with a policy of giving the customer 'more for his money' was an example of this changing situation.[95] Many of the owners of other department stores on

the street resented this but the fires of 1920, according to William Roche's associate Pat Fitzgerald:

> helped to wipe out the superiority complex possessed by our bigger competitors ... and from being newcomers and interlopers in the trade we became overnight 'Brothers in Distress' and all started from scratch in the wooden premises.[96]

Thus, the 'Burning of Cork' helped to create an equalisation in commerce in the city in the early years of the Free State, an equalisation that continued following the reconstruction of the street.

That the event became known as the 'Burning of Cork' is itself a perspective on what happened of the night of 11 December 1920 – the

perception by subsequent generations of Cork people that although only 248 yards of the street were destroyed (as well as the City Hall and the Carnegie Library), such was the impact of this destruction that to Cork people, the heart of Cork itself was destroyed. This is testimony that St Patrick's Street was synonymous with Cork; even its partial destruction was Cork's destruction. This, however, is not the full story. While broad histories of the period give little mention to the event and recent publications give in depth both the context and the details of the burning, they do not complete the story.[97] Because from the ashes of destruction in which much of the old St Patrick's Street, its traditions and its legacy died, a new street was born and a new legacy created which was passed on once more to future generations of Cork people.

Given the absence of trams and indeed tracks, it is possible this photograph was taken from the top of a tram-pole after 1931. (Courtesy Michael Lenihan)

10 Twentieth-Century Developments

An early bus at the Statue.

The War of Independence had taken its toll in Cork, not least in the destruction of St Patrick's Street. So too had the Civil War which followed, with Cork being one of the last bastions of republicanism to fall. But from then a new era dawned – a New Ireland was born and Cork took its place as the nation's second city. Plans were drawn up that would finally see the end of the slums in the old medieval core, with the people living there being rehoused to areas such as Gurranabraher. Ever-improving public transport brought them to and from the city centre and as the population of the city grew, these people of Cork developed their own twentieth-century culture, often best seen on the main street of the city – St Patrick's Street.

The Omnibus Wars

If the 1920s was the decade that saw the rebirth of Cork city's main street, it was also the decade that saw the beginning of the end for the electric tram transportation system. Ever-increasing numbers of bicycles were having an impact on their existence; so also was the arrival of the automobile, even before a more significant arrival on the street – that of the omnibus.

In 1926, Captain A. P. Morgan, an ex-British army officer who had been running a bus service in London for over three years, applied to city manager Philip Monahan for a licence to introduce a similar service to Cork.[1] Having received the licence, he immediately imported five Daimler double-decker forty-four seat omnibuses and introduced a service that ran from the Bon Secours Convent on College Road to St Luke's Cross on the north side, via a central point at the Statue. The service was an instant success, with crowds gathering at the bus stops, not alone to avail of the new initiative, but for many, to marvel at this new cosmopolitanism that had arrived on the main street of the city. Such was the success that quickly new routes were added, though not necessarily with the same level of success. A route from the Statue to Blackrock was stopped due to the poor condition of the road and another from the Statue to Turner's Cross lasted only a week. Sunday evening specials, especially to Glanmire, were a success however.

Within a year Captain Morgan was followed into the transportation business by another former army officer, Colonel Bennett, who started a single-decker service between Blackpool and Magazine Road, again via St Patrick's Street. He was quickly followed by the Southern General Omnibus Co., Triumph Motor Co., Southern Motorways, Rapid Transport Co. and the Rocksavage Omnibus Co. owned by Gerry Dwyer. Competition was fierce and not all the companies could possibly survive. Such was the nature of the competition that it was not uncommon for buses from rival companies to race each other along St Patrick's Street in an attempt to get to the next stop first and secure the waiting passengers. A speed limit of 20 miles per hour was introduced but it mattered little to the racing bus drivers. Rapid turnaround too was required in order to return to the lucrative city centre bus stops quickly. Enterprising law enforcement was called for and a scheme was developed whereby two officers of the law would mark an exact distance of one mile and synchronise their timepieces. Taking marks when a 'flying' bus passed each in turn, back at the station and employing some mathematical endeavour, they soon calculated just how fast the bus was travelling and could proceed with prosecution. The competition inevitably resulted in the demise of a number of the services. With fares dropping to an unsustainable level, for some the writing was on the wall.

The Irish Omnibus Company (IOC) was the established agent of the Great Southern Railways to run bus services throughout the country. In the latter years of the 1920s they moved into Cork and bought out all the independent companies except one: Gerry Dwyer's Rocksavage Omnibus Co. still flew the independent flag. He was supported vigorously by many of the local politicians now serving on the Corporation which had been reinstated under the Cork city Management Act of 1929. Philip Monahan, who supported the IOC, was appointed city manager and he wanted to see that company operating all services in the city.[2] When the trams ceased in September 1931, the only competition to the IOC monopoly was Gerry Dywer's company. Lord Mayor Frank Daly and many others on the Corporation attacked Monahan for holding his position and while the IOC was being granted licences to run certain routes by the city manager, at the same time Gerry Dwyer was being granted other licences by the Corporation. Inevitably money won out at the end of the day and in March 1932, the Rocksavage Omnibus Co. ran for the last time before it too was swallowed up by the IOC which in time became part of CIÉ – Coras Iompair Éireann – which took over transport for the entire state.

From the Statue one could journey to Blackrock for 3½d; to Douglas for 3d or the South Gate Bridge for 1½d. The Statue remained the central point for the buses, with the fireman's hut of old and tram central point for over thirty-one years, becoming for the busmen their information office, tea room, shelter, waiting room and general all-round essential part of Cork's main street until its removal with the renewal of the street at the start of the twenty-first century.

Eucharistic Procession

It is only with great difficulty that one can define the uniqueness of a local culture at any time in the history of a place. Customs, achievements, dress, language, sport, art and music are but a few of the many elements that make up just such an independent local culture. Another is the faith of the community and it is with this element that one of the earliest manifestations of Cork's twentieth-century culture can be seen.

In 1926, a Cork-based solicitor and lecturer in law at University College Cork, C. K. Murphy, organised that on Corpus Christi Sunday, there would be a procession to the city centre from the Cathedral comprising the men and boys from all the city's churches, with the Blessed Sacrament being carried by the Bishop and at the end of which there would be public benediction. It would be the greatest ever public demonstration of the Catholic faith and it began a tradition that still remains to this day in Cork city. The event was described by the newspapers on the following day as a 'Marvellous Cork Demonstration' and the procession as being 'Miles Long'.[3] In fact the procession took over two and a half hours to pass a given point, with an estimated 60,000 taking part and many more thousands of women and children lining the streets.

As the crowds processed down Mulgrave Road, Camden Quay, Bridge Street, MacCurtain Street, across Brian Boru Bridge and up the South Mall to the altar at the end of the Grand Parade, they were joined by many others from areas to the northeast and the south side. It was close to seven o'clock when all the participants had arrived in the city at which time Bishop Coholan presided at the benediction. The army band played 'Faith of our Fathers', bringing proceedings to a close and the Blessed Sacrament was then processed back to the Cathedral via St Patrick's Street. 'It was an occasion that will long linger in the hearts and minds of Cork's citizens and the numbers outside Cork itself who had the privilege of witnessing so glorious a sight.'[4]

Such was the success of the event that it was immediately decided to hold it again the following year and Mr Jim Barry of Evergreen Road was appointed the Chief Marshall.[5] Not only did it take place with equal success that following June of 1927, but over eighty years on it still continues, though not with the numbers that attended the first occasion in 1926. Over the years changes have taken place. For example the route of the procession was soon changed from that of the first event. The shorter route of Mulgrave Road, Camden Quay, St Patrick's Bridge, St Patrick's Street and the Grand Parade was soon decided upon. This was also facilitated by the fact that the rebuilding of sections of the southern side of St Patrick's Street was now complete, the Roches Stores block having reopened in January 1927. In 1941 the altar was moved to the other end of the Grand Parade, at Daunt Square. This was 'due to the erection of a line of air-raid shelters at the National Monument end of the Grand Parade'.[6]

The only year in which the procession did not take place was 1932. That year the Eucharistic Congress was held in Dublin and many thousands of Cork people travelled to the Phoenix Park on that Corpus Christi Sunday to join with their countrymen and women in a national demonstration of their faith. The Cork spectacle resumed again in 1933 when:

at the moment when the Blessed Sacrament was raised in solemn benediction – the crowd who augmented the processionists to join in the concluding ceremony must have been in the neighbourhood of 35,000 people, making public testimony of their living faith.[7]

Jim Barry again acted as Chief Marshall and continued to do so until 1955. The following year the position was taken up by his son Michael.[8]

Generations of Cork people well remember the excitement in the week leading up to the procession as shrines were placed in the windows of the houses; flags were flown from almost every roof or window; St Patrick's Street was spruced up to a high degree in anticipation of the great event about to take place; speculation was rife as to whether it would be wet or dry, cold or hot; should one take a coat or not? Boys marched proudly with their fathers and grandfathers. The bands played; the people sang and the Cork citizens of the twentieth century continued the tradition of procession on the city's main street as their forebears had done a century before. In the 1820s people had marched with O'Connell for the right to live their faith. In the 1920s people marched – living their faith.

Cinema

The immense crowds that gathered for the Eucharistic processions was a manifestation of the place which the Catholic Church held in the lives of the people of Cork. Emerging from nearly 800 years of colonialism, the populace were anxious to show to a watching world their beliefs and their culture. So also would they be influenced by the wider world, and even before political independence there opened on St Patrick's Street a place that would bring that wider world into the lives of the Cork people. Cinema had begun in the early years of the twentieth century in America with the first Irish picture house being opened in Dublin in 1909 by James Joyce.[9] On Thursday 10 March 1921, there opened at Nos. 80–81 St Patrick Street the Pavilion Cinema and Restaurant Ltd, in the premises where Harrington's druggists and Pennington's auctioneers had operated up to the 1880s and part of which had once been known as Beethoven House when B & T Atkins operated a music and pianoforte saloon there during the 1890s.[10]

Owned by the Tallon family from the Rochestown Road and managed by Fred Hartford, a well-known actor from Dublin, the opening drew huge

crowds to the street at a time when such assemblies could be dangerous. Those who gained admittance were treated to a showing of D. W. Griffith's *The Greatest Question* featuring Lilian Gish and Bobby Harron. Also shown were a Burton Holmes travel feature and a comedy entitled *It's a Boy*.[11] For many on that opening night, however, the films were merely items of curiosity. The rest of the evening's entertainment was what dominated. Signor Grossi played 'a delightful violin solo' and the orchestra, under Dr Eveleigh played magnificently. 'Indeed the musical contributions to the entertainment yesterday would almost have proved sufficient programme without any films.'[12]

The new form of entertainment became ever more popular as the months and years passed by, particularly when the 'talkies' arrived. Prior to that the choice of musical accompaniment to the silent films was of crucial importance, requiring an understanding not only of the films themselves, but also of the audience and how it would react to the various scenes. Indeed the wrong choice could well destroy the experience for the viewing public. In the Pavilion this task fell to Sheila Healy and cinema-goers fondly remember her choices and how she would research her work in advance, listening to her selected band of advisers but never for a minute giving away any of the plot-lines. That would be totally unacceptable. Her role ended in 1929 when the Pavilion installed a sound system to bring to the audience picture *and* sound.

The newspapers of Monday 17 February screamed a headline to the people of Cork. To those who had not already heard, a 'Destructive Morning Outbreak in Cinema' had destroyed the Pavilion.[13] At about half past ten the previous morning, a guard named Booth, while on duty on St Patrick's Street, heard the sound of breaking glass from within the cinema building and upon investigation saw smoke coming from inside. He immediately alerted the fire services and although they were quickly on the scene under the command of Captain Ring, dense smoke was soon billowing from the roof. Locked doors prevented them from gaining immediate access. When, after about five minutes, they did enter the building, flames were raging fiercely in the area of the screen. It took over an hour to bring the inferno under control by which time the screen, a room housing a dynamo and the sound equipment were completely destroyed. Plasterwork on the ceiling and walls was ruined and the front rows of seats were beyond recovery. The good news, however, was that upon examination the exterior of the building was undamaged. Nevertheless, the cinema closed and the people wondered if the 'Pav' as it had come to be known, would ever open again.

To the delight of everybody it reopened within five months of the devastating fire. On Sunday 8 June 1930, the Pavilion Cinema on Cork's St Patrick's Street opened its doors once more for business. It was now described as 'one of the most beautiful and comfortable talking picture theatres in Ireland'.[14] The interior refurbishment was done by local firm J. A. O'Connell from Washington Street, and the *Evening Echo* described that the 'beautiful colour scheme is harmonious in every respect, strikingly effective and at the same time designed in quiet tones that please the eye and give a most impressive effect generally'.[15] The feature screened at the reopening of the cinema was *Paris*, starring Irene Bardoni and Jack Buchanan.

Throughout the remaining sixty or so years of the 'Pav's' existence as a cinema, thousands of people frequented the place. Memories were made there, each as individual as those who call them to mind with warmth, affection and love. It was a place where children saw the films of Danny Kaye; where couples courted while watching *Gone with the Wind* or Nelson Eddy and Jeanette MacDonald in *Rose Marie*; where the finest of meals could be obtained in a restaurant that afforded a spectacular view of St Patrick's Street. Each and every person who went there had their own special memories.

Denis O'Callaghan, the well-known clock and watchmaker from Oliver Plunkett Street, recalls – apart from any courting that he did – that his was the job of looking after the clock that stood on the cinema wall for many years. On one occasion, not long after the war, the clock stopped late in the afternoon and he was called to duty to get the problem sorted before the evening showing. He immediately made his way from his home on Blarney Street to the cinema. What he did not realise was that because it was a Sunday night, the cinema was packed to capacity ... early. (At the time many people had their own regular places and despite advance booking often went to the 'Pav' very early to secure their place.) Access to the clock was gained by climbing on to the front wall of the balcony and edging along it as far as the clock. Needless to say this provided the greatest imaginable entertainment to those seated below waiting for the film. Quite a number of them knew Denis personally and shouted their expert advice to him from their seats below.

One shouted: 'Denis boy, do you want a hand?'

Immediately the reply came from another: 'The big one or the small one' and the place erupted in laughter.

For weeks afterwards the talk among the 'Pav' goers was not of the main feature film, but of the entertainment beforehand. It was typical of Cork humour that the management were asked if they couldn't have the clock break down every Sunday night.

The doors of St Patrick's Street Pavilion cinema closed in August 1989 with a final showing of *Indiana Jones and the Last Crusade*. Cruelly, the modern world and the cultural changes that it wrought on society were in many ways responsible for the closure of beloved places that themselves had ushered in the modern era. Perhaps in the case of the cinemas, their own big screens brought to the developing Ireland values that in time led to the demise of those self same cinemas.

The popularity of the 'Pav' paved the way for further developments in the unique twentieth-century entertainment that was the cinema. The people of Cork, having come through the long and difficult nineteenth century and the traumas of the War of Independence and the Civil War, embraced it and made it their own. During the 1920s the name of the Savoy appeared on the city's main street as a restaurant at No. 112, taking over from Mrs O'Connell's High Class Luncheon Rooms. On Thursday 12 May 1932, the name was taken over by a new entertainment venture built just four doors further up the street. The Savoy Cinema was born and now, with the 'Pav' at one end of the street and the Savoy at the other, St Patrick's Street had changed yet again, truly reflecting not just the local culture of the city, but of the entire western world.[16]

Denis O'Callaghan, the well-known watch and clockmaker, whose job it was to repair the clock in the Pavilion and who entertained the crowds in the process. (Courtesy sandraocallaghan.com)

The iconic frontage to the Savoy.
(Courtesy sandraocallaghan.com)

In the lead-up to the opening of the Savoy, various advertisements had appeared in the local papers outlining the progress of a venture that at its peak employed over 1,000 people in construction and development. When the day arrived for the opening ceremony to take place, thousands of people congregated on St Patrick's Street and since there was no advance booking for gaining access to the ceremonies, the Gardaí had a difficult time controlling the crowds.

The Lord Mayor in 1932 was Frank J. Daly and he made an impassioned speech, during which he declared to tumultuous applause that with a theatre worthy to grace the capital of Ireland, that it was not too much to expect that Cork would one day be the capital of Ireland. He then went on to thank the builders, Meagher & Hayes of Cork, not least for spending over £130,000 of the total cost of £148,000 in the city. Sharing in the opening ceremony was the Chairman of the Harbour Board Mr Richard Wallace and he presented to the Lord Mayor a cheque for £100 from the directors of the theatre for the poor of the city.

The Lord Mayor then cut with a golden scissors the ribbon binding the curtain before the cinema screen, amid great applause. He was then presented with the scissors in a golden casket by the manager.[17]

Immediately after this a sound that became synonymous with St Patrick's Street and with Cork was heard for the first time. Fred Bridgeman struck up the national anthem on the famous Compton organ that the people of Cork would grow to love, almost as the 'national instrument of Cork'.

> The console or manual is situated immediately in front of the stage and is visible to the audience, It is operated by electricity and differs from the ordinary church organ in as much as it is capable in addition of providing the music of a symphony orchestra or a dance band at the discretion of the player.[18]

Over the years, the performance on the organ given by Fred Bridgeman was as popular as the films shown in the Savoy. He and the organ would rise up from beneath the stage on an electric platform and he played a wide variety of music from classical to the most modern popular pieces. Though not a Corkman – he was originally from Reading – the people took to him as one of their own and when he retired in 1967 it was a sad day for the patrons of the Savoy who had been entertained by Fred for thirty-five years.

Just like the 'Pav', the Savoy was soon a beloved institution of Cork's St Patrick's Street and not just for films either. Many live performances were held there with famous names such as Beniamino Gigli and Paul Robeson performing on its stage. Always, on these occasions, the theatre was packed to capacity, all 2,249 seats occupied and many more outside seeking a glimpse of the stars or a snatch of sound from an open door.

It is not for the famous live performing stars that the Savoy will be most remembered however. Rather its place in history is secured as the home of the Cork International Film Festival which grew from an initiative in the early 1950s called *An Tóstal* designed to boost Ireland and Irishness to the international world. *An Tóstal* began in 1953 and ran from 5–26 April that year. A series of events, including an industrial exhibition and a performance of Handel's *Messiah* were held and such was its success that it was decided to host it again the following year. The first Film Festival was held two years after that in 1956 with the help of the International Federation of Film Producers.

The festival opening was held in the Savoy on 21 May 1956 with the screening of *A Town Called Alice*, starring Peter Finch and Maureen Swanson and both stars attended the screening. 'No Comparison between Cork and Cannes' and 'All was a Shambles at French Resort' were among the complimentary headlines on the *Evening Echo* which also reported that hundreds gathered at the railway station for the arrival of the 'Star Express', the train that brought a host of film stars to the city for the occasion.[19] Over the following years the festival got bigger and better and soon it was in the diary of even the world's greatest film stars. Yet again St Patrick's Street was the stage for these performers and thousands gathered to see their heroes. Film-going became one of the most popular entertainments in the city and when *Mary Poppins* opened at the Savoy in 1965 vast numbers of people went to see it during its run there.

But as always, times were changing. Television, alternative life interests and economic factors all had a bearing on the demise of the great Savoy cinema which closed its doors to a sad Cork public in 1974. The Film Festival lives on; the Savoy building lives on too. So also does its name in the language of Cork people. To all, the Savoy means more than a place or a group of shops. It is another connection between generations of people. Savoy is a word that encompasses nostalgia and warm memories. When spoken it creates a feel-good factor and can often prompt a night of storytelling and recollection, pastimes beloved of the Corkonian.

The Choral and Dance Festival

The Film Festival was not the only Cork festive institution to emerge from *An Tóstal* during the 1950s. Even before the 1956 emergence of the Film Festival, a choral and dance event had been organised in 1954 under the driving force of such famous Cork people as Jenny Dowdall (who became Lord Mayor in 1959), Gus Healy (who held that office in 1964 and 1975) and Pa McGrath, First Citizen in the formative years of the festival in the early 1950s. The earliest meetings regarding the Choral and Dance Festival took place in a single room above Fitzgerald's at No. 25 St Patrick's Street, the location of Cork's first tourist office. With all the preparations in place, the first festival was opened by Erskine Childers, Minister for Posts and Telegraphs, on 30 April 1954 and has continued to grow in status throughout its history. With choirs and dance troupes travelling from all over the world, a highlight of the event every year are the open air performances held at various locations throughout the city, the most prominent of which have always been the dancing and singing that takes place on St Patrick's Street. Truly, the Choral Festival is an event that all Cork people believe is a part of Cork.

In 1964, however, it was not without controversy. In that year the organisers asked the President, Éamon de Valera, to open the festival. After consulting with his advisers he declined the invitation, which did not go down too well. Three ministers were then asked but all gave the same reply. Finally it was decided to ask the Earl of Rosse, who had opened a painting exhibition in the city the previous year. A member of the Arts Council, he was delighted to accept the invitation. General Tom Barry, a hero of the War of Independence, however, believed that it was unthinkable for a relative of the British royal family to be asked and he began a campaign calling on people to disrupt the proceedings of the opening night. Some weeks before the opening ceremony, Barry organised a public meeting on St Patrick's Street and denounced the festival committee as 'imperialists and snobs'. The committee would not be bullied and following consultation with the Earl, it was decided to proceed. Shouts and banners greeted the Earl on his arrival at City Hall and a letter of protest was handed to the festival organisers. Nevertheless the proceedings went ahead without any difficulties, with the Earl in his speech declaring that 'if he were not an Irishman, there wasn't an American in the USA as his family were resident in Birr since before the Pilgrim Fathers sailed to the new world'.[20] So ended the events of 1964 and probably the most dangerous episode in the festival's history.[21]

The wonderful singing and dancing that graced St Patrick's Street and the various other places throughout the city each year provided a street entertainment for the people of Cork that was second to none. Sadly, on each occasion, as the colourful spectacle that was the Choral Festival came to a close, the streets fell silent and Cork returned to the daily grind of life. But not for long; by next morning messenger boys on their bicycles, working men and women en route to their places of employment, the children going to school, all enthused with the singing of the week before, could be heard humming great choral pieces, singing great arias, whistling a happy tune.

Other Entertainments

Although the decades following independence were difficult ones in many ways, nevertheless for many people life was improving. Notwithstanding continued poverty in the lowest strata of society with a consequent high level of emigration and other social problems, many people were trying

to create for themselves lives of happiness and meaning. Crucial in this endeavour were the entertainments through which people met and enjoyed themselves, the cinema being one of the most obvious. Other forms of entertainment, too, grew up in the city and it was to the heart – St Patrick's Street – that many people ventured for such pastimes.

Snooker was very popular over the decades in Cork. Upstairs at No. 3, overlooking the Statue, the Sovereign Rooms were located with 'Doc' Walsh in charge. He controlled, in fact, two floors of full slate tables, provided the cues and charged 1s per table per session. A popular game during the 1930s was known as 'who shall?' Simply it meant the best of three frames and the loser was the one 'who shall' pay the shilling. Further up the street, over Burton's, another snooker hall, the Regal, was located.

Card drives, in particular whist, became very popular in the city – as they are to this day – and on St Patrick's Street the commercial travellers held their whist drives above Thompson's during the 1950s. It was open to the public and was but one of a number of whist drives held on the city's main street. Upon arriving at the door and paying the entrance money of a shilling, a ticket was obtained which indicated your seat number. Inside there were sixteen tables along the wall; the ladies sat on the inside and the men on the outside. You took your place and the man or woman opposite you was your partner for the game. At the completion of each game, the ladies moved one direction while the men moved the other. Thus a new partner was ensured for every game. Stewards kept a check on every individual's score or number of tricks won. At the end of the night the individual with the most tricks was the winner and won a share of the door money. A good score, considered to have a good chance of winning, would have been 150 tricks. At Christmas time the prizes changed to the much more valuable commodities of hams or bottles of whiskey. There was always also a booby prize, a small sum for the person getting the least number of tricks.

Outside on the street, as people queued for the cards or cinemas, local characters such as Gerry Bruton entertained them. Gerry's party piece – many say his only piece – was 'Let's All Go Down to the Marina'. Gerry was but one of many street entertainers to grace St Patrick's Street down through the decades. Often people arrived into St Patrick's Street to the strains of Michael and Christy Dunne, as much a part of Cork as the Statue itself, many would say. Christy Dunne was a blind violinist and along with his brother Mick, who played the banjo, they were among the first 'famous' Cork buskers. Usually playing outside the English Market, they also had a pitch outside Roche's Stores or the Munster Arcade. Although they travelled widely, playing on the continent during the summer months, when they arrived back in Cork, whether it was from Galway or Paris, they quietly slipped into position and just as if they had never been gone, passers-by would drop a few coins into the shoebox on the ground.

'Morning Mick, morning Christy.' They rarely responded if playing. Two shy gentlemen and wonderful musicians, beloved of Cork. A huge sadness was felt throughout the city when one day Christy arrived alone. His music was sweeter than it had ever been, but melancholic. The minor keys were more accentuated and all too soon he too came no more. The city mourned two men, not least because most people realised they did not even know where the brothers had come from.

The street entertainers or buskers are now as much a part of the life of St Patrick's Street as any of the shops or businesses operating there or indeed the people who daily journey through the city centre. Where once traditional Irish music and song was the sound that permeated the air, today it is mingled with the sounds of many different places, sounds from all corners of the globe. Pianists from Eastern Europe, pan pipes from South America, drummers from Africa, all add their distinctive harmonies to the sound that is St Patrick's Street, reflecting the global world in which we now live.

Michael and Christy Dunne, much loved street musicians who played to Cork people from their pitch on St Patrick's Street. (Courtesy sandraocallaghan.com)

11 Past, Present and Future St Patrick's Street

Twenty-first-century St Patrick's Street is a space both changed and changing. Just over 100 years since its foundation, the iconic Roches Stores is no more, replaced by Debenhams, a British department store where once the London House held sway. Much of the street from Academy Street to William Street has changed dramatically to modern blocks of high street stores, though the preservation of some of the frontages retains for future generations some of the street's former identity. How long more the identifying and unique irregular building lines of the street will survive is a matter for the city authorities and the planning department. It is to be hoped that those charged with planning the city's future will fully appreciate the part that St Patrick's Street plays in the life of Cork and Cork people. The street was, is and will remain the centre of almost every aspect of Cork life. It is where the people have always come and continue to come together to pray and to praise or protest; to celebrate and to shop; to mingle and to mourn. It is a repository of memories, collective and individual.

Apart from its name, there is no physical evidence to indicate that St Patrick's Street emerged from a time and a context in which the revival of things Celtic dominated Irish society and the patron saint was declared by all to represent their brand of Irishness. However, using contemporary newspaper sources, this book places the emergence of the street to dates in May 1783 and by showing that Cork was a part of the broad context in which St Patrick was honoured by all in society at that time, locates the naming of the new street after the patron saint in that context. Among the characteristics that have come down to us from the earliest emergence of the street are its distinctive curved shape, the irregular building lines and some of the earliest buildings on the street. From this physical evidence and also through contemporary written accounts as well as newspapers, the emergence of a commercial street from merchant beginnings is demonstrated. As the commercial profile grew to overshadow those of merchant, artisan, professional and manufacture on the street, trade directories mapped the changes. By the end of the twentieth century, St Patrick's Street was over 80 per cent retail.

Commodities traded on the street were in the luxury category as evidenced by the newspaper advertisements and customer account ledgers examined. The trade directories also reveal that almost a quarter of the businesses on the street retained their core business for over a century while almost half retained theirs for between 50 and 100 years. With this analysis, it is shown that elements of tradition and legacy played a fundamental role in the street's history. Physical characteristics of the streetscape changed with time and culture and this aspect of the street's history is also examined through contemporary written accounts, the trade directories and other historical writings. What is revealed is that St Patrick's Street became the centre of developing transport systems; lighting, communications and advertising developments impacted on the street; the nature of the shops themselves changed in keeping with developments during the nineteenth and twentieth centuries.

Yvonne Whelan's work on modern Dublin contributes to a conceptual framework used in an earlier part of this book. In that work she says that 'landscape is now conceived as being … shaped and reshaped … by people.'[1] The chapter on the 'People of St Patrick's Street', how they were recorded in the trade directories and the 1911 census returns, reveals how the street reflected the gender roles in urban society: women were the servants and the assistants; men were the apprentices and the masters. That chapter also introduced, among others, two famous personages associated with the street, both styled 'apostles', both of whom sought better conditions for the less well off in society – but they are remembered in very different ways. The most famous person associated with the street, temperance apostle Fr Theobald Mathew, is commemorated by the iconic monument in Cork, known simply as the Statue. The story of its unveiling in 1864 is an example of how Cork people take possession of their main street in mass gathering to make a statement to the wider world. While the Statue was unveiled less than a decade after Fr Mathew's death, over 175 years after the death of the 'earliest Irish apostle of the social revolution', William Thompson, the William Thompson Commemorative Committee hope to have a plaque erected in his honour on the site of his former home, No. 4 St Patrick's Street.[2]

With Cork having been the most violent county in the country between 1917 and 1923, it was inevitable that the city's main street would sustain damage during the War of Independence.[3] Throughout 1920, violence and tension rose as the year progressed and on the night of 11 December, twenty premises on the street, totalling 248 yards, were completely destroyed by fire in a British retaliation for ambushes that had occurred at Kilmichael weeks previously and at Dillon's Cross on the same night. The reconstruction of the street took more than six years. This book follows the reconstruction story using contemporary newspaper accounts and the minutes of the Corporation's Reconstruction Committee. What is revealed is that financial difficulties associated with the broader national situation, the Civil War and tensions within Cork society itself, contributed to delays in the street's reconstruction. Nevertheless, the aspiration of the city engineer in 1920 that a commercial heart consisting of buildings worthy of their place in the centre of the city was achieved and this also led to a unifying of diverse commercial attitudes, such that from then on, the street served all of the people of Cork.[4]

Some characteristics of St Patrick's Street have remained unchanged throughout its history. Amongst these are the most fundamental aspect of its identity: its name; its distinctive curved shape; the irregular building lines; its place as the commercial heart of the city; its place as centre stage for the performance of a variety of acts by the native people such as processions and mass gatherings. These permanent characteristics are the foundation upon which the identity of the street is laid and have passed from generation to generation, as indeed they will to future generations, a legacy in brick and stone.

Other characteristics of the street, however, have changed with time, reflecting the adoption of ideas and values stemming from outside influences. Thus, for example, the nature and appearance of shops and transport, the products traded and the fashions worn, the iconography of the street, have all varied throughout its history. This 'change consequent upon influence' is itself part of the street's identity and adds elements of tradition and culture to the legacy. This facet of identity is by its nature

Work on the redevelopment of St Patrick's Street during 2003.
(Courtesy sandraocallaghan.com)

fluid, differing with each succeeding generation that adds its signature to the legacy, before passing it on again. The statue of 1864 was one signature of that period; the post-1920 reconstruction another example; the most recent Beth Gali renewal is an example of an embracing of European cultural influences, both through the nationality of Beth Gali herself and through the modelling of her design on streetscapes in other European countries.

As the first decade of the new millennium came to an end, sections of the street from Academy Street to William Street were completely rebuilt. No longer do the offices of the *Cork Examiner* grace the street; the bow-fronted buildings of the Gentlmens' Quarters, however, have been preserved. The developments comprised two separate projects; the first was by Cork property developer Owen O'Callaghan and as well as the frontages on St Patrick Street, the €500-million project encompassed

Crowds on St Patrick's Street at the opening of Dunnes Stores in 1944.
(Courtesy Dunnes Stores)

the former Faulkner's Lane, renamed Opera Lane, and stretches as far as Emmet Place. The project, according to O'Callaghan, will provide a 'high street' for a much wider region.[5]

The second development was undertaken by Dunnes Stores. Ben Dunne began trading at number No. 105 St Patrick's Street on 31 March 1944. Later developments saw the business expand to incorporate numbers Nos. 102–104 also. This block has now been completely revamped, though the fascia of the previous structures has been retained. When Ben Dunne opened his business in March 1944, he approached a friend, William Dan Barrett, asking if he would leave his job with Roches Stores and join him in the endeavour. Willie Dan took the leap and over the years was present as the business thrived and expanded. It is he who had the honour of reopening Dunnes Stores on St Patrick's Street on the morning of Thursday 10 September 2009 and said to those assembled there that 'there will always be a Dunnes Stores at No. 105 St Patrick's Street'. At the opening, daughter of Ben Dunne, Margaret Hefffernan, recalled working

The newly refurbished original Dunnes Stores which was opened on 10 September 2009.
(Courtesy sandraocallaghan.com)

there in her younger days and said that the St Patrick's Street store was very close to the family's hearts. With her were son, Michael, and daughter, Ann. Both were very aware of the place Dunnes Stores holds in the history of Cork's main street and as the new generation driving the company, were delighted to be retracing their grandfather's steps. At a private function for family and friends to celebrate the reopening, a cake decorated with a picture of the original store was cut for the occasion. Over 1,000 people passed through the doors of the reopened premises in the first two minutes and in a matter of hours more than 10,000 made their way to the heart of the city to greet an old friend and welcome him back to the street.

St Patrick's Street is the centre and the heart of Cork city. It is a legacy in brick and stone which succeeding generations mould and shape in keeping with their own time before passing it on again. Thus shaped, St Patrick's Street is a repository of memory, culture and tradition and is itself an icon of Cork.

St Patrick's Street for a new generation. Trees being planted on the completed pavement.
(Courtesy sandraocallaghan.com)

Appendices

Appendix 1
Wide Street Commissioners, 1783

From the legislation 5 Geo. III, Ch.24, Sect. XII, those serving as Wide Street Commissioners in 1783 would have included the Mayor, Richard Kellett, the Aldermen Owgan, Wrixon, Swete, Wetherall, Bury, Philpott, Kellett, Webb, Baker, Carelton, Travers, Butler, Allen, Kent who had just completed his term as Mayor, Shaw and Waggett. As well as these, others who would have been on the Commission, but not listed as attending Corporation meetings, were the Right Honourable John Hely Hutchinson Esq., William Ponsonby Esq., Henry Sheares Esq., Hugh Lawton Esq., Francis Carelton Esq., Stephen Denroch Esq., Riggs Falkiner Esq., Bayle Rogers Esq., Walter Travers Esq., William Verling Esq., Simon Dring Esq., Luke Grant Esq., Kevan Izod merchant, Godfrey Baker merchant, Henry Wrixon Esq. and William Butler Esq. or their descendents.

(Richard Caulfield, *The Council Book of the Corporation of the City of Cork, from 1609–1643 and from 1690–1800* (Guilford, 1876))

Appendix 2 – Report from the Hibernian Chronicle, 1 October 1789

Cork

On Tuesday the Key-stone of the last arch of the new bridge was laid by the Ancient and Honourable Society of Free Masons of this city. The morning was ushered in with the ringing of bells; an immense crowd assembled in the principal streets before the hour of eleven. About twelve the procession of the different Lodges, dressed with their jewels and the insignia of the respective orders, preceded by the band of the 51st regiment, began in the following manner:
Army Lodge,

Grand Tyler with drawn sword,
Grand Almoner bearing a chalice of wine.
Two Grand Deacons, the Bible supported by two other Grand Deacons,
The Chaplain of the Grand Lodge,
Lord Donoughmore, Grand Master of All Ireland,
Joseph Rogers esq. Provincial Grand Master of Munster attended by two Grand Wardens, secretary etc.
Tyler of Lodge No.1.
Two Deacons of do.
Master, Wardens Secretary etc. of do.
After whom followed 14 Lodges with their Masters and Wardens in regular order.

The procession moved from the Council chamber amid the acclamation of the rejoicing multitude, through Castle Street, down the new street called St Patrick's Street, and advanced to the foot of the new bridge, which was decorated on the occasion with the Irish standard, the Union flag, and several other ensigns – here they were saluted with nine cannon, the workmen dressed in white aprons lining each side of the bridge; the procession advanced up to the centre of the last arch where they were received by the Commissioners and the Architect. The last key-stone which was previously suspended; and which weighed 47 hundred, was then instantly lowered into its berth – and the Bible laid upon a scarlet velvet cushion adorned with tassels and gold fringe was placed upon it – His Lordship, as Grand Master, thereupon, in due form gave three distinct knocks with a mallet; the Commissioners were then called upon to mention the name intended for the new bridge, which being communicated, the Grand Master emptied his chalice of wine upon the key-stone and the Grand Master, in the name of the Ancient and Honourable Fraternity of the Free and Accepted Masons of the Province of

Munster, proclaimed it St Patrick's Bridge. The whole body of Masons, composed of upwards of 400 of the most respectable gentlemen of city and county gave a salute three times three which was returned by nine cheers of the populace and the firing of nine cannon. After this the procession marched over the bridge and its portcullis, surveyed them, and were again saluted with nine cannon. They then returned back in the same order to the Council chamber.

Appendix 3 – Specifications for the Surface of St Patrick's Street

Pedestrian Areas: 100mm thick stone
    12.5mm joints with 30 N/mm2 mortar on
    40mm bedding on
    200mm rough concrete slab

Traffic Areas: 150mm thick stone
    12.5mm joints with 30 N/mm2 mortar on
    40mm bedding on
    200mm rough concrete slab
    or
    45mm HRA on
    55mm bitmap basecourse on
    200mm rough concrete slab

(Simon Brewitt, 'Redevelopment of St Patrick's Street', Paper presented to the Institute of Engineers of Ireland, Cork, 15 November 2005)

Appendix 4 – Tolls authorised by Parliament in 1786 to be collected on St Patrick's Bridge (26 Geo. III, C.28, Sect. XXVL)

	s	d
For every coach, chariot, berlin, chaise, chair or calash drawn by six or more horses	1	1
For every coach, chariot, berlin, chaise, chair or calash drawn by less than six but more than two horses		6½
For every coach, chariot, berlin, chaise, chair or calash drawn by two horses or mules		3
For every wagon, wain, car, cart, or carriage of burthen or other carriage with four wheels drawn by four or more beasts	1	1
For every wagon, wain, car, cart, or carriage of burthen or other carriage with two wheels drawn by more than one horse or other beast		3
For every wagon, wain, car, cart, or carriage of burthen or other carriage with two wheels drawn by one horse or other beast		½
For every horse, mule or ass, laden or unladen and not drawing		½
For every drove of oxen, cows or net cattle – by the score and so in proportion for any greater or lesser number not less than four		5
For every score of calves, hogs, sheep or goats		½
For every score of lambs		½
For every passenger passing over the bridge – each		½

except such person or persons as shall be driven in any coach, chariot, berlin chaise, chair or calash, and the driver or drivers thereof, servant or servants thereof, standing behind the same.

(William O'Sullivan, *The Economic History of Cork City from the Earliest Times to the Act of Union* (Cork, 1937), p. 352)

Appendix 5 – List of properties 99 years or more in the same business

No. 3   clockmaking from 1856–1976
No. 4   grocer and vintner from 1824–1925
No. 5   bakery tradition from 1844–1976
No. 6   tobacco from 1844–1945
No. 7   apothecary and chemist from 1856–1976
No. 18 department store from 1844–
No. 19 as above
No. 20 as above
No. 21 as above
No. 27 department store 1925–
No. 28 as above
No. 29 as above
No. 30 as above
No. 32 silver, jewellery, ecclesiastic goods
            1886–1986
No. 35 hotel 1803–
No. 60 drapery 1856–1867 and 1907–
No. 64 grocery/wine/spirit 1844–1976
No. 68 drapery 1856–1976
No. 69 drapery 1844–1945
No. 70 printing stationery 1844–1945
No. 83 watches and jewellery 1867–
No. 86 seeds 1844–1945
No. 87 guns 1844–
No. 88 banking 1907–
No. 92 travel 1907–
No. 93 vintner/wine/spirit 1844–
No. 95 newspaper 1841–2005
No. 99 grocery/wine/spirit 1844–1945
No. 107 chemist 1875–1975
No. 125 grocery/wine/spirit 1844–1945

Total of 99 years or more – 30

Fifty-nine premises kept their core businesses for between 50 and 99 years. These were Nos. 1, 2, 9, 10, 11, 12, 13, 14, 15, 16, 17, 22, 24, 25, 26, 31, 34, 36, 37, 38, 39, 40, 41, 44, 47, 48, 49, 51, 52, 53, 54, 58, 59, 63, 65, 66, 67, 71, 73, 74, 75, 80, 84, 85, 89, 90, 91, 94, 103, 106, 108, 109, 110, 113, 112, 117, 120, 121, 124.

(These statistics are based on each premises being accounted for in its own right regardless of whether it formed part of a business that also occupied other premises.)

Acknowledgements

It was while working on strands of history programming for Radio Teléfis Éireann, Ireland's national broadcaster, that I first met Professor Dermot Keogh, Head of the History Department at University College Cork. During his many visits to the studio we came to know each other and he became aware of my interest in Cork's local history. When I asked his opinion on whether or not I should consider pursuing a master's degree in history at the college, he immediately recommended that I do so. Since then his advice and interest in my studies has been of enormous help to me. I would like to take this opportunity to thank him for all his help and support.

I cannot thank enough Dr Dónal Ó Drisceoil. His knowledge on Cork's history, his interest in my work and his advice on everything from source material to photographic records of the street to approaching difficult aspects of the subject matter, were second to none. I really appreciated his encouragement and reassurances that my work was worthwhile and interesting. I continue to value his friendship and advice. Buíochas mór duit, a Dhónal.

I also want to say a special thank you to Dr Dave Edwards. As co-ordinator of the course I was undertaking at the university, his was the unenviable task of finding time for many students. Nevertheless he was always ready with advice – and always with a sense of encouragement and humour. I was proud to shake his hand at the end of it all.

During my research I spent many hours in the Local Studies Department at the Cork City Library, the County Library, the Cork Archives Institute and the Special Collections Department of University College Cork. I wish to thank all the staff in these institutions, especially Kieran Burke, Mary Sorrensen, Mary O'Leary, Caroline Long Nolan, Yvonne O'Connor and Niamh Cronin. A special thanks to Brian Magee who spent much time digging for materials about St Patrick's Street for me in the archives and city archaeologist Ciara Brett for all her help. Also to three other people who believed in me, Séan Scully, Paul O'Flynn and Tom MacSweeney. Thank you also to Amy and Chris Ramsden of The Day Photographic Collection and DeBurca Rare books for all their help. One of the pleasures in doing a project such as this is time spent with fellow historians discussing and debating Cork's colourful past. I spent many happy hours with Michael Lenihan, searching his collections of Cork memorabilia and photographs and for this I am deeply in his debt.

I also want to thank some of my friends and fellow travellers in pursuit of the master's degree in history. To James, Kevin, Brian, Mícheál and Kim who, while researching their own subjects, managed to find material pertaining to mine on occasions also. Beyond anyone else, a special thanks to fireman Pat. When all sources failed in pursuit of some obscure aspect of the city's history, Pat Poland had the answer or the route to it. We blazed an email trail and drank copious cappuccinos while discussing our favourite subject, the history of Cork.

Finally I want to thank my family for living with the history of Cork's St Patrick's Street for a number of years now. To my children, Lorna and Brenton, your support, not least in historical and technical matters was invaluable. To the love of my life, my wife Sandra, your encouragement, support and love helped me to fulfil a lifelong dream. My thanks and love always.

Notes and References

Abbreviations
CE – Cork Examiner
HC – Hibernian Chronicle
JCHAS – Journal of the Cork Historical and Archaeological Society

Introduction
1 Simon Brewitt, 'Redevelopment of St Patrick's Street', Paper presented to the Institute of Engineers of Ireland, Cork, 15 November 2005.
2 This framework is developed using the work of Roland Barthes, Jacques LeGoff and Susan Sontag as outlined in the Hanno Hardt paper 'Pierced Memories on the Rhetoric of a Bayoneted Photograph', www.indiana.edu/~rhetid/hardt.htm [accessed 18 October 2005].

Chapter 1: Early History
1 The existence of Finbarr has been debated in recent times following Professor Padraig O'Riain's suggestion that it was a localised manifestation of the *wanderkult* of Finnian of Moville. See Padraig O'Riain, 'St Finbarr: a study in a cult', *Journal of the Cork Historical and Archaeological Society (JCHAS)*, 72 (1977); Henry Alan Jefferies in *Cork Historical Perspectives* (Dublin, 2004), among others, has debated this issue. Whether or nor Finbarr existed, his name has come down to us through the generations.
2 William O'Sullivan, *The Economic History of Cork City from the Earliest Times to the Act of Union* (Cork, 1937), p. 7; John Bradley and Andrew Halpin, 'The Topographical Development of Scandinavian and Anglo-Norman Cork', in Patrick O'Flanagan and Cornelius Buttimer (eds.), *Cork: History and Society* (Dublin, 1993), p. 16; Jefferies, *Cork Historical Perspectives* (Dublin, 2004), p. 14.
3 *The Four Masters Annals of the Kingdom of Ireland from the Earliest Times to the Year 1616*, Vol. 1 (3rd edn, Dublin, 1990), p. 287.
4 Donnchadh Ó Corráin, 'Prehistoric and Early Christian Ireland', in Roy Foster (ed.), *The Oxford Illustrated History of Ireland* (London, 1991), p. 13.
5 Evelyn Bolster, *A History of the Diocese of Cork from the Earliest Times to the Reformation*, (Shannon, 1972), p. 37; G. F. Mitchell, 'Prehistoric Ireland', in T. W. Moody and F. X. Martin (eds.), *The Course of Irish History*, (Dublin and Cork, 1980), p.45.
6 Bolster, *Diocese of Cork*, p. 37.
7 *Ibid.*, p. 38; Ó Corráin, 'Prehistoric and Early Christian Ireland', p. 14.
8 Bolster, *Diocese of Cork*, p. 41; Rev. John Ryan, *Irish Monasticism: Origins and Early Development*, (Dublin and Cork, 1931), p. 316.
9 Ó Corráin, 'Prehistoric and Early Christian Ireland', p. 13.
10 Ó Corráin, 'Ecclesiastical Power Struggle', *Cork Examiner (CE)*, 16 January 1985.
11 Jefferies, *Cork Historical Perspectives*, p. 15.
12 Ó Corráin, 'Ecclesiastical Power Struggle'; Bolster, *Diocese of Cork*, p. 24.
13 *Ibid.*, p.46; Bradley and Halpin, 'Topographical Development', p.16; Jefferies, *Cork Historical Perspectives*, p. 34.
14 Ó Corráin, 'Prehistoric and Early Christian Ireland', p. 33.
15 Liam de Paor, 'The Age of the Viking Wars', in Moody and Martin, *The Course of Irish History*, p. 97; Ó Corráin, 'Prehistoric and Early Christian Ireland', p. 40.
16 De Paor, p. 102; Edmund Curtis, *A History of Ireland from the Earliest Times to 1922*, (London, 2002), p. 30.
17 O'Sullivan, *Economic History*, p. 12.
18 Jefferies, *Cork Historical Perspectives*, p. 36.
19 *Ibid.*, pp. 40–1.
20 John de Courcy Ireland, *Ireland and the Irish in Maritime History*, (Dublin, 1986), p. 53.
21 Brian Ó Cuív, 'Ireland in the Eleventh and Twelfth Centuries', in Moody and Martin, *The Course of Irish History*, p. 111.
22 Bradley and Halpin, 'Topographical Development', p. 15.
23 O'Sullivan, *Economic History*, p. 12.
24 Bradley and Halpin, 'Topographical Development', p. 23.

25 A. F. O'Brien, 'The Development of the Privileges, Liberties and Immunities of Medieval Cork and the Growth of an Urban Autonomy c. 1189–1500' in *JCHAS*, 90 (1985), pp. 46–64.

26 John Barry, 'The Rise of the Medieval City', *CE*, 2 January 1985.

27 Brian Graham, 'Urbanisation in Ireland during the High Middle Ages', in Terry Barry (ed.), *A History of Settlement in Ireland* (London, 2000), p. 128.

28 Barry, 'The Rise of the Medieval City'; see also O'Brien, 'Privileges, Liberties and Immunities'.

29 O'Sullivan, *Economic History*, pp. 24–6.

30 *Ibid.*, p. 31.

31 Jefferies, *Cork Historical Perspectives*, p. 63.

32 *Ibid.*, p. 66.

33 B. J. Graham, 'The Towns of Medieval Ireland', in R. A. Butlin (ed.), *The Development of the Irish Town* (London, 1977), p. 50; Jefferies, *Cork Historical Perspectives*, p. 70.

34 *Ibid.*, pp. 71, 73.

35 Francis Tuckey, *The County and City of Cork Remembrancer* (Cork, 1980) gives a number of examples. One is listed for 1376, 'the King, in aid of the repairs of the walls of Cork, then stated to be in great dilapidation, being by the hostile incursions of the Irish enemy, almost totally destroyed … allowed them a remission', p. 26.

36 Bradley and Halpin, 'Topographical Development', p. 27.

37 Gina Johnson, *The Laneways of Medieval Cork* (Cork, 2002), p. 5; Bradley and Halpin, 'Topographical Development', p. 28.

38 See for example the *Pacate Hibernia* Map 1585–1600 in Eugene Carberry, 'The Development of Cork City', *JCHAS*, 48 (1943).

39 Mark McCarthy, 'Historical Geographies of a Colonised World: the Renegotiation of New English Colonialism in Early Modern Urban Ireland, *c.* 1600–10', *Irish Geography*, 36, 1 (2003), pp. 66–9.

40 Jefferies, *Cork Historical Perspectives*, p. 124; Rev. C. B. Gibson, *The History of the County and City of Cork*, Vol. 2, (London, 1861), p. 82.

41 David Dickson, *Old World Colony: Cork and South Munster, 1630–1830* (Cork, 2005), p. 39.

42 Jefferies, *Cork Historical Perspectives*, p. 126.

43 Seamus Pender, *A Census of Ireland circa 1659*, (Dublin, 1939), p. 191. The final figures differ slightly from Jefferies, *Cork Historical Perspectives*, p. 127, because he quotes the use of a multiplier of three and then adds the figures for military based in the city. I have used the parish figures only.

44 For a detailed account of the siege of Cork see Diarmuid Ó Murchadha 'The Siege of Cork in 1690', *JCHAS*, 95 (1990).

45 Jefferies, *Cork Historical Perspectives*, p. 132.

46 The thrust of Mark McCarthy's unpublished PhD thesis in 1997 was 'The Historical Geography of Cork's transformation into an Atlantic European port', UCC (1997); In his paper on 'Historical Geographies of a Colonised World', pp. 66–9, he also refers to Cork's economy not suffering post 1603; O'Sullivan's *Economic History* describes the inhabitants having the opportunity to restore their flocks, p. 103; David Dickson, *Old World Colony*, describes the effects of the transport revolution and its consequences in south Munster.

47 O'Sullivan, *Economic History*, p. 294.

48 *Ibid.*, p. 106.

49 Customs returns for Cork more than doubled between 1664 and 1683. Diarmuid Ó Drisceoil and Donal Ó Drisceoil, *Serving a City: The Story of Cork's English Market* (Cork, 2005), p. 16.

50 The population increases begun at this time continued through the eighteenth century and have been well recorded by historians. Angela Fahy says that by latter half of the seventeenth century it was up to 17,595. 'A social geography of nineteenth century Cork', unpublished MA thesis, UCC (1981), p. 61; Michael Gough says that by 1750 it was 74,000 and by 1775 80,000, 'A history of the physical development of Cork city', unpublished MA thesis UCC, (1973), pp. 153, 175; O'Sullivan similarly traces the pattern using a number of sources in *Economic History*, p. 224.

51 Dickson says that this project was agreed to by the newly formed revenue commissioners 'because of the greatness of trade in the port' and describes it as one of a number of 'key decisions'. *Old World Colony*, p. 116.

52 *Ibid.*, p. 117.

53 Tuckey, *Cork Remembrancer*.

54 For details on the leasing of the eastern marsh to Dunscombe see *JCHAS*, 10 (1904) pp. 128–131.

55 The best account of the Hoare family that I

have been able to locate, other than those accounts in local histories such as O'Sullivan and Dickson, is Capt. Edward Hoare, *Early History & Genealogy of the Families of Hore and Hoare* (London, 1883). The account is spread throughout almost the entire book which traces the family chronologically. Capt. Edward Hoare, the compiler of the history, was with the North Cork Rifle brigade.

56 Dickson, *Old World Colony*, p. 116.

57 Gough, 'Physical development of Cork City', p. 325.

58 Marshlands to the west were also being reclaimed at this time.

59 Irish Manuscripts Commission, Registry of Deeds, Dublin, *Abstracts of Wills Vol.1 1708–45* (Dublin, 1956), pp. 28, 172, 265. This last will goes on to say 'set by lease to her father, John Cartwright of said city, gentlemen, deceased, by Alderman George Wright,' indicating that an Alderman of the city was the property holder at the outset.

60 McCarthy, 'Historical Geography', p. 516.

61 O'Sullivan's *Economic History* and Dickson's *Old World Colony* trace the economic history throughout the period.

62 Hoare Bank Ledger, UCC Archives, UC/HB/U31/1.

63 Some histories refer to this as Colville's Quay.

64 For an account of the developments in Dublin and other cities in the eighteenth century see Dickson, 'Large Scale Developers and the Growth of Eighteenth Century Irish Cities', in Butel and Cullen (eds.), *Cities and Merchants, French and Irish Perspectives in Urban Development 1800–1900* (Dublin, 1986), pp. 109–122.

65 O'Sullivan, *Economic History*, pp. 74, 144.

66 Dickson, *Old World Colony*, p 117; W. E. H. Lecky, *A History of Ireland in the Eighteenth Century* (Chicago, 1972), p. 100.

67 *Ibid.*, p. 78.

68 *Ibid.*, p. 90.

69 Dickson, *Old World Colony*, p. 275.

70 *Ibid.*, p. 437.

71 McCarthy, 'Historical Geography'; 'Historical Geographies of a Colonised World', p. 72.

72 Dickson, *Old World Colony*, p 118.

Chapter 2: Place and Identity

1 Ewan Morris, *Our Own Devices* (Dublin, 2005), p. 111.

2 A number of historians have referred to the Union of 1801 as not being between the two nations, Britain and Ireland, but rather between elite elements within the respective societies. See for example R. F. Foster, *Modern Ireland 1600–1972* (London, 1989), p. 283 quoting Grattan; Alvin Jackson, 'The Survival of the Union', in Joe Cleary and Claire Connolly (eds.), *Modern Irish Culture* (Cambridge, 2005), p. 28.

3 Peter Alter, 'Symbols of Irish Nationalism', *Studia Hibernica*, 14 (1974), pp. 104–123 describes how the flag was not accepted as representing the entire nation but only of a definite portion of the population. Latterly the union flag was an expression of Unionist and Protestant sympathies.

4 Curtis, *A History of Ireland*, (London, 2002), p. 300. Some Catholics, including some of the bishops, supported the Union in the belief that it would lead to Catholic Emancipation. See James H. Murphy, *Ireland: A Social, Cultural and Literary History, 1791–1891* (Dublin, 2003), p. 20. For details regarding Bishop Francis Moylan's (Cork) support for and correspondence regarding the Union see Bolster, *A History of the Diocese of Cork From the Penal Era to the Famine* (Cork, 1989), pp. 168–9.

5 The term 'Irish' was no longer synonymous with Catholic and from the early to mid-eighteenth century, educated Protestants had a new attitude to their Irish cultural inheritance. See Sean Connolly, 'Ag Déanamh Commanding': Elite Responses to Popular Culture, 1660–1850', in J. S. Donnolly and Kerby A. Miller (eds.), *Irish Popular Culture 1650–1850* (Dublin, 1999), p. 6; See also S. J. Connolly, 'Culture, Identity and Tradition, Changing Definitions of Irishness', in Brian Graham (ed.), *In Search of Ireland: A Cultural Geography* (London, 1997), p. 48 describing the development of a new sense of identity for the 'new English' during the eighteenth century. See also Jacqueline R. Hill, 'National Festivals, the State and 'Protestant Ascendancy' in Ireland, 1790–1829', *Irish Historical Studies*, 24, 93 (1984) in which she says 'if the Irish were not to lose their identity in the [post-Union] British Parliament, they too needed a national tradition'.

6 For a detailed study of the changing place of St Patrick in Irish society during the eighteenth century see Bridget McCormack, *Perceptions of St Patrick in Eighteenth-Century Ireland* (Dublin, 2000).

7 Edward Relph, *Place and Placelessness* (London, 1976), p. 34.

8 Yvonne Whelan, *Reinventing Modern Dublin: Streetscape, Iconography and Politics of Identity* (Dublin, 2003), p. 22.

9 *Ibid.*, pp. 1–29 for a detailed account of the groundwork upon which her work was based and through which this brief framework is developed.

10 *Ibid.*, p. 234.

11 *Ibid.*, p. 57. For more detailed accounts of the eighteenth-century Dublin developments, see Siobhan Kilfeather, *Dublin: A Cultural and Literary History* (Dublin, 2005); L. M. Cullen, *Life in Ireland* (London, 1968), Chapter 4; Dickson, 'Large Scale Developers', pp. 109–123.

12 Whelan, *Reinventing Modern Dublin*, pp. 6–21.

13 Named after Daniel O'Connell in 1924. See Whelan, *Reinventing Modern Dublin*, p. 224 for a map of the Dublin changes in the decades following independence.

14 O'Sullivan, *Economic History*, p. 142.

15 *Volunteer Journal or Independent Gazetteer*, 31 March 1783, p. 3.

16 *Ibid.*, dates as listed.

17 *Ibid.*, 1 May 1783, p.4, col. 4. The provision for monies from Assizes to be used in this way dates to 13 November 1781, Richard Caulfield, *The Council Book of the Corporation of the City of Cork, from 1609–1643 and from 1690–1800* (Surrey, 1876), p. 970. The Crooked Billet was where Academy Street is today, see Connor's map of 1774.

18 *Volunteer Journal or Independent Gazetteer*, 5 May 1783. At the time two different groups were advertising for subscriptions towards the surveying and mapping of the city. One was headed by Daniel Murphy who claimed to be working for the Society of Arts and Sciences; the other by Francis Cottrell and Patrick Aher who did not cite any commissioning agency. (See the *Hibernian Chronicle (HC)*, 3 April 1783 for an example of the former and 1 May 1783 for the latter.) Within a fortnight of the above quoted letter appearing in the *Journal*, another letter appeared decrying the actions of a copycat group seeking to muscle in on the hard work of the legitimate surveyors of the city for their own personal gain. This dispute is of no consequence in the story herein being told; however, it does serve to underline that the issue of street improvements and in particular the naming of the streets was to the fore in the minds of the readership of the contemporary newspapers.

19 *Volunteer Journal or Independent Gazetteer*, 22 May 1783, p. 3, col. 4.

20 There is one exception to this statement. On Thursday 12 June, 'the printers hereof' sought two apprentices for their printing works at No. 9 on the Long Quay. One possible explanation for this could be that in seeking employees, given the newness of the St Patrick's Street name, potential candidates from beyond the city would be more familiar with the old name as the place to apply to. The previously quoted letter seeking identification of the streets with name signs could be seen as additional weight this argument.

21 *HC*, 8 May 1783.

22 *Ibid.*, 10 July 1783.

23 That the name first appeared in the *Journal* as opposed to other publications such as the *HC* associated the naming of the street with movements such as the Volunteers which identified with St Patrick at this period. See the next section on the context of the naming.

24 *HC*, 21 July 1783.

25 *Ibid.*, dates as cited.

26 *Ibid.*, 3 January 1780.

27 Curtis, *A History of Ireland*, p. 259.

28 See O'Sullivan's *Economic History*, p. 151 for an account of trade embargoes during the 1750s and 1760s as they affected Cork city.

29 Murphy, *Ireland: A Social, Cultural and Literary History*, p. 12.

30 Patrick Fagan, *Catholics in a Protestant Country: the Papist Constituency in Eighteenth-Century Dublin* (Dublin, 1998), p. 184.

31 J. C. Beckett, *The Making of Modern Ireland, 1603–1923* (London, 1981), p. 209. This is an example of the purchasing of elections which was engaged in at the time.

32 *Ibid.*, p. 196. The Patriot Movement is dealt with in a number of histories of this period. Beckett's

account is comprehensive; so also is David Dickson's in *New Foundations Ireland, 1660–1800* (Dublin, 2000). Foster, *Modern Ireland*, gives a sevenfold interpretation of patriotism as applicable to the period. It comprises the rights of Irish Protestants, constitutional redress, legislative independence, personal freedom, regulation without foreign control, beneficial economic measures and gentry' nationalism, pp. 247–8.

33 Connolly, 'Culture, Identity and Tradition', p. 49.

34 Lecky, *A History of Ireland*, p. 114.

35 McCormack, *Perceptions of St Patrick*, p. 72.

36 *Ibid.*, p. 74.

37 Hill, 'National Festivals', p. 32.

38 McCormack, *Perceptions of St Patrick*, p. 74

39 Foster, *Modern Ireland*, p. 194.

40 McCormack, *Perceptions of St Patrick*, p. 29.

41 William Henry, *Love of our Country: a sermon preached in the Cathedral Church of St Patrick, Dublin, March 17 1756, being the anniversary of the festival of St Patrick* (Dublin, 1761), pp. 28–9.

42 Rev. Arthur W. Edwards, 'Historical Sketch of the Church of Ireland', in *Essays on The Irish Church by Clergymen of the Established Church in Ireland* (Oxford, London and Dublin, 1868), p. 99.

43 McCormack, *Perceptions of St Patrick*, p. 87.

44 Foster, 'Ascendancy and Union', in Foster, *Oxford Illustrated History of Ireland*, p. 166.

45 McCormack, *Perceptions of St Patrick*, p. 16.

46 Poetry, music and the formation of the Royal Irish Academy in 1785 were all other aspects of the first Celtic revival. See Connolly, 'Elite responses to popular culture', pp. 1–24.

47 Beckett, *Making of Modern Ireland*, p. 213.

48 Foster, *Modern Ireland*, p. 246.

49 Peter Galloway, *The Most Illustrious Order of Saint Patrick* (Chicester, 1983), p. 4.

50 Connolly, 'Culture, Identity and Tradition', p. 49.

51 In fact the creation of an Order was first suggested in May 1768 and again in 1777, so this was the third addressing of the issue. For details see Galloway, *The Most Illustrious Order of Saint Patrick*, pp. 3–5.

52 Historical Manuscripts Commission, *The Manuscripts of J. B. Fortescue Esq.*, Vol. 1, (London, 1892), p. 177. Lord Charlemont, however, one of the leading Patriots, had been concerned that 'it might in some degree tend to increase the influence of the Crown' and 'he might not wish to be associated with some of the candidates', from Historical Manuscripts Commission, *The Manuscripts and Correspondence of James, First Earl of Charlemont, Vol.1, 1745–1783* (London, 1891), pp. 151–2. Following reassurances from Earl Temple, however, he agreed to be nominated. Charlemont's acceptance indicates that the constituency of the Irish people accepted and welcomed the principle of the Order.

53 Historical Manuscripts Commission, *Manuscripts of J. B. Fortescue Esq.*, Vol. 1, p. 189.

54 *Ibid.*, pp. 190, 195–6, 201.

55 *HC*, 24 March 1783, p. 1.

56 *Volunteer Journal or Independent Gazetteer*, 20 March 1783, p. 3.

57 *Corke Journal*, 15 March 1758.

58 Dickson, *Old World Colony*, p. 276.

59 Tuckey, *Cork Remembrancer*, p. 150.

60 Dickson, *Old World Colony*, p. 442.

61 *Ibid.*, p. 421.

62 Examples taken from just one page of the *Corke Journal*, 18 November 1756 include teas of many sorts, refined and raw sugars, a wide assortment of spices, shoe, knee and stock silver buckles, spoons, salvers and locket rings, choice London porter, cherry and raspberry brandy, culgee handkerchiefs at Dublin prices.

63 Jefferies, *Cork Historical Perspectives*, p. 142. For a more detailed account of the Committee of Merchants see O'Sullivan, *Economic History*, pp. 256–279.

64 Dickson, *Old World Colony*, p. 367.

65 Gibson, *History of the County and City of Cork*, Vol. II, pp. 217–230; Dickson, *Old World Colony*, p. 445.

66 *HC*, 28 March and 3 June 1782. In the latter edition the Culloden Volunteers and the Cork Union adopted a similar resolution.

67 *Volunteer Journal or Independent Gazetteer*, 17 March 1783.

68 Dickson, *Old World Colony*, p. 446.

69 *HC*, 24 March 1783, p. 1.

70 Angela Fahy, 'Residence, Workplace and Patterns of Change: Cork 1787–1863', in Butel and Cullen, *Cities and Merchants*, p. 41.

71 Ian d'Alton, *Protestant Society and Politics in Cork, 1812–1844* (Cork, 1980), p. 93. Ian d'Alton's account of the Friendly Club tells its history up to the changes that occurred in Cork politics with Catholic enfranchisement and the changed composition of the Corporation following on the 1841 elections, see pp. 93–101. For another account of how the city voted, particularly with an emphasis on the sectarian divide, see Peter Jupp and Stephen Royle, 'The social geography of Cork City elections, 1801–30', *Irish Historical Studies*, 29, 113 (1994), pp. 13–43.

72 Ian d'Alton, *Protestant Society* p. 93; O'Sullivan, *Economic History*, p. 227.

73 Henry Alan Jefferies, *Cork Historical Perspectives*, p.162.

74 Caulfield, *Council Book of the Corporation of the City of Cork*, pp. 970, 1001. The Corporation's involvement in matters pertaining to streets is also illustrated in an entry in Tuckey, *Cork Remembrancer*, p. 197, where it is recorded for 22 September 1787 that 'an order of the council was passed empowering the mayor to have the different streets, lanes, alleys, quays etc. named and the houses numbered'.

75 Dickson, *New Foundations*, (Dublin, 2000), p. 184; O'Sullivan, *Economic History*, p. 142.

76 *Ibid.*, p. 142.

77 Kevin Hourihan, 'The Evolution and Influence of Town Planning in Cork', in O'Flanagan and Buttimer, *Cork: History and Society*, p. 946; Ó Drisceoil and Ó Drisceoil, *Serving a City*, p. 24; Jefferies, *Cork Historical Perspectives*, p. 151.

78 *The Statutes At Large Passed in the Parliament held in Ireland*, Vol. IX (Dublin, 1786), p. 423.

79 *HC*, 20 March 1783.

80 *Volunteer Journal or Independent Gazetteer*, 5 May 1783.

81 Caulfield, *Council Book*, pp. 794–989. The Aldermen were those persons who had already served as Mayor and according to d'Alton 'natural process usually meant that at any given time there were about fifteen'. D'Alton, *Protestant Society and Politics in Cork*, p. 91.

82 *HC*, 30 July 1787.

83 *Ibid.*, 11 January 1787.

84 Fahy, in 'A social geography of nineteenth century Cork', unpublished MA thesis, UCC (1983), p. 101, says that 'By 1801, Patrick Street was now the major thoroughfare and was terminated in Patrick's Bridge'.

85 From information held by the Freemasons at their rooms at Tuckey Street in Cork city. The dining room has many historic artefacts in display cases and documents mounted on the walls pertaining to the history of the Masons in Cork; for example an account of a grand committee held at the house of Brother John Hodnett, Globe Tavern at which Lodges Nos. 1,27,28,67 and 95 debated the validity of Lodge No. 1. The names of some representatives from the Lodges are legible on the document. There is also historical information about some of the Lodges at the website http://homepage.eircom.net/~masons/95_1.htm, [accessed 25/10/2006]. This says that the original documentation about St Patrick's Lodge has been lost.

86 *HC*, 1 October 1789. For full text of this article see Appendix 2. A full history of St Patrick's Bridge can be found in Antóin O'Callaghan, *Of Timber Iron and Stone: A Journey through Time on the Bridges of Cork* (Cork, 1989), pp. 22–36.

87 *HC*, 18 January 1787.

88 *Ibid.*, 17 September 1801.

89 *Ibid.*, 30 October 1807.

90 *Constitution*, 10 December 1825.

91 The early maps of Cork, drawn prior to the creation of St Patrick's Street, illustrate that the river channel shape is consistent with the street shape shown on maps subsequent to the street's creation.

92 Use of the term 'confinement' is based on Mayor Samuel Rowland's statement that prior to the arching in of the river channels they flowed 'open and unconfined'. *HC*, 18 January 1787.

93 Tim Cadogan, *Cork in Old Photographs* (Dublin, 2003), p. 31. This latter operation was undertaken shortly after the removal of the electric tram tracks following the closure of the tram service in 1931.

94 Report on 'Cork Main Drainage Scheme: Archaeological monitoring of the laying of services at St Patrick's Street, Cork City: May–October 1999'. Licence no: 96E157.

95 I am indebted to Ms Ciara Brett, Cork City Archaeologist, for giving to me these as yet unpublished details about the findings beneath St Patrick's Street. Interview with Ms Brett took place at her offices in Navigation House on 29 August 2006.

96 I am indebted to Mr Kevin Terry, City Engineer in Cork, for the information in this section of the book and for giving me access to documentation

pertaining to the development of the street. Among those utilised in this section are 'St Patrick's Street Development Brief', Cork Corporation, August 2001; Brewitt, 'Redevelopment of St Patrick's Street'.

97 The use of a black surface would minimise the effect; the cost of replacement in the event of such being necessary was also a factor.

98 Brewitt, 'Redevelopment of St Patrick's Street'. For the full specifications used in the final road surface see Appendix 3.

99 O'Sullivan, *Economic History*, p. 352.

100 See Appendix 4 for the full set of tolls imposed. The calash was a low-wheeled carriage with a removable hood; the chaise, a two-wheeled, open-topped horse-drawn carriage for one or two persons while a wain was a type of goods wagon.

101 Coleman O'Mahony, *In the Shadows: Life in Cork, 1750–1930* (Cork, 1997), p. 33.

102 Fahy, 'The Spatial Differentiation of Commercial and Residential Functions in Cork City, 1767–1863', *Irish Geography*, 17 (1984), p. 20.

103 Fahy, 'Residence, Workplace and Patterns of Change', in Butel and Cullen, *Cities and Merchants*, p. 46.

104 Fahy, 'Spatial Differentiation', p. 18 says that 'at the close of the eighteenth century, three of Cork's wealthiest merchants, Rogers, Dunscombe and Newenham had built houses two or three miles outside the city'.

105 Fahy, 'Residence, Workplace and Patterns of Change', pp. 47–8.

106 The best account of both the horse-drawn and electric trams in Cork is Walter McGrath, *Tram Tracks through Cork* (Cork, 1991) from which much of this information has been obtained.

107 William Martin Murphy of Dublin lockout fame was responsible for the construction of the street track and brick paving associated with it. He later became chairman of the Electric Tramways Company, see McGrath, *Tram Tracks*, p. 33.

108 Sylvester O'Sullivan, 'Cork's Much Loved Tram Service Faces its Doom', *Evening Echo*, 23 August 1976, p. 6.

109 McGrath, *Tram Tracks*, p. 36.

110 *Ibid.*, p. 38.

111 *Ibid.*, p. 29. *CE*, 18 December 1900 carries an advertisement for Russell's, 4 Patrick Street, which asks that its address be noted as 'opposite tram terminus'.

112 O'Sullivan, 'Cork's Much Loved Tram Service Faces its Doom'; see also O'Sullivan 'The Battle of the Busses', *Evening Echo*, 30 August 1976, p. 5.

113 There was a considerable dispute between The Irish Omnibus Company and the Rocksavage Omnibus Company owned by Jerry Dwyer, before the latter finally sold. For a detailed account of this dispute see Aodh Quinlivan, *Philip Monahan, A Man Apart* (Dublin, 2006), pp. 125–9.

114 For many years a hut served as the control centre – effectively an on-street office for the bus inspector – at the Statue. It had been the location of a fire ladder during the nineteenth century. An on-street office is now located further down St Patrick's Street, following the recent redevelopments.

115 The story of the Statue and its place as an icon of identity is told in a later section of this book.

116 O'Sullivan, 'The Battle of the Busses'.

117 O'Mahony, *In the Shadows*, p. 35.

118 *Ibid.*

119 John Windele, *Windele's Cork: Historical and Descriptive Notices of the City of Cork* (Cork, 1973), p. 77; O'Sullivan, *Economic History*, p. 141.

120 Jefferies, *Cork Historical Perspectives*, p. 208.

121 Joachim Fisher and Grace Neville (eds.), *As Others Saw Us: Cork through European Eyes* (Cork, 2005), p. 253.

122 Brewitt, 'Redevelopment of St Patrick's Street', p. 3.

123 Brewitt also says that this array is supplemented with another lamp known as the Pitmit Lamp. Arup, a group of specialist lighting engineers, were appointed to assist with the technical development of the light.

124 *Irish Examiner*, 23 September 2004, p. 9.

125 As mentioned previously, the name Caldwell appears on Smith's map of 1750. The Crooked Billet Dock is seen to join Traver's Quay – the same quay as Smith's Caldwell's – on Connor's map of 1774. The name also features prominently in a recently drawn sketch-map by Dr Martin Pulbrook based on papers found in the gallery of the Unitarian meeting house on Prince's Street, gathered by an unidentified member of the congregation in 1923 and based on

deeds and land grants *c*. 1714. This drawing is an excellent illustration of the water channel at this location.

126 In the 'St Patrick's Street: Development Brief', issued by Cork City Council, these buildings are detailed and listed for protection.

127 The 1793 date is based on a plaque above the door. As identifiable premises they are first listed in *Pigot's Directory* of 1824. No. 92 is listed to a Daniel Flynn, operating as a vintner, spirit and porter store and continued in that business under the listings of James Moloney and Mathias O'Keefe, until it changed to Barter's travel shop in the early twentieth century which is still operating to this day. No. 93 is also first clearly identified in *Pigot's Directory* of 1824 when Thomas Caldwell operated a books and stationery shop. By 1844 it had changed to Grocery, Wine and Spirits under Thomas Morgan, a trade continued by John Morgan Smith from *c*. 1863. From *c*. 1907 it is listed as The Chateau and it came into the Reidy family's possession in the 1930s.

128 Nos. 99–101 St Patrick's Street ('St Patrick's Street: Development Brief').

129 Fahy described this as the 'dual commercial residential function of property' and says that 'residential use was common on St Patrick's Street', 'A social geography', pp. 107, 113.

130 A number of others were similarly built during the nineteenth century, for example part of Woodford Bournes and No. 66 next door to it.

131 *HC*, 12 November 1795.

132 *Cork Mercantile Chronicle*, 23 January 1804.

133 *Holden's Triennial Directory, 1805–7* (London, 1807), pp. 63–75.

134 Cornelius Kelly, *The Grand Tour of Cork* (Cork, 2003), p. 55.

135 Sean Rothery, *The Shops of Ireland* (Dublin, 1978), pp. 20 and 89.

136 Fisher and Neville, *As Others Saw Us*, p. 37. While a certain amount of conjecture is involved in applying these descriptions to St Patrick's Street, given that the street is never actually mentioned, both writers say their accounts pertain to the recently in-filled areas. As such the descriptions could apply to Grand Parade and the South Mall of today also. I am inclined to the view that as travellers they would undoubtedly have visited St Patrick's Street and so feel it is justifiable to use the descriptions.

137 Henry Heany (ed.), *A Scottish Whig in Ireland, 1835–1838; the Irish Journals of Robert Graham of Redgorton* (Dublin, 1999), p. 132.

138 Archibald G. Stark, *The South of Ireland in 1850; being the Journal of a tour in Leinster and South Munster* (Dublin, 1850), p. 72.

139 *Ibid.*, p. 73.

140 *Aldwell's County and City of Cork Post Office Directory 1844–5*, St Patrick's Street listings.

141 *Slater's Royal National Commercial Directory of Ireland 1856*, listings for Carmichael & Co.18–19 and William Treacy & Co 56–57; *Robert H. Laing's Cork City Mercantile Directory for 1863*, Carmichael & Co. 18–21, McCormack's Victoria Hotel 35–37, Arnott & Co. 52–54, Treacy & Co. 56–57, Barnardo & Son 59–60, Dan Sheehan 109–110; *Francis Guy's County and City of Cork Directory for the years 1875–6*, pp. 573–4, Carmichael & Co. 18–21, Crystal Palace 27–28, Munster Arcade 29–30, Wilson's Victoria Hotel 35–37, Newsom & Son 40–41, Grant & Co. 52–54, William Treacy & Co. 56–57, Barnardo & Son 59–60, Daniel Sheehan 109–110; *Francis Guy's City and Suburban Directory 1891*, pp. 258–9, Atkins Bros. London House 14–15, Cash & Co. 18–21, Munster Arcade 29–30, Wilson's Victoria Hotel 35–37, Newsom & Son 40–41, Grant & Co. 52–54, William Treacy & Co. 56–57, Bernard Alcock 74–75, TR Lester 106–107, Daniel Sheehan 109–110; *Francis Guy's Cork City and Suburbs, 1893*, pp. 222–3, Atkins Bros. London House 14–15, Cash & Co. 18–21, Munster Arcade 29–30, W. Egan & Son 32–33, Wilson's Victoria Hotel 35–37, Newsom & Son 40–41, Grant & Co. 52–54, William Treacy & Co. 56–57, Woodford Bourne & Co. 64–65, Bernard Alcock 74–75, TR Lester 106–107, Daniel Sheehan 109–110; *Francis Guy's Postal Directory Cork City and Suburbs 1907*, pp. 524–5, London House Ltd 14–15, Cash & Co. 18–21, Munster Arcade 29–30, Royal Victoria Hotel 35–37, Newsom & Son 40–41, Grant & Co. 52–54, William Dennehy & Sons 60–62, Woodford Bourne & Co. 64–65, F. H. Thompson & Son Ltd 71–72, Bernard Alcock 74–75, Cork Chemical and Drug Co. Ltd 80–81, John Perry & Son Ltd 89–90, TR Lester 106–107, Daniel Sheehan 109–110.

142 The Woodford Bourne building on St Patrick's

Street was designed by Henry Hill (1806–87) and construction was completed in the 1840s. Today the premises are occupied by a fast food outlet. It was and still is a favourite meeting place, not quite as iconic as the Statue but nevertheless popular. A recent publication on the history of Woodford Bourne is David Nicholson with Philip MacKeown, *The Story of Woodford Bourne: Wine Importers Established 1750* (Cork, 2005).

143 Hourican, 'The Evolution and Influence of Town Planning in Cork', in O'Flanagan and Buttimer, *Cork: History and Society*, p. 958.

144 David Hennessy, 'The making of a modern street; St Patrick's Street in the twentieth century', unpublished paper for the UCC Geography Department, p. 11, Local Studies, Cork City Library.

145 *Ibid.*, pp. 14–16.

146 *Shop Fronts and Advertisements Guidelines, 1990*, Cork Corporation, (January 1990), p. 5. Under these guidelines, fascias, pilasters, stall-risers, windows, entrance doors, materials and colour, security screens, canopies, advertising signs, directional signs and bank cash machines or ATM's – a new physical feature on St Patrick's Street – would also be controlled. See pp. 11–18.

147 The effect of these guidelines was reiterated in the *August 2001 Cork Corporation St Patrick's Street Development Brief*, wherein among other facades declared valuable were No. 98, a four-storey Georgian building; Nos. 106–107, a pair of late nineteenth-century commercial buildings now forming Quill's drapery shop; No. 108, the former Savoy Cinema with an art-deco facade built in the 1930s.

148 In fact the 1990 guidelines document pointed out that 'refurbishment of shop-fronts can often offer an opportunity to strip away later additions and to re-establish the proportions and details of the original framework', p. 5.

Chapter 3: St Patrick's Bridge

1 Many works detail the city's economic expansion at this time. See for example, O'Sullivan, *Economic History*; Dickson, *Old World Colony*.

2 O'Callaghan, 'St Patrick's Street, Cork: Historical Perspectives', unpublished MA thesis, UCC (2007).

3 T. F. McNamara, *A Portrait of Cork* (Cork, 1981),

p. 77.

4 *Holden's Triennial Directory 1805–7*.

5 An excellent account of the events surrounding the destruction and subsequent reconstruction of the first St Patrick's Bridge can be read in the *Cork Examiner* reportage of the opening of the second St Patrick's Bridge, in the edition of Thursday 12 December 1861.

6 McNamara, *Portrait of Cork*, p. 209.

7 *CE*, 12 December 1861.

8 *HC*, 1 October 1789.

9 Tuckey, *Cork Remembrancer*, p. 217 says that the tolls of St Patrick's Bridge were sold for a period of twelve months at public auction on 7 September 1801, the sum involved being £1,400.

10 *Cork Mercantile Chronicle*, 13 August 1806.

11 *Ibid.*, 10 September 1806.

12 *Ibid.*, 13, 15, 19 August 1806.

13 McNamara, *Portrait of Cork*, p. 33.

14 *Ibid.*, p. 242.

15 *CE*, 4 May 1849.

16 *Ibid.*, 2 November 1853 gives a detailed account of the events under the headline 'Fearful Inundation in the City: Destruction of Patrick's Bridge and Loss of Life'.

17 *Ibid.*, 12 December 1861.

18 *Ibid.*, 13 January 1854.

19 *Ibid.*, 18 January 1854.

20 *Ibid.*, 28 January 1854.

21 *Ibid.*, 15 March 1854.

22 The announcement of the Corporation's intention to seek replacement of the bridge was posted in the *Cork Examiner* of 18 November 1853. A letter to the editor in the edition of 21 November demanded that swivel bridges be constructed to allow for shipping to once more travel upstream of the St Patrick's Bridge site. The author of the letter, one William Fitzgibbon of London, claimed that the removal of the facility to allow shipping to travel upstream of the bridge discriminated against businesses located on those quays.

23 A general meeting of Builders and Stonemasons took place at Mary Street on Monday 19 April 1858 at which the members made their feelings known that stone should be the material used in the bridge construction project. See *CE*, 21 April 1858.

24 *Ibid.*, 12 December 1861.

25 *Ibid.*, 5 May 1854.

26 *Ibid.*, 10 May 1854.

27 *Ibid.*, 14 July 1854.

28 A full copy of the report appears in *ibid.*, 28 January 1854.

29 *Ibid.*, 20 April 1855.

30 *Ibid.*, 25 April 1855.

31 *Ibid.*, 4 May 1855.

32 *Ibid.*, 1 October 1855.

33 *Ibid.*, 30 November 1855.

34 *Ibid.*, 5 December 1855.

35 *Ibid.*

36 *Ibid.*, 7 January 1856.

37 *Ibid.*, 5 March, 9 May 1856.

38 *Ibid.*, 29 March 1858.

39 *Ibid.*, 9 April 1858.

40 *Ibid.*, 21 April 1858.

41 *Ibid.*, 17 June 1859.

42 *Ibid.*, 22 August 1859.

43 *Ibid.*, 11 November 1859.

44 *Ibid.*

45 *Ibid.* There was also placed in the cavity 'a specimen of every coin in the realm'.

46 The silverwork was done by Mr Hawkesworth, Silversmith, Grand Parade.

47 *CE*, 12 December 1861.

48 *Ibid.*, 23 April 1858.

49 *Cork Constitution*, 26 May 1859.

50 Much of the story of the rebuilding of St Patrick's Bridge and the footbridge built by Barnard is told humorously in a poem by John Fitzgerald, Bard of the Lee, entitled 'The Bridge that Barnard Built'.

51 *CE*, 25 May 1859.

52 *Ibid.*, 12 December 1861, as mentioned previously, gives a detailed account of events in the bridge story.

53 McNamara, *Portrait of Cork*, p. 210.

Chapter 4: People of St Patrick's Street

1 *Holden's Triennial Directory 1805–7*, pp. 63–75.

2 Dickson, *Old World Colony*, pp. 273 and 583.

3 Tim Cadogan and Jeremiah Falvey, *A Biographical Dictionary of Cork* (Dublin, 2006), pp. 119–120.

4 Grace Lawless Lee, *The Huguenot Settlements in Ireland* (London, 1936), p. 47.

5 *Constitution or Cork Advertiser*, 15 February 1838.

6 *Southern Reporter*, 20 March 1827.

7 By the end of the twentieth century, many businesses were listed by name, for example A-Wear or The Bijou Box. The above extractions refer to where women were clearly identifiable and named as the entry in the directory, for example Kay Cogan who ran a childcare centre. As such they only indicate a trend.

8 Cork City and County Archives, Dowden's Records, B500/13/1, box 7, Lady Customers, 1857–1860.

9 Cork City and County Archives, B500/13/4, Account Book to Purchases by Gentlemen Customers, May 1884 – March 1887.

10 Census of Ireland, 1911, Form A, Return of the members of this family and their visitors, boarders, servants etc, who slept or abode in this house on the night of Sunday 2 April, 1911; Form B1, House and Building return; Form N, Enumerator's abstract for Townland or Street.

11 Of the 340 listed as residents on the street, 143 were male and 197 female. 251 were returned as Roman Catholic, 52 as Church of Ireland and 37 as other denominations including Presbyterian and Jewish.

12 Richard Lucas, 'The Cork Directory for the year 1787', *JCHAS*, 72 (1967), pp. 135–159.

13 *HC*, 26 May 1791.

14 *Ibid.*, 25 July 1791.

15 *Ibid.*, 6 April 1795.

16 *Ibid.*, 15 September 1805.

17 *Ibid.*, 12 November 1795.

18 *Holden's Triennial Directory 1805–7*, pp. 63–75.

19 *HC*, 10 November 1800.

20 *Ibid.*, 23 January 1804.

21 *Ibid.*, 2 October 1804.

22 *Mercantile Chronicle*, 25 January 1805.

23 Davis and Mary Coakley, *Wit and Wine, Literary and Artistic Cork in the Early Nineteenth Century* (Dublin, 1985), p. 15.

24 *Ibid.*, p. 16.

25 *Ibid.*, p. 50.

26 *Pigot's Directory, 1824.*

27 *Freeholder*, 31 December 1816.

28 Biographical information in this section is based on Rosemary Folliott's article 'Biographical Notes on some Cork Clock and Watch Makers', *JCHAS*, 69 (1964), pp. 38–55 and on trade directories for the city. Some information comes from descendants

and members of families involved, such as the O'Callaghans and the O'Sullivans.

29 Cork Corporation, *Restoration of Shandon Steeple Clock, Church of St Ann, Shandon; a contribution to the European Year of the Environment* (Cork, 1987).

30 Story told by Denis O'Callaghan who worked as a watch and clockmaker in the city for over sixty years between 1933 and the 1990s.

31 O'Mahony, *In the Shadows*, p. 116.

32 James Connolly, *Labour in Irish History* (London, 1987), p. 104.

33 Fintan Lane, *In Search of Thomas Sheahan, Radical Politics in Cork, 1824–36* (Dublin, 2001), p. 14.

34 Richard Pankhurst, *William Thompson, 1775–1833, Pioneer Socialist* (London, 1954), p. 2.

35 Dolores Dooley, *Equality in Community, Sexual Equality in the writings of William Thompson and Anna Doyle Wheeler* (Cork, 1996), p. 7.

36 Desmond Fennell, 'Irish Socialist Thought', in Richard Kearney (ed.), *The Irish Mind: Exploring Intellectual Traditions* (Dublin, 1985), p. 188.

37 Dooley, *Equality in Community*, pp. 5–6.

38 Pankhurst, *William Thompson*, p. 3; see also J. W. Boyle (ed.), *Leaders and Workers*, from the Thomas Davis Lecture series (Cork), p. 12.

39 Fennell, 'Irish Socialist Thought', p. 189.

40 Connolly, *Labour in Irish History*, p. 95.

41 *Ibid.*, p. 98.

42 Fennell, 'Irish Socialist Thought', p. 189.

43 Dooley, *Equality in Community*, p. 17.

44 Fennell, 'Irish Socialist Thought', p. 189.

45 A William Thompson commemorative committee is seeking to have a plaque mounted in his honour at the site of his home at No. 4 St Patrick's Street.

46 Fr Augustine, OFM Cap, *Footprints of Fr Theobald Mathew* (Dublin, 1947), p. 58.

47 Many wealthier Catholics were buried in St Joseph's Cemetery in its early stages but during the Famine years it became the last resting place for thousands of the destitute poor.

48 Fr Augustine, *Footprints*, p. 91.

49 *Connaught Journal*, 19 March 1840, 'the Very Rev T Mathew, who has been (and not undeservedly) styled the great Apostle of Temperance'; *Freeman's Journal*, 30 March 1840, 'the celebrity of the great apostle'; Paul A. Townend, *Father Mathew, Temperance and Irish Identity* (Dublin, 2002), p. 4,

'By the spring of 1840 … Father Mathew was styled as the great 'Apostle of Temperance' when he was not being described as a second coming of Saint Patrick'. The phrase 'Apostle of Temperance' is carved into the plinth on which the statue in his honour stands.

50 For a detailed analysis of Fr Mathew and the temperance crusade – its successes and its failures – see Townend, *Father Mathew*.

51 Maura Cronin, *Country, Class or Craft?* (Cork, 1994), p. 206.

52 Richard T. Cooke, *Cork's Barrack Street Band* (Cork, 1992), p. 20.

53 *CE*, 28/29 March 1842.

54 For an account of the political dimension of the alliance between Fr Mathew and Daniel O'Connell and how it may have been orchestrated by the repeal leader, see Townend, *Father Mathew*, pp 192–234.

55 *CE*, 22 May 1843.

56 *Ibid.*

57 *Ibid.*

58 *Ibid.*, 30 August 1841.

59 O'Mahony, *In the Shadows*, p. 151.

60 *Ibid.*, p.152.

61 *CE*, 27 January 1847.

62 *Ibid.*, 14 May 1847.

63 *Ibid.*

64 *Ibid.*

65 *Ibid.*, 11 October 1847.

66 *Ibid.*, 31 December 1847.

67 Fr Augustine, *Footprints*, pp. 466–503.

68 *CE*, 10 October 1864.

69 Fr Augustine, *Footprints*, p. 534.

70 John Fitzgerald, *Legends, Ballads and Songs of the Lee* (Cork 1913), pp. 34, 64.

71 *CE*, 10 October 1864. These were among those listed travelling in the committee members' carriages.

72 The statue is in bronze and was crafted by John Foley. However the contract was originally awarded to the famous sculptor Hogan. Foley undertook the project following the death of Hogan. The *Cork Examiner* account of the unveiling proceedings carried a synopsis of the project – 10 October 1864. Details on this can also be found in Ken Inglis, 'Father Mathew's Statue: the Making of a Monument in Cork', in Oliver McDonagh and W. F. Mandle (eds.), *Ireland and Irish-Australia: Studies in Cultural*

and Political History (London, 1986), pp. 119–136.

73 *CE*, 10 October 1864.

74 *Ibid.*

75 Inglis, 'Father Mathew's Statue', p. 124.

76 *Ibid.*, p. 121.

77 *CE*, 10 October 1864.

78 *Ibid.*

79 *Ibid.*

80 *Ibid.*

81 *Ibid.*

82 *Ibid.*

83 *Evening Echo*, 13 July 2000.

84 *Ibid.*, 21 July 2000.

85 *Ibid.*, 13 November 2000.

86 In a description of the business in *Strattens Directory* of 1892, John Arnott is described as a pioneer of the Monster Warehouse system, p. 173.

87 Ronald Nesbitt, *At Arnotts of Dublin, 1843–1993* (Dublin, 1993), p. 7.

88 James N. Healy, *Roches Stores* (Cork, 1981), p. 7.

89 *Ibid.*, p. 12.

90 *Ibid.*, p. 16.

91 From information supplied by John Porter, Manager, Dunnes Stores, Merchant Quay complex, St Patrick's Street, Cork.

92 Peter Burke, *Popular Culture in Early Modern Europe* (Aldershot, 1998), p. 182.

93 Gary Owens, 'Nationalism without Words: Symbolism and Ritual Behaviour in the Repeal 'Monster Meetings' of 1843–45', in Donnelly and Miller, *Irish Popular Culture*, pp. 247–8, 256.

94 Peter Jupp and Eoin Magennis (eds.), *Crowds in Ireland, 1720–1920* (London, 2000), pp. 14–31.

95 Owens, 'Nationalism without Words', pp. 257, 255.

Chapter 5: Commerce on the Street

1 O'Mahony, *In the Shadows*, pp. 58–9.

2 *Report of the Pipe Water Commissioners 1809*, pp. 35–6 and 53–4 (Local Studies, Cork City Library). The south side is that of Nos. 1 to 63 today and the west that of Nos. 64 to 125.

3 *Griffith's Valuation of Rateable Properties in Ireland* (Local Studies, Cork City Library).

4 This figure was reached by dividing the total valuation for the relevant side by 63, the number of properties, as opposed to the number of individual entries.

5 Valuation Office [accessed 28 September 2006] www.valoff.ie

6 Of those on the South Main Street, twenty were 'vacant', 'ruins' or 'building ground' rated at 0. Excluding these the average was €135.66.

7 Dickson, *Old World Colony*, p. 413; O'Sullivan, *Economic History*, pp. 165–224.

8 Dickson, *Old World Colony*, pp. 366, 427.

9 Andy Bielenberg, *Cork's Industrial Revolution 1780–1880: Development or Decline?* (Cork, 1991), p. 3.

10 RTÉ Cork Library, SS3 9/10/11. Interview with presenter Rob Vance recorded in Morrissey's of Abbeyleix, Saturday, 1 October 2005. Programme transmitted, with extracts from the interview, on 28 March 2006.

11 Cormac Ó Gráda, *Ireland, A New Economic History, 1780–1939* (Oxford, 1994), pp. 239, 265.

12 Lucas, 'Cork Directory for the year 1787'. pp. 135–159.

13 Some of the directory listings used in this section were compiled by Kieran Burke, Librarian, Local Studies Department, Cork City Library, for a website on Cork history, www.corkpastandpresent.ie/places. His methodology was to use residential listings in those directories where street indices were not included in the directories but to use the street indices where they were available. Where his listings were employed, sample cross-checking with the original directories was undertaken.

14 For example Wine and Spirit merchants are classified in the merchant group but grocery wine and spirit falls into the retail category.

15 Maura Murphy, 'The Economic and Social Structure of Nineteenth Century Cork', in David Harkness and Mary O'Dowd (eds.), *The Town in Ireland* (Belfast, 1981), p. 130, notes that 'the accuracy of these directories is questionable'. Her concerns are that they ignore many of the small backstreet businesses and also that the different publishers sometimes contradict each other. As this book is solely concerned with St Patrick's Street, however, and given that she later goes on to say that 'the trade directories remain our best source of information on the city's employer numbers and business structure', the ensuing analysis is valid with

these points in mind. At least one example of a potential discrepancy will be quoted.

16 *Holden's Triennial Directory, 1805–7*, pp. 63–75. Seven individuals were named without profession constituting the remaining 9.46 per cent. Of these two were traceable. George Goold was a merchant on St Patrick's Street in 1787 and previous to that he was listed in Mallow Lane in 1758. (See 'A brief directory of the city of Cork, 1758', *The Irish Genealogist*, 8 (1940)). Sir Vesian Pick was a wine merchant on St Patrick's Street in 1787.

17 O'Mahony, *In the Shadows*, p. 41. The significance of this point is twofold. Firstly, it serves as a warning that analysis such as that undertaken here provides trends only; beginning after 1787 and being gone before 1805, these directories did not register the charity shop's existence. Thus much more detailed research is needed before any analysis can be declared absolute. Secondly, the demise of a charity shop on the street is an early indication as to the developing nature of the street as one of a higher class nature.

18 William West, *Cork Directory 1809–10* (Cork, 1810).

19 *1820–22 Commercial and Residential Directory*.

20 *Pigot's Directory, 1824*.

21 A brief examination of advertisements follows which will further substantiate this point.

22 *Aldwell's Directory, 1844–45*; *Slater's Directory, 1856*.

23 *British Parliamentary Papers, 1851 Census of Ireland, Part VI General Report* (Shannon, 1970), pp. 228–234, lists 2,819 males and 3,590 females of fifteen years or upwards and 85 males and 139 females of under fifteen years of age as 'ministering to clothing' in the occupations category, (total 6,633). The total number given for the city in this source is 35,421 making the clothing industry 18.72% of that total. Unfortunately, figures for the individual streets are not given.

24 For example, tailors were more commonly employed in workrooms associated with bigger retailing outfits such as Dowden's or Fitzgerald's, than in tailoring rooms per se. Similarly with jewellery, craftsman were more commonly employed in firms such as Egan's.

25 *Constitution or Cork Advertiser*, 19 December 1840.

26 *CE*, 18 December 1850.

27 *Ibid.*, 19 December 1860.

28 *Ibid.*, 19 December 1870.

29 *Ibid.*, 18 December 1880, 18 December 1890.

30 *Ibid.*, 18 December 1900.

31 Cronin, *Country, Class or Craft*, pp. 28–9.

32 Murphy, 'The Economic and Social Structure of Nineteenth-Century Cork', pp. 132–3.

33 Later Roches Stores also acquired No. 15.

34 Ó Gráda, *New Economic History*, p. 270.

35 O'Leary PR and Marketing, 'Roches Stores Press Statement', issued 8 August 2006. See also *Irish Examiner*, p.18, 8 August 2006.

36 *CE*, 23 December 1846.

37 O'Mahony, *In the Shadows*, p. 181.

38 *JCHAS*, (1996), p.16.

39 O'Mahony, *In the Shadows*, p. 247.

40 *CE*, 16 September 1873.

41 Stratten & Stratten, *Stratten's Dublin, Cork and South of Ireland: A Literary, Commercial and Social Review, Past and Present* (London, 1892), p. 208.

42 *Ibid.*, p. 160.

43 I am grateful to Hugh Burke for his time and his memories which unfortunately are not recorded anywhere. The conversation took place at his home on 7 March 2006.

44 *Stratten's Review*, p. 154.

45 *Ibid.*, p. 167.

46 The information on this firm is obtained from a file held in the Local Studies Department of Cork City Library. See also David Nicholson and Philip MacKeown, *The Story of Woodford Bourne, Wine Importers Established 1750* (Cork, 2005).

47 I am grateful to Rory Cobbe, a relative of the McOstrichs, for information on the family.

48 *Stratten's Review*, p. 216.

49 Nesbitt, *At Arnotts of Dublin*, p. 5.

50 *CE*, 8 October 1847, p.1 for Fogaty and Co., No. 91 St Patrick's Street and 14 May 1847, for the Linen Drapery Co. at No. 110 on the street, are two early examples.

51 Cronin, *Country, Class or Craft*, p. 38.

52 *Stratten's Review*, p. 173.

53 *Ibid.*, p. 162.

54 *Ibid.*, p. 229.

55 *Ibid.*, pp. 213–14.

56 *Ibid.*, p. 228.

57 *Ibid.*, p. 206.

58 *Ibid.*, p. 164.

59 It must not be forgotten that *Stratten's Review* was a commercial publication and so comparison should be made between this glowing account of 'relaxation' for employees and the experiences of William Roche encountered in the earlier chapter on people.

60 The information in the following paragraphs is taken from *Stratten's Review*.

61 Wife of the Rev. Gibson who wrote *A History of Cork* in 1861.

Chapter 6: Violence on the Street

1 For a detailed analysis of this see Cronin, *Country, Class or Craft*.

2 *CE*, 8 March 1867.

3 *Ibid.*, 9 March 1867.

4 See R. V. Comerford, *The Fenians in Context* (Dublin, 1985).

5 Murphy, 'Cork Commercial Society 1850–1899: Politics and Problems', in Butel and Cullen, *Cities and Merchants*, p. 241. See also Murphy, 'Fenianism, Parnellism and the Cork Trades, 1860–1900', *Saothar*, 3 (1979), pp. 27–38.

6 Much of the information in this section is taken from Sean Daly, *Cork; A City in Crisis* (Cork, 1978).

7 *CE*, 23 June 1870.

8 Daly, *A City in Crisis*, p. 41.

9 *CE*, 23 June 1870.

Chapter 7: St Patrick's Street and the March of a Nation

1 McGrath, *Tram Tracks*, p. 15. This book is undoubtedly the most authoritative on trams in Cork and most of the information in this section is taken from this source.

2 Fahy, 'Place and Class in Cork', in O'Flanagan and Buttimer, *Cork: History and Society*, p. 808.

3 *Ibid.*

4 *CE*, 15 September 1880.

5 *Ibid.*, 7 April 1880.

6 *Ibid.*, 4 October 1880.

7 *Ibid.*

8 *Ibid.*,

9 *Ibid.*, 29 December 1884.

Chapter 8: A Changing Streetscape

1 Mary Leland, *The Lie of the Land, Journeys Through Literary Cork* (Cork, 1999), p. 207.

2 Seán Ó Faoláin, *Vive Moi* (London, 1993), p. 11, 29.

3 Mike Cronin and Daryl Adair, *The Wearing of the Green; A History of St Patrick's Day* (London and New York, 2002) contains a detailed history of St Patrick's Day parades worldwide.

4 *Cork Constitution*, 19 March 1900.

5 William Martin Murphy of the Dublin lockout fame was responsible for the construction of the street track and brick paving associated with it. He later became chairman of the Electric Tramways Company (McGrath, *Tram Tracks*, p. 33).

6 O'Sullivan, 'Cork's Much Loved Tram Service Faces its Doom', p. 6.

7 McGrath, *Tram Tracks*, p. 36.

8 *Ibid.*, p. 29. *Cork Examiner*, 18 December 1900 carries an advertisement for Russell's, 4 Patrick Street which asks that its address be noted as 'opposite tram terminus'.

9 Notification of this appeared in the *Cork Examiner*, 27 April 1900.

10 *CE*, 3 August 1903.

11 *Ibid.*

12 *Ibid.*

13 In conversation with this writer.

14 Local Studies Department, Cork City Library.

15 *Strattens' Review*, p. 179.

16 Peter Hart, *The IRA and Its Enemies: Violence and Community in Cork, 1916–1923* (Oxford, 1998), p. 48. For a detailed account of the events in Cork during Easter week 1916 see *Why the Guns Remained Silent in Rebel Cork*, documentary shown on RTÉ, December 2005, director Conal Creedon.

17 *CE*, 29 April 1916.

18 *Ibid.*

19 Hart, *The IRA*, p. 50.

Chapter 9: Destruction and Reconstruction

1 See Chapter 6.

2 Hart, *The IRA*, pp. 50–1.

3 *Ibid.*, p. 240.

4 Gerry White and Brendan O'Shea, *The Burning of Cork* (Cork, 2006), p. 13.

5 Seán Ó Faoláin, *Vive Moi!*, p. 140.

6 White and O'Shea, *The Burning of Cork*, pp. 54–103, gives a detailed account of events throughout this period.

7 Tom Barry, *Guerrilla Days in Ireland* (Dublin, 1981), pp. 36–52; Hart, *The IRA*, pp. 21–38. Peter Hart's modern analysis of the previously largely accepted version of the ambush as penned by Tom Barry has led to a very public dispute with, among others, Meda Ryan. Much of this dispute was through the organ of *History Ireland* magazine during 2005.

8 Irish Labour and Trade Union Congress, *Who Burnt Cork City?* (Dublin, 1921), witness 29, p. 38, witness 31, p. 40.

9 *Ibid.*, witness 11, p.29.

10 *Ibid.*, witness 13, p. 30.

11 White and O'Shea, *The Burning of Cork*, gives a detailed account of the events of the night, including the burning of the City Hall and the Carnegie Library as well as the witness reports of Black and Tan and Auxiliary interference with the efforts of the fire services.

12 Extracts from *The Burning of Cork*, a radio documentary broadcast on Radio Éireann, 18 April 1960. The contributors were not identified and it should be acknowledged that these were accounts given from memory. Some were taken from *Who Burnt Cork City* booklet.

13 *CE*, 13 December 1920.

14 White and O'Shea, *The Burning of Cork*, p. 207.

15 Healy, *Roches Stores*, p. 22–3.

16 *CE*, 13 December 1920.

17 *Ibid.*, 14 December 1920.

18 *Ibid.*

19 *Ibid.*, 20 December 1920.

20 *Ibid.*, 17 December 1920.

21 *Ibid.*, 21 December 1920.

22 *Ibid.*, 24 December 1920.

23 *Ibid.*, 20 December 1920.

24 *Ibid.*, 29 December 1920.

25 *Ibid.*, 14 December 1920.

26 Zones 5 and 7 included the City Hall, Carnegie Library and parts of Oliver Plunkett Street.

27 *CE*, 16 February 1921.

28 House of Lords Record Office, Lloyd George Papers (LG) ref. F/180/5/18, undated.

29 *CE*, 14 December 1920.

30 *Ibid.*, 16 December 1920.

31 Healy, *Roches Stores*, p. 23.

32 *Ibid.*, p. 25.

33 *CE*, 20 January 1921.

34 *Constitution*, 7 January 1921.

35 Healy, *Roches Stores*, p. 27. Enquiries would subsequently show that Cash's and Munster Arcade claimed a similar situation – that limited monies received from insurance sources covered only stock and the erection of temporary premises, *CE*, 8 February 1922. At a Chamber of Commerce meeting held on 2 February 1922 it was stated that 'no firm was fully covered for stock and buildings', *CE*, 3 February 1922.

36 *CE*, 8 February 1921.

37 *Ibid.*, 19 February 1921. Details of other awards granted, appear in *CE* dated 23, 24, February; 1, 2, 3, 5, 10, 11, 12, 14, 18, 23 March.

38 *Ibid.*, 28 February 1921. The committee was to consist of a representative of each ward as well as representatives of the Employers Federation, trades bodies directly affected and the Industrial Development Association.

39 *Ibid.*, 30 August 1921.

40 *Ibid.*, 26 November 1921.

41 *Ibid.*, 24 February 1922. Michael Collins was Minister for Finance from the first Dáil when he replaced Eoin Mac Neill, until July 1922, Andrew McCarthy, 'Michael Collins, Minister for Finance 1919–22', in Gabriel Doherty and Dermot Keogh (eds.), *Michael Collins and the Making of the Irish State* (Cork, 1998), p. 52.

42 *CE*, 24 February 1922.

43 This approach was consistent with how Michael Collins conducted the national financial affairs whereby he asked for an estimate every month from each government department stating what they required for the following month. McCarthy, 'Michael Collins, Minister for Finance', p. 62.

44 *CE*, 25 February 1922.

45 The conditions included that the Corporation would have no liability, that any monies paid were part of the decrees and not in the form of a loan, that monies would only be paid out on certified expenditure, that monies received would be divided equally between decree holders and that the Corporation would not subsequently be liable for

the monies paid provided they did not give more that the decreed amount to any person, *CE*, 6 March 1922.

46 McCarthy, 'Michael Collins, Minister for Finance', p. 65.

47 *CE*, 24 March 1922.

48 Diarmuid Fawsitt (DF) to City Treasurer; DF to All Members; Cork Reconstruction Finance Committee minutes, Local Studies, Cork City Library. The funds would be held in an account in the Munster and Leinster Bank.

49 DF to Town Clerk, 13 May 1922, Cork Reconstruction Finance Committee minutes, Local Studies, Cork City Library.

50 *CE*, 9 May 1922.

51 All except one, that of the Munster Arcade, had been undefended at the original compensation claim hearings and so were subject to the commission's hearings.

52 *CE*, 2 June 1922.

53 *Ibid.*, 25 April 1922 gives an account of the support for the Labour initiative in Cork. Helen Litton, *The Irish Civil War* (Dublin, 1995), pp. 57–80 is one brief account of the lead-up to and the bombardment of the Four Courts in Dublin.

54 *CE*, 19 August 1922.

55 *Ibid.*, 22 August 1922.

56 DF to Town Clerk, 30 March 1922, Reconstruction Finance Committee minutes.

57 *CE*, 29 July 1922.

58 The progress of the Civil War as it affected Cork is beyond the scope of this chapter. *CE*, 14 August 1922, contains a detailed account of the decisive operation where Free State forces took control of the city, having landed by boat at Rochestown and winning the Battle of Douglas. The anti-Treaty forces left the city but continued to harass the Free State troops. For example on Friday 8 September, a soldier stationed at Moore's Hotel was fired at, *CE*, 11 September 1922.

59 DF to Secretary, Reconstruction Committee, 4 August 1922, Reconstruction Finance Committee minutes.

60 *CE*, 28 October 1922.

61 Report from City Treasurer, 1 December 1922, Reconstruction Finance Committee minutes.

62 Litton, *The Irish Civil War*, p. 120.

63 *CE*, 5 January 1923.

64 *Ibid.*, 24 January 1923.

65 On 24 May, Eamonn de Valera 'proclaimed a definitive cease-fire' (Beckett, *The Making of Modern Ireland*, p. 459). He was arrested at an election rally in Ennis, County Clare in August. For a report on the arrest see *CE*, 16 August 1923.

66 *CE*, 15 January 1923.

67 *Ibid.*

68 *Ibid.*, 23 February 1923.

69 *Ibid.*, 25 June 1923.

70 *Ibid.*, 3 March 1923.

71 *Ibid.*, 10 March 1923.

72 *Ibid.*, 24 May 1923.

73 *Ibid.*, 4 June 1923.

74 *Ibid.*, 9 June 1923.

75 *Ibid.*, 26 November 1923.

76 *Ibid.*, 15 December 1923.

77 As well as this but not included in this report, Saxone had reopened for business on 28 March, *CE*, 15 April 1924. A further report was issued on progress on 24 June 1924.

78 *CE*, 16 February 1924.

79 The other advantages were the economics of its local availability, Sicilian marble more porous than limestone, the colour of limestone was a beautiful dove, limestone exceptionally durable and hard wearing, the polish on Sicilian marble when exposed would not last, *CE*, 3 March 1924.

80 The Cork Progressive Association was formed in 1923 to address dissatisfaction with the running of municipal affairs. Many business owners were members of the Association. For a detailed account see Quinlivan, *Philip Monahan*, pp. 59–60.

81 *CE*, 14 June 1924.

82 *Ibid.*, 1 November 1924.

83 *Ibid.*, 10 January 1925.

84 Healy, *Roches Stores*, p. 31.

85 *CE*, 7, 16 March (as seen in pictures).

86 *Ibid.*, 29 January 1926.

87 Cork City and County Archives, Chillingworth and Levie File, refs ARC 1/547; ARC 1/394; ARC 1/548; ARC 1/1678.

88 *CE*, 25 January 1927.

89 Healy, *Roches Stores*, p. 29.

90 Hourihan, 'The Evolution and Influence of Town Planning in Cork', p. 957–8. Cork Town Planning

Association, *Cork – A Civic Survey* (Liverpool, 1926).

91 *Cork – A Civic Survey*, pp. 24–5.

92 *CE*, 22 June 1922. For Dublin see 'City of Dublin, new town plan' in P. Abercrombie, S. Kelly and A. Kelly, *Dublin of the Future* (Dublin, 1922). The similarity lies in the position of dominance given to the prominent buildings. In Cork's case this was the New Municipal Building at Sullivan's Quay facing the Grand Parade with lesser streets radiating from it; in Dublin it was the Parliament Building faced by the Central Station again with lesser streets radiating therefrom. There was also another plan for Dublin published in December 1922 by the Greater Dublin Reconstruction Movement. Neither of the Dublin plans nor the Cork one were implemented.

93 Patrick Abercrombie was born in 1880. In 1915 he was appointed Professor of Civic Design at the Liverpool School of Architecture. In 1916 he was the winner of a Civics Institute of Ireland competition for a new town plan for Dublin and the 1922 plan was based largely on this. He died in 1957.

94 See the commercial portrait section in Chapter 5 for a more detailed account of these trends. The carriage trade was where people came to the street from the suburbs in their carriages and were served by shop assistants who brought items to them in their carriages for approval.

95 Healy, *Roches Stores*, p. 12.

96 *Ibid.*, p. 26–7.

97 F. S. L. Lyons, *Ireland Since the Famine* (London, 1973), p. 420, is one example of a broad history's treatment of the event. White and O'Shea, *The Burning of Cork*.

Chapter 10:
Twentieth-Century Developments

1 O'Sullivan, 'The Battle of the Busses'. This was one of a series of articles during the summer of 1976 which detailed aspects of Cork's transport history.

2 For a detailed account of this dispute see Quinlivan, *Philip Monahan*, pp. 125–9.

3 *CE*, 7 June 1926.

4 *Ibid.*

5 *Evening Echo*, 4 June 1990.

6 *CE*, 16 June 1941.

7 *Ibid.*, 19 June 1933.

8 *Evening Echo*, 4 June 1990.

9 John McSweeney, *The Golden Age of Cork Cinemas* (Cork, 2003), p. 4.

10 *CE*, 11 March 1921.

11 *Ibid.*

12 *Ibid.*

13 *Ibid.*, 17 February 1930.

14 *Evening Echo*, 9 June 1930.

15 *Ibid.*

16 *Ibid.*, 13 May 1932.

17 *Ibid.*

18 *Ibid.*

19 *Ibid.*, 21 May 1956.

20 Ruth Fleischmann, *Cork International Choral Festival, 1954–2004: A Celebration* (Germany, 2004), p. 27–8.

21 *Ibid.*

Chapter 11: Past, Present and Future St Patrick's Street

1 Whelan, *Reinventing Modern Dublin*, p. 12.

2 Connolly, *Labour in Irish History*, p. 104.

3 Hart, *The IRA*, p. 51.

4 Report on Cork Corporation Reconstruction Committee Proceedings, *CE*, 3 May 1922.

5 *Irish Examiner*, 9 July 2009.

Bibliography

Primary Sources

Brewitt, Simon, 'Redevelopment of St Patrick's Street', paper presented at the Institute of Engineers of Ireland, Cork Region night lecture series, 15 November 2005.

Census of Ireland, 1911.

Cork Corporation Reconstruction Committee Minutes File, Local Studies Department, Cork City Library.

Cork Corporation, *Shop Fronts and Advertisements Guidelines, 1990* (January, 1990).

Chillingworth & Levie Files, Cork City and County Archives, ARC 1/547; ARC 1/394; ARC 1/548; ARC 1/1678.

Dowden Papers, Cork City and County Archives, B500/ 1/10-11/13.

Griffith's Valuation of Rateable Properties in Ireland, Local Studies Department, Cork City Library.

Hoare Ledger 1742–96, University College Cork, Department of Archives, UC/HB/U31/1.

Hoare Papers, Cork City and County Archives, U150.

Lloyd George Papers (LG) F/180/5/18, undated, House of Lords Record Office, London.

O'Leary PR and Marketing, 'Roches Stores Press Statement', 8 August 2006.

Report on 'Cork Main Drainage Scheme; Archaeological monitoring of the laying of services at St Patrick's Street, Cork City; May–October 1999.' Licence no: 96E157.

Report of the Pipe Water Commissioners 1809, Local Studies Department, Cork City Library.

Radio Éireann, *The Burning of Cork*, radio documentary broadcast 18 April 1960.

RTÉ Cork Library, Interview tapes SS3 9/10/11.

St Patrick's Street Development Brief', Cork Corporation, August 2001.

The Statutes At Large Passed in the Parliament held in Ireland, Vol. IX, (Dublin, MDCCLXXXVI).

Irish Manuscripts Commission

Abstracts of Wills Vol. 1 1708–45 (Dublin, 1956).

Pender, Seamus, *A Census of Ireland circa 1659* (Dublin, 1939, 2002).

The Manuscripts of J. B. Fortescue Esq. Vol. 1 (London, 1892).

The Manuscripts and Correspondence of James, First Earl of Charlemont, Vol. 1, 1745–1783 (London, 1891).

Newspapers/Periodicals

Connaught Journal, 1840
Corke Journal, 1756–8
Cork Constitution, 1845–1920
Cork (Irish) Examiner, 1841–2006
Cork Mercantile Chronicle, 1804
Evening Echo, 1975–2006
Freeman's Journal, 1780–1845
Hibernian Chronicle, 1780–1805
Southern Reporter, 1827
Volunteer Journal or Independent Gazetteer, 1783–1786

Trade Directories

Holden's Triennial Directory, Fourth Edition for 1805, 1806, 1807 (London, Glendinning, Calvert, Barnard and Sultzer, Stowers, Spilsbury, Wilks and Hart, 1805)

Pigot's National Commercial Directory of Ireland 1824 (Dublin, 1824)

Aldwell, Alexander, *The County and City of Cork Post Office General Directory, 1844–45* (Cork, 1844)

Slater's Royal National Commercial Directory of Ireland, 1856 (Manchester, 1856)

Laing, Robert H., *Cork Mercantile Directory for 1863* (Cork, 1863)

Henry & Coughlan, *General Directory of Cork for 1867* (Cork, 1867)

Guy's County and City of Cork Directory 1875–76 (Cork, 1875)

Guy's Directory of Munster for 1886 (Cork, 1886)

Guy's Cork Almanac, County and City Directory 1925 (Cork, 1925)

Guy's Cork Almanac, County and City Directory 1935 (Cork, 1935)

Guy's Cork Almanac, County and City Directory 1945 (Cork, 1945)

Thoms Commercial Directory (Dublin, 1976)

Thoms Commercial Directory (Dublin, 1997)

Secondary Sources

Abercrombie, P. S. Kelly and A. Kelly, *Dublin of the Future* (Dublin, 1922).

Alter, Peter, 'Symbols of Irish Nationalism', *Studia Hibernica*, 14 (1974).

Barry, Anthony, *No Lovelier City, A Portrait of Cork* (TK Publications, Kilkenny, 1995).

Barry, John, 'The Rise of the Medieval City', *Cork Examiner*, 2 January 1985.

Barry, Terry, (ed.), *A History of Settlement in Ireland* (Routledge, London, 2000).

Barry, Tom, *Guerrilla Days in Ireland* (Anvil Books Ltd, Dublin, 1981).

Beckett, J. C., *The Making of Modern Ireland, 1603–1923* (Faber & Faber, London, 1981).

Bielenberg, Andy, *Cork's Industrial Revolution 1780–1880: Development or Decline?* (Cork University Press, Cork, 1991).

Bennett, Richard, *The Black and Tans* (Spellmount, Kent, 2001).

Bolster, Evelyn, *A History of the Diocese of Cork from the Earliest Times to the Reformation* (Shannon, 1972)

Bradley, John and Andrew Halpin, 'The Topographical Development of Scandinavian and Anglo-Norman Cork' in Patrick O'Flanagan and Cornelius Buttimer, (eds.), *Cork: History and Society* (Geography Publications, Dublin, 1993).

Burke, Peter, *Popular Culture in Early Modern Europe* (Wildwood House, 1988).

Butel P. and L. M. Cullen, (eds.), *Cities and Merchants: French and Irish Perspectives on Urban Development 1500–1900* (Dublin, 1986).

Butlin, R. A., (ed.), *The Development of the Irish Town* (Croom Helm, London, 1977).

Cadogan, Tim, *Cork in Old Photographs* (Gill & Macmillan, Dublin, 2003).

Cadogan, Tim and Jeremiah Falvey, *A Biographical Dictionary of Cork* (Four Courts Press, Dublin, 2006).

Carberry, Eugene, 'The Development of Cork City', *JCHAS*, 48 (1943)

Caulfield, Richard, *The Council Book of the Corporation of the City of Cork, from 1609–1643 and from 1690–1800* (Surrey, 1876).

Chandler, Edward, *Photography in Ireland, The Nineteenth Century* (Edmund Burke Publisher, Dublin, 2001)

Cleary, Joe and Claire Connolly, (eds.), *The Cambridge Companion to Modern Irish Culture* (Cambridge University Press, Cambridge, 2005).

Connolly, James, *Labour in Irish History* (Bookmarks, London, 1987).

Connolly, Sean, 'Elite responses to popular culture', in J. S. Donnelly & Kerby A. Miller, (eds.), *Irish Popular Culture 1650–1850* (Irish Academic Press, Dublin,1999).

Cork Town Planning Association, *Cork – A Civic Survey* (Liverpool, 1926).

Creedon, Conal (Director), *Why the Guns Remained Silent in Rebel Cork*, Television Documentary broadcast 25 December 2005.

Cronin, Maura, *Country, Class or Craft, The Politicisation of the Skilled Artisan in Nineteenth-Century Cork* (Cork University Press, Cork, 1994).

Cronin, Mike and Daryl Adair, *The Wearing of the Green: A History of St Patrick's Day* (Routledge, London and New York. 2002).

Croker, T. Crofton, *Researches in the South of Ireland, 1812–1822* (Irish Academic Press, 1981, first published 1824).

Curtis, Edmund, *A History of Ireland From the Earliest Times to 1922* (Methuen & Co. Ltd, 1936; Routledge edition, New York, 2002).

d'Alton, Ian, *Protestant Society and Politics in Cork, 1812–1844* (Cork University Press, Cork, 1980).

Daly, Sean, *Cork: A City in Crisis* (Tower Books, Cork, 1978).

de Courcy Ireland, John, *Ireland and the Irish in Maritime History* (Glendale Press, Dublin, 1986).

dePaor, Liam, 'The Age of the Viking Wars', in T. W. Moody & F. X. Martin, (eds.), *The Course of Irish History* (Mercier Press, Cork/Dublin, 1980).

Secondary Sources (continued)

Dickson, David, *Old World Colony, Cork and South Munster 1630–1830* (Cork University Press, Cork, 2005).

—, *New Foundations Ireland 1660–1800*, 2nd edn, (Irish Academic Press, Dublin, 2000).

Doherty Gabriel, and Dermot Keogh, (eds.), *Michael Collins and the Making of the Irish State* (Mercier Press, Cork, 1998).

Donnelly, J. S. & Kirby A. Miller, (eds.), *Irish Popular Culture 1650–1850* (Irish Academic Press, Dublin, 1999).

Dooley, Dolores, *Equality in Community, Sexual Equality in the writings of William Thompson and Anna Doyle Wheeler* (Cork University Press, Cork, 1996).

Edwards, Rev. Arthur W. 'Historical Sketch of the Church of Ireland', in *Essays on The Irish Church by Clergymen of the Established Church in Ireland* (Oxford, London and Dublin, 1868).

Edwards, Owen Dudley and Bernard Ransom, (eds.), *James Connolly, Selected Political Writings* (Jonathan Cape Ltd, London, 1973)

Ellis, Alan J., *The Burning of Cork: an eyewitness account* (Aubane Historical Society, Millstreet, Cork, 2004).

Echoes of the Past, A Trip Down Memory Lane (Evening Echo, Cork, 2001).

Fisher, Joachim & Grace Neville, *As Others Saw Us, Cork through European Eyes* (The Collins Press, Cork, 2005).

Fagan, Patrick, *Catholics in a Protestant Country: the Papist Constituency in Eighteenth-Century Dublin* (Four Courts Press, Dublin, 1998).

Fahy, Angela, 'A social geography of nineteenth century Cork', unpublished MA thesis, UCC (1981).

—, 'Residence, workplace and patterns of change: Cork 1787–1863, in Paul Butel and L. M. Cullen, (eds.), *Cities and Merchants: French and Irish Perspectives on Urban Development 1500–1900* (Dublin, 1986).

—, 'Place and Class in Cork', in O'Flanagan & Buttimer, *Cork: History and Society* (Geography publications, Dublin, 1993)

Fennell, Desmond, 'Irish Socialist Thought', in Richard Kearney, (ed.), *The Irish Mind: Exploring Intellectual Traditions* (Wolfhound Press, Dublin, 1985).

Fitzgerald, John, Legends, *Ballads and Songs of the Lee* (Guy and Co. Ltd, Cork 1913).

Fleischmann, Ruth, *Cork International Choral Festival, 1954–2004: A Celebration* (Glen House Press, Germany, 2004).

Foster, R. F., *Modern Ireland 1600–1972* (Penguin Books, 1989).

Foster, R. F., (ed.), *The Oxford Illustrated History of Ireland* (BCA, London, 1991).

Fr Augustine, O.F.M. Cap., *Footprints of Father Mathew* (M. H. Gill and Son Ltd, Dublin, 1947).

Galloway, Peter, *The Most Illustrious Order of Saint Patrick* (Phillimore & Co. Ltd, Chicester, 1983)

Gibson, Rev. C. B., *The History of the County and City of Cork in Two Volumes* (Thomas C. Newby, London, 1861).

Gough, M., 'A history of the physical development of Cork city', unpublished MA thesis, UCC (1973).

Graham, Brian, 'The Towns of Medieval Ireland' in R. A. Butlin, *The Development of the Irish Town*.

Guilbard, G.Massard, 'The Genesis of an Urban Identity, The Quartier de la Gare in Clermont Ferrand, 1850–1914', *Journal of Urban History*, 25, 6 (1999).

Hardt, Hanno, 'Pierced Memories on the Rhetoric of a Bayoneted Photograph', [cited 18 October 2005] <www.indiana.edu/~rhetid/hardt.htm.

Harkness, David and Mary O'Dowd, (eds.), *The Town in Ireland*, Historical Studies XIII (Appletree Press, Belfast 1981).

Hart, Peter, *The I .R .A. & its Enemies, Violence and Community in Cork 1916–1923* (Clarendon Press, Oxford, 1998).

Healy, James N., *Roches Stores* (Roches Stores, Cork, 1981).

Heaney, Henry, (ed.), *A Scottish Whig in Ireland, The Irish Journals of Robert Graham of Redgorton* (Four Courts Press in association with The National Library of Ireland, Dublin, 1999).

Hennessy, David, 'The Making of a Modern Street, St Patrick's Street in the Twentieth Century', Local Studies Dept., Cork City Library.

Henry, William, *Love of our Country: a sermon preached in the Cathedral Church of St Patrick, Dublin, March 17, 1756, being the anniversary of the festival of St Patrick* (Dublin, 1761).

Hill, Jacqueline R., 'National Festivals, the State and Protestant Ascendancy in Ireland, 1790–1829', *Irish Historical Studies*, 24, 93 (1984).

Hoare, Capt. Edward, *Early History & Genealogy of the Families of Hore and Hoare* (London, 1883).

Hourihan, Kevin, 'The Evolution and Influence of Town Planning in Cork', in O'Flanagan and Buttimer, *Cork: History and Society* (Geography Publications, Dublin, 1993).

Inglis, Ken, 'Father Mathew's Statue: the Making of a Monument in Cork', in Oliver McDonagh and W. F. Mandle, (eds.), *Ireland and Irish-Australia: Studies in Cultural and Political History* (Croom Helm, London, 1986).

Jackson, Alvin, 'The Survival of the Union' in Joe Cleary and Claire Connolly, (eds.), *Modern Irish Culture* (Cambridge, 2005).

Johnson, Gina, *The Laneways of Medieval Cork* (Cork City Council, Cork, 2002).

Jupp, Peter and Eoin Magennis, (eds.), *Crowds in Ireland, c.1720–1920* (Macmillan Press, London, 2000).

Jupp, Peter and Stephen Royle, 'The social geography of Cork City elections, 1801–30', *Irish Historical Studies*, 29, 113 (1994).

Kearney, Richard, (ed.), *The Irish Mind: Exploring Intellectual Traditions* (Wolfhound Press, Dublin, 1985).

Kelly, Cornelius, *The Grand Tour of Cork*, (Cailleach Books, Cork, 2003).

Keogh, Dermot, *Twentieth-Century Ireland, Nation and State* (Gill & Macmillan, Dublin, 1994).

Kilfeather, Siobhán, *Dublin: A Cultural and Literary History* (The Liffey Press, Dublin, 2005).

Lane, Fintan, *In Search of Thomas Sheahan, Radical Politics in Cork, 1824–36* (Irish Academic Press, Dublin, 2001).

Lawless Lee, Grace, *The Huguenot Settlements in Ireland* (Longmans Green and Co., London, 1936).

Lecky, W. E. H., *A History of Ireland in the Eighteenth Century* (University of Chicago Press, Chicago, 1972).

Leerssen, Joep, *Hidden Ireland, Public Sphere* (Arlen House, Galway and Dublin, 2002).

Lewis, Samuel, Lewis' Cork, *A Topographical Dictionary of the Parishes, Towns and Villages of Cork City and County* (The Collins Press, Cork, 1998).

First published as part of *A Topographical Dictionary of Ireland* by S Lewis & Co. (London 1837).

Lincoln, Colm, *Steps and Steeples, Cork at the Turn of the Century* (O'Brien Press, Dublin, 1980).

Lucas, Richard, 'The Cork Directory for the Year 1787', *JCHAS*, 72 (1967).

Lyons, F. S. L., *Ireland Since the Famine* (Fontana Press, Great Britain, 1986). First published 1971.

McCarthy, Andrew, 'Michael Collins, Minister for Finance 1919–22', in Gabriel Doherty and Dermot Keogh, (eds.), *Michael Collins and the Making of the Irish State* (Mercier Press, Cork, 1998).

McCarthy, Mark, 'The historical geography of Cork's transformation from a late medieval town into an Atlantic seaport, 1600–1700', unpublished PhD thesis, UCC (1997).

McCormack, Bridget, *Perceptions of St Patrick in Eighteenth-Century Ireland* (Four Courts Press, Dublin, 2000).

McDonagh, Oliver and W. F. Mandle, (eds.), *Ireland and Irish-Australia: Studies in Cultural and Political History* (Croom Helm, London, 1986).

McGrath, Walter, *Tram Tracks Through Cork* (Tower Books of Cork, 1981).

Mitchell, G. F., 'Prehistoric Ireland', in T. W. Moody & F. X. Martin, (eds.), *The Course of Irish History* (Mercier Press, Cork/Dublin, 1980).

Moody, T. W. and F. X. Martin, (eds.), *The Course of Irish History* (Mercier Press, Cork/Dublin, 1980).

Morris, Ewan, *Our Own Devices: National Symbols and Political Conflict in Twentieth Century Ireland* (Irish Academic Press, Dublin, 2005).

Murphy, James H., *Ireland: a social, cultural and literary history, 1791–1891* (Four Courts Press, Dublin, 2003).

Murphy, Maura, 'The Economic and Social Structure of Nineteenth Century Cork', in David Harkness and Mary O'Dowd, *The Town in Ireland* (Appletree Press, Belfast 1981).

Nolan, William and Thomas P. Power, *Waterford: History and Society* (Geography Publications, Dublin, 1992).

O'Brien, A. F., 'The Development of the Privileges, Liberties and Immunities of Medieval Cork and the Growth of an Urban Autonomy. c.1189–1500', *JCHAS*, 90 (1985).

Secondary Sources (continued)

Ó Corráin, Donnchadh, 'Prehistoric and Early Christian Ireland', in Roy Foster, (ed.), *The Oxford Illustrated History of Ireland* (BCA, London, 1991).

—, 'Ecclesiastical Power Struggle', *Cork Examiner*, 16 January 1985.

Ó Cuív, Brian, 'Ireland in the Eleventh and Twelfth Centuries', in T. W. Moody & F. X. Martin, (eds.), *The Course of Irish History* (Mercier Press, Cork/Dublin, 1980).

O'Donnell, E. E., *Fr Browne's Cork, Photographs 1912–1954* (Wolfhound Press,1995).

Ó Drisceoil, Diarmuid & Donal Ó Drisceoil, *Serving a City: The Story of Cork's English Market* (The Collins Press, Cork, 2005).

Ó Faoláin, Seán, *Vive Moi!* (Sinclair-Stephenson, London, 1993).

O'Flanagan, Patrick and Cornelius G. Buttimer, (eds.), *Cork: History and Society* (Geography Publications, Dublin, 1993).

O'Flanagan, Patrick, 'Three Hundred Years of Urban Life: Villages and Towns in County Cork *c.*1600–1901', in O'Flanagan and Cornelius Buttimer, *Cork: History and Society* (Geography Publications, Dublin, 1993).

Ó Gráda, Cormac, *Ireland, A New Economic History 1780–1939* (Clarendon Press, Oxford, 1994).

O'Mahony, Coleman, *In the Shadows: Life in Cork 1750–1930* (Tower Books, Cork, 1997).

Ó Murchadha, Diarmuid, 'The Siege of Cork in 1690', *JCHAS*, 95 (1990).

O'Riain, Padraig, 'St Finbarr: a study in a cult', *JCHAS*, 82 (1977).

Sylvester O'Sullivan, 'Cork's Much Loved Tram Service Faces its Doom', *Evening Echo*, 23 August 1976.

—, The Battle of the Buses', *Evening Echo*, 30 August 1976.

O'Sullivan, William, *The Economic History of Cork City from the Earliest Times to the Act of Union* (Cork University Press, Cork, 1937).

Ó Tuathaigh, Gearóid, 'Language, ideology and national identity', in Joe Cleary and Claire Connolly (eds.), *Modern Irish Culture* (Cambridge, 2005).

Owens, Gary, 'Nationalism without Words: Symbolism and Ritual Behaviour in the Repeal 'Monster meetings' of 1843–5', in Donnelly J. S. & Kerby A. Miller, *Irish Popular Culture 1650–1850*.

Pankhurst, Richard, *William Thompson, 1775–1833, Pioneer Socialist* (Pluto press, London, 1954).

Picture That, Cork through the Ages (Cork Examiner Publications, 1996).

Quinlivan, Aodh, *Philip Monahan, A Man Apart* (Institute of Public Administration, Dublin, 2006).

Relph, E., *Place and Placelessness* (Pion Ltd. London, 1976).

Rothery, Sean, *The Shops of Ireland* (Gill & Macmillan, Dublin, 1978).

Rouse, Sarah, *Into the Light: An Illustrated guide to the Photographic Collections in the National Library of Ireland* (National Library of Ireland, 1998).

Rynne, Colin & Billy Wigham, *Forgotten Cork, Photographs from the Day Collection* (The Collins Press, Cork, 2004).

Stark, Archibald G., *The South of Ireland in 1850; Being the Journal of a tour in Leinster and South Munster* (James Duffy, Dublin, 1850).

Stratten & Stratten, *Strattens' Dublin, Cork and South of Ireland; A Literary, Commercial and Social Review, Past and Present* (London, 1892).

The Four Masters Annals of the Kingdom of Ireland from the Earliest Times to the Year 1616, Third Edition, Vol. 1 (deBúrca Rare Books, Dublin, 1990).

Townend, Paul A., *Father Mathew, Temperance and Irish Identity* (Irish Academic Press, Dublin, 2002).

Tuckey, Francis, *Cork Remembrancer* (Tower Books, Cork, 1980). First published in 1837.

Whelan, Yvonne, *Reinventing Modern Dublin, Streetscape, Iconography and Politics of Identity* (UCD Press, Dublin, 2003).

White, Gerry and Brendan O'Shea, *The Burning of Cork* (Mercier Press, Cork, 2006).

Windele, John, *Windele's Cork, Historical and Descriptive Notices of the City of Cork*, 'Revised, Abridged and Annotated by James Coleman, MRSAI' (Fercor Press, Cork, 1973).

Who Burnt Cork City? (Irish Labour Party and Trade Union Congress Jan 1921). (Facsimile published by South Gate Books, Cork, 1978. Local Studies Department, Cork City Library.)

Index